WHY
PARENTS
MATTER

WHY
PARENTS
MATTER

❖ ❖

Parental Investment and Child Outcomes

Nigel Barber

Bergin & Garvey
Westport, Connecticut • London

Library of Congress Cataloging-in-Publication Data

Barber, Nigel.
    Why parents matter : parental investment and child outcomes / Nigel Barber.
      p. cm.
    Includes bibliographical references and index.
    ISBN 0–89789–725–0 (alk. paper)
    1. Parenting.   2. Parent and child.   I. Title.
  HQ755.8.B3723   2000
  649′.1—dc21   99–055886

British Library Cataloguing in Publication Data is available.

Library of Congress Catalog Card Number: 99–055886
ISBN: 0–89789–725–0

First published in 2000

Bergin & Garvey, 88 Post Road West, Westport, CT 06881
An imprint of Greenwood Publishing Group, Inc.
www.greenwood.com

Printed in the United States of America

The paper used in this book complies with the
Permanent Paper Standard issued by the National
Information Standards Organization (Z39.48–1984).

10 9 8 7 6 5 4 3 2 1

This book is dedicated to Trudy and David.

Contents

CONTENTS

Preface

There has been a recent academic controversy over whether parental child-rearing has any real effect on how offspring turn out. Ordinary people seem far ahead of the brightest minds in psychological research in their intuitive knowledge that parental attention and solicitude matter a great deal for the happiness and social success of children. They know that if parents, rich or poor, spend little time with their offspring they can reasonably expect resentment and disturbing behavioral problems.

This controversy was begun by behavior geneticists who found that personality differences are strongly influenced by genes. Moreover, they concluded that, regardless of shared genes, siblings raised in the same home are no more similar in personality than any two individuals chosen at random from the population. These results have caused many academics to jump to the conclusion that parents have little role to play in how their children turn out. Yet, a closer look at the actual research findings makes it clear that this conclusion should not be drawn.

Personality traits like extroversion and anxiety are determined by brain biology, and they would have to be influenced by genes. We cannot expect parents to alter substantially such basic biological traits of their children, and the behavior geneticists are telling us that in fact they do not. What parental influence can do is to intervene between biologically based behavioral tendencies and what the child actually does. For example, Jerome

Kagan, a developmental psychologist at Harvard University, has shown that children who are very fearful and averse to taking risks can be encouraged by parents to be more venturesome. The same point is even more obvious in the case of impulsive aggression. Parents who give in to aggressive control tactics practiced on them by a toddler should not be surprised to discover that they have raised a bully. Parents do not change basic biology; they change the manner in which impulses get expressed.

One reason that the importance of parental influence has been called into question is that a lot of the research evidence dealing with parental socialization efforts is flawed. To take a simple, and widely known, example, if parents often slap their children, it has been found that the children grow up to be more aggressive. Is this the result of being beaten by their parents, or is it due to the fact that they have inherited their parents "aggressive" genes? In all probability, both influences matter considerably, but current evidence does not allow us to distinguish between the relative importance of each. In the past, socialization researchers have simply ignored the possibility of genetic influence, assuming, like Christopher Columbus, that if they had discovered it, it must be theirs.

Given the softness of much of the socialization evidence in favor of parental influence, it is important to focus on research, which establishes parental effects without ambiguity. Ideally, this is done by means of formal experiments. In this book, I have chosen to assemble a comprehensive collection of the experimental evidence establishing that parental treatment affects child outcomes. Also included are natural experiments, as in the case of children raised in intellectually and emotionally impoverished circumstances in orphanages. (We refer to these psychologically impoverished circumstances as a natural experiment because they are not arranged by a researcher.) Orphans raised in institutions are not only deprived of parental interaction but often lack the basic sensory and social stimulation necessary for normal brain development. No one doubts that such extreme parental deprivation hinders intellectual development and socialization. Some behavior geneticists have concluded, however, that if home life is neither frankly abusive or neglectful, it matters little for a child's outcome. If the home environment is "good enough," according to Sandra Scarr, then children will be more the result of their genetic potential, and how parents treat a particular individual is quite irrelevant to how the child turns out. Ten years ago this might have seemed like a safe generalization. Recently, behavior geneticists have collaborated with developmental psychologists to produce compelling evidence that the fine nuances of how parents treat one child relative to another have major consequences regarding which child grows up to be delinquent or to suffer from depression. Once again, the state of the art in psychological research is breathing on the heels of what we all intuitively know: that the happiness of children in a family can be greatly affected by whether parents perceive them as favorites or as the black sheep of the family.

Experimental evidence supporting the impact of parental behavior on children's psychological development is not voluminous, but it does coalesce to produce a compelling overall picture. Beginning at a child's birth (and possibly even earlier), the quality of the mother's voice, whether she is depressed or not, can affect the capacity of the young brain to learn. Experiments conducted in the first year of life have shown that mothers can be trained to be more sensitively responsive to their infants and that this training may induce a warmer, more secure relationship between mother and child that colors all future emotional relationships, including romantic ones. Maternal responsiveness to infants also boosts intelligence. Head Start programs, which are often mistakenly thought of as failures, can produce lasting enhancement of IQ scores but only if they are begun by the first year of life. Programs begun later in life only boost intelligence temporarily, but they do produce lasting improvements in academic motivation and performance. The burning question of what generates antisocial behavior in children has also yielded to experimental work conducted by family researchers who modified family interaction patterns in the case of out-of-control boys, teaching parents and children to interact in more cooperative and less hostile ways. Ten years later, the behavior of the treated children, now adolescents, was indistinguishable from that of a control group who had never had conduct problems.

Why Parents Matter is not just an issue of evidence showing that what parents do affects their children. Beneath this phenomenon is a more fundamental issue. Why don't all parents strive to raise the kind of bright, happy, and hard-working individuals who succeed in our society? The prevailing view in the social sciences is that some parents do not perform up to these criteria because they are disorganized or pathological. An alternative perspective, which is developed in this book, is that parents are preparing children to succeed in the kind of world in which they currently find themselves, as opposed to their dreams for the future. Thus, the American inner city is a kind of modern Sparta, in which the widespread use of corporal punishment actively encourages children to be aggressive, rather than the Athens of learning and civilization represented by mainstream America (at least in comparison).

For a young man who happens to be making a living distributing narcotics, a high school diploma isn't going to increase his income. Moreover, a reputation for culture and sensitivity is not going to improve his social success in a street gang. Tragic though the consequences may be, there is a clear logic to the phenomenon of harsh, insensitive parenting producing offspring who are tough and antisocial, whereas sensitive, responsive parenting produces children who are bright, altruistic, and open to others.

The rationale is that parental behavior helps children to fit in with and succeed in whatever kind of social environment they find themselves.

Parental investment is of great practical importance because it explains some of the main inequities in our society, such as the fact that children born to poor parents are less likely to be occupationally successful and more likely to exhibit delinquent behavior, to be addicted to drugs, to have accidents, and to be in poor health. These outcomes are all predicated on reduced parental investment, which is more likely in poorer homes. Likelihood is not certainty. Many poor children do not develop serious social problems. In addition, there have been many recent incidents in which children raised in affluent homes have committed horrifying crimes. We may never know all of the precipitating circumstances behind such comparatively rare events, but the level of disconnection between the daily lives of parents and children accepted as normal in many of these households is as chilling as the atrocities themselves.

Chapter 1

The Big Picture: Societal Differences in Parenting

You can tell a great deal about a student by the contents of his book bag. Sometimes, this reveals even more about his parents, and even the society in which he lives. One of my most vivid memories of high school, or "secondary school" as it was called in Ireland, was the day that Kieran D., a strapping country lad of 14 years, opened his remarkably tiny school bag, divulging its entire contents, as I walked behind him in the corridor that separated a pair of prefabricated classrooms. Actually it was a shiny little case of the kind that children used to carry in first grade. Snapping open the single clasp, Kieran removed a notebook and a pencil. Left inside was a huge lunch box and nothing else. With a shock, I realized that he had brought no textbooks. At the same moment, it occurred to me that the reason why his book bag was so small was that he had actually never obtained any of the required textbooks. Moreover, his parents must have been complicit in his textless state. In another context, such privation would be construed as neglectful parenting. In rural Ireland, circa 1968, here was a carefree lad with no interest in books who was whiling away his last pointless year in school before moving on to a future in agriculture.

Instead of seeing parents as either bad or good, it is more useful to recognize that their level of investment in children varies greatly. Low-investing parents are not necessarily bad parents but people whose parenting style helps children to fit in with difficult social or economic conditions, whether this is the arduous life of a small farmer or the dangerous world of an inner city slum. Unfortunately, this may not prepare children to make their way as happy, productive members of the complex society in which we live. Either they have difficulty acquiring an education and establishing themselves in careers, or they get in trouble with the law, or they are personally unhappy and leave a trail of emotional wreckage in their close relationships.

CAUSES OF DIFFERENCES IN PARENTAL INVESTMENT ACROSS AND WITHIN SOCIETIES

Parental investment varies continuously but is best understood in terms of extremes. In addition to the reliable provision of good food and shelter, high investing parents have some distinguishing characteristics:

- a warm, trusting relationship with children;
- minimal use of punishment and scolding and a corresponding reliance on explanation as a method of control;
- provision of intellectually stimulating activities and toys;
- spending time talking to and listening to children; and
- an emotional commitment to each other.

Low-investment parenting is the major cause of all kinds of social problems. This is strong language, academically speaking, but there is a compelling body of scientific evidence that allows this conclusion to be drawn. The evidence is brought together for the first time in an accessible form in this book.

The effects of low parental investment can be appreciated in terms of the connection between poverty and social problems. Social problems, which have often been attributed to poverty or to race, are really produced by reduced parental investment. Lower parental investment increases the probability that children will be delinquent, do poorly at school, become addicted to drugs, or have children outside wedlock. The association between poverty and social problems makes much more sense when you realize that poverty is the epicenter of numerous influences that strike at families and tend to reduce parental investment. Poverty is a complex stressor that disrupts family life and makes it more difficult for parents to raise happy productive children. No matter how bleak the physical surroundings may be, children who have a close relationship with at least one adult are much more likely to avoid developing behavior problems.[1, 2]

For poor people, education is an important key to social mobility. If so, then many are liable to encounter a permanently locked door. Welfare children tend to do appallingly badly in school, even after the curriculum has been deliberately "dumbed down" for political reasons in order to give them a fighting chance. This means that they are locked in a cross-generational cycle of poverty. Another way of stating it is to say that they are locked in a cross-generational cycle of low parental investment. Low academic performance in poor children is linked to an intellectually impoverishing early environment that stunts academic promise as manifested in reduced IQ scores.

Why do children raised in poverty score as much as ten points lower in IQ than those raised in affluent homes?[3] One view is that the differences may be entirely due to genetics. This conclusion seems unlikely in view of evidence that children's IQ scores may be permanently boosted by enriched environments of the kind produced by Head Start programs, at least if these are begun in the first year of life.[4] Perhaps the strongest evidence against the genetic argument is the finding that gaps between blacks (who are more likely to be poor) and whites in standardized tests of academic ability have virtually halved in recent decades, despite the fact that there has been no time for genetic changes to occur in the population.[5] Such evidence points to the critically important role of environmental factors like parental investment in academic performance.

The cycle of low academic attainment, poverty, violence, criminality, drug addiction, psychological disorders, and social problems in American inner cities seems obscene in comparison to the lifestyle enjoyed by ordinary middle-class Americans. An even more telling contrast is between the United States (and other developed nations) and underdeveloped countries, particularly the poorest states of Africa. In terms of most objective criteria, being poor and living in a backward African country is much worse than being poor and living in an American ghetto. For instance, in some countries, populations may average as low as 70 on IQ tests (which may reflect problems with the test as well as low academic potential).[6] Crime rates may be ten times as high as they are here. Health care is primitive, so that many children die before reaching maturity. Thousands die of hunger each year. Women and children are sold into slavery. Young children are forced to fight in wars.

In some ways, the grim reality of life for children in some poor African countries may be more reflective of the broad sweep of human history than is true for current conditions in America and the rest of the West. In the past, before the age of scientific medicine, children often died before reaching maturity, even in the "civilized" countries of western Europe. This meant that parents could not have formed such close relationships with all of their children as they do today, when most children survive and when far fewer children are being produced in Western families. Since far fewer children are being produced, it is possible to invest a great deal more in each of them.

The possibility of increased investment in children has led to a sort of cult of the child. Families today are much more child-centered than the rather authoritarian family system that held sway early in the twentieth century. There is a great deal of emphasis on catering to the emotional needs of children and providing intellectually enriching activities from an early age.[7] In that respect, we are living in a golden age for children. Children have never had greater opportunities for intellectual and emotional growth. On the other hand, these opportunities are not evenly distributed. Poverty is one force that tends to undermine parental investment. Unfortunately, while the average amount of money per child in affluent homes has continued to increase, the number of children growing up in poverty has not fallen, hovering around 10 percent to 11 percent of families from 1970 to 1995.[8] Another influence that tends to reduce parental investment in children, particularly by fathers, is marital instability. The divorce rate has increased at a staggering rate this century (doubling between 1964 and 1975, for example [9]), so that living apart from one parent for some part of childhood is about to become the norm. It is not marital dissolution, as such, that undermines parental investment in children, but rather the more fundamental lack of commitment between husbands and wives, which makes it difficult for them to cooperate on a permanent basis for the purpose of raising children.

The central theme of this book is that even though circumstances are much worse for children in Africa than in the worst American slums, both show the same pattern of social problems converging on the poor, and the root cause of this pattern is low parental investment. Parental investment in children is reduced in various ways by poverty and by marital instability, and it is also reduced when parents bring large numbers of children into the world, as still happens in underdeveloped countries, since this reduces the amount of care they can hope to give to each.

WHAT IS PARENTAL INVESTMENT?

Parental investment is a term drawn from biology. It was defined by Robert Trivers[10] as anything done by a parent for the offspring that increases its chances of survival while diminishing the parent's capacity to invest in other offspring (whether already born or not). This means that, all other things being equal, parental investment will be lower in a large family because parental resources are divided and thus diminished for each child. It will also be lower in poor families. Marital instability tends to reduce parental investment because children are denied access to the noncustodial parent for much of the time. Divorced families are also poorer, unless and until remarriage takes place.

Although parental investment includes a large range of goods and services provided by parents to children, including affection and emotional support, there is nothing iffy or "touchy-feely" about it. All of these goods and services are not only measurable in principle; many actually have been

4

measured. Moreover, there is now abundant evidence that parental investment has substantial effects on child outcomes, such as educational and occupational success, teen pregnancy, and antisocial behavior, including
serious crimes, as described in detail in later chapters of this book. Parental
investment includes but is not limited to services and resources such as
time; attention; discipline; instruction; emotional support; material resources such as food, housing, toys, and intellectually stimulating items in
the home; and, of course, wealth and money, which can be used to provide
all of the above, including the emotional support that infants can expect in a
good day-care facility.

Since harsh, insensitive, or neglectful parental behavior increases the
likelihood of problem behavior in young adults, it is a negative contribution to parental investment. There are many potential causes of emotionally
abrasive parental behavior. One is the experience of having had insensitive
parents. Another is conflict and hostility between the sexes, which hinges
on marital instability.

SIBLING COMPETITION AS A TRAGEDY OF THE COMMONS

When parental investment is viewed from a cross-species perspective,
some spine-tinglingly unpleasant phenomena come to the surface. Take for
instance the bizarre reproductive system of eagles. Two eggs are laid several days apart. When the eaglets hatch, they do so at different times so that
the older chick tends to be much larger than the younger one. What happens next is gruesome and puzzling. The older chick systematically batters
its sibling to death with its bill. This phenomenon was particularly
perplexing to biologists because it defied their expectation that close relatives should tend to help each other because the genetic basis for such altruism is likely to be shared by the relative who is helped, thereby creating an
unthinking mechanism by which relatives tend to help each other. This
principle is known as kin selection.[11] Even more astonishing is the behavior
of the parents. Instead of intervening to save their weaker chick, they remain aloof, ignoring the horrific sequence as though it was of no consequence to them.

Research on egrets and other species has begun to provide an explanation for these strange and disturbing events.[12] One conclusion that can be
quickly drawn is that eagles are not alone in hatching an excessive number
of chicks. Among the egrets, which have larger clutches, it is common for
the brood to begin with around five chicks, one of which may be killed off
by its brothers and sisters. The mechanism by which this happens is a fascinating example of adaptive design, which provides an important clue to
the whole ghastly phenomenon. A well-fed egret chick is drowsy and
peaceful. When the food supply is diminished, the young egrets wake up

and get annoyed. They begin fighting amongst themselves. Eventually they all pick on the smallest, weakest chick and batter it to death. Following this clutch reduction, there is more food to go around, the chicks revert to being sleepy and peaceful, and everything goes back to its previous state.[13]

The story of the egrets certainly does not apply in any direct sense to humans. The killing of a sibling in human families is rather rare, although not unprecedented. Nevertheless, all parents with more than one child have witnessed destructive impulses directed by one sibling against another, often without immediate provocation. For instance, a younger child who is jealous of the attention received by an older sibling may lash out at the older child without warning.

For humans, as for egrets, the course of interactions among siblings is mixed. Much of the time relations may be relaxed and friendly. However, if there is a reason for competition, or merely a suspicion of such a reason, bitter hostilities may break out at the drop of a hat. As biologist Robert Trivers pointed out almost thirty years ago, children are designed by natural selection to compete fiercely over parental investment. The fundamental reason for this is that a unit of parental investment that could have gone to an individual and gets diverted to a sibling is "wasted" to the tune of 50 percent as far as that individual is concerned. This is because a unit invested in me favors my genes by 100 percent whereas a unit invested in my brother or sister favors my genes by only 50 percent. According to Trivers's theory of parental investment, siblings have no choice but to compete with each other when important items of parental investment are in short supply.[14]

This may lead to some rather unpleasant results, such as constant fighting among siblings. While this may be distressing to parents and difficult for the children themselves, it may not be easy to avoid. One important principle of a competitive social environment is that individuals who are "nicer" or more altruistic than their companions will tend to get taken advantage of. Similarly, the benefits to a child of hostility towards his or her siblings can guarantee that this occurs even though conflict often makes the children in a household quite miserable. Moreover, the worse the social environment a child is exposed to both inside and outside the home, the more likely it is that selfishness and aggression will prevail. For humans, as for egrets, when the going gets tough, the tough get going.

If the social environment during childhood is harsh and abusive, then individuals who are selfish and aggressive will fare better than those who are meek and altruistic. In part, this is true because they are more successful in competing for material resources, such as food, and other kinds of parental investment that are provided by parents and other care givers. In part, it may be due to an emotional strategy of manipulating care givers and monopolizing their attention. It is interesting that when children have something to compete over, it tends to bring out their most aggressive and undisciplined behavior. For example, I used to walk two eight-year-olds to school. If I ignored them, they chattered happily together. If I took an interest in the conversation, they were liable to begin a heated argument about whose turn it was to speak. Apparently, their readiness to compete over the attention of an adult sucks them into a bitter and pointless dispute, which results in both of them becoming quite upset, apparently over nothing.

As the number of children in a family increases, realistic causes for competition increase, since there is less of everything to go around, and the motivation for selfish and obnoxious actions is exacerbated. It can thus be argued from first principles that the civility of the home will tend to decline with the number of siblings present. Consistent with this view, it has been found that competitiveness among siblings increases with family size.[15] When a person needs a vital organ, such as a kidney transplant, it turns out that the fewer the number of siblings he or she has, the more likely it is that one of them will serve as a donor. This result is contrary both to common sense and to probability, but it can be explained as due to less competition over parental investment in a small family compared to a larger one.[16] Since the children in a small family generally have less objective reason for competing with each other, they can be mellower, like egrets in small clutches.

Parents evidently struggle to maintain as high a level of civility in their homes as possible. They do everything in their power to curb the antisocial, entropic forces unleashed by the inevitable conflict between siblings over parental investment. This endeavor is quite easy in a home with only one child but is more difficult in homes with two siblings and tends to increase in difficulty as a direct function of family size. This is not to say that parents cannot be successful in restraining sibling hostilities in large families but merely that it is more difficult and requires a higher level of parental effort per child (because children are liable to provoke each other more and spend more time fighting with each other).

When the family reaches a certain size, older children may be recruited to fulfill some parental functions. This may be a mixed blessing since young people who are poorly socialized themselves cannot be relied upon to inculcate rules of expected conduct. At the end of the day, children raised in larger families are more likely to be delinquent, even when you take account of the fact that larger families are more likely to live below the poverty line.[17, 18, 19]

Reduced parental investment is thus conducive to social problems. Conversely, children who grow up in loving, supportive homes (or homes with high parental investment) develop altruistic attitudes and behaviors and reflect this altruism back on their communities in adulthood by becoming law-abiding, productive citizens who invest a great deal in their children, particularly in respect to educating them and inculcating rules and values of appropriate conduct.

Parents are not merely passive observers of the unwinding of their socialization efforts in adverse environments. Harsh and abusive parents actively contribute to the undermining of civility in their homes. Parental favoritism can be a major cause of conflict and leads to social problems. For instance, one study found that 60 percent of differences in adolescent anti-social behavior could be accounted for by conflictual and hostile behavior directed at an individual by parents.[20] Ironically, harsh parental behavior directed only at a sibling had a protective effect, suggesting that some children may benefit when their brothers and sisters get into trouble. Parental favoritism can thus be of great importance in determining which children grow up to become problematic adults.

According to the parental investment approach to child socialization, individuals who contribute to social problem statistics (crime, teen pregnancy, high school dropout, unemployment) do so partly because they receive reduced parental investment. This results in difficulty with impulse control, politeness, altruism, and the ability to feel selfless affection for others.

Of course, some children are more difficult to socialize than others, and there is a genetic influence on problem behaviors. Still, with the exception of the small fraction of the population who are antisocial personalities and therefore pose a difficult problem (about 3 percent of men and 1 percent of women), it seems reasonable to assume that all children can be socialized. This impression is supported by societies with extremely low, or zero, crime rates. Even in the case of antisocial individuals, it appears that only about half are incarcerated for criminal activity, suggesting that they too can be socialized to follow rules of expected conduct.[21]

SOCIETAL DIFFERENCES IN THE MARRIAGE MARKET AND PARENTAL INVESTMENT

Of the many influences on parental investment among different societies and at different historical periods, two stand out as being critically important. The first is the number of children born into a family, which clearly affects the amount of parental effort that can be invested in each child (for humans as much as for egrets). The other is the relationships between the sexes. Where these are hostile and strained, it is difficult for stable marriages to exist since marriages are founded on a basis of trust.

Of the many advantages of modern medicine, perhaps none is more striking than reduced mortality of infants and children. For example, a woman living in late medieval England, between A.D. 900 and 1500 could expect to produce approximately five children in her lifetime. This number was considerably reduced by breast-feeding, which suppressed ovulation and thereby increased birth intervals to around thirty months. Noble families, which employed wet nurses, often produced twice as many children.[22]

Since the majority of women reproduced, although probably not as many as today, each woman needed to produce only slightly more than two children, on average, in order for the population to be maintained.[23] This suggests that the English medieval population must have been growing at a very rapid rate. In fact, it hardly grew at all. The inescapable conclusion to be drawn from these numbers is that approximately half of the children born never survived to maturity.

To put this in context in terms of infant mortality in the United States today, the risk of any mother losing a child in the first, and riskiest, year of postnatal life is less than 1 in 100.[24] In medieval England, the average mother might expect to lose at least one infant. There are few events more traumatic to parents than the loss of a child, but the reality of high mortality rates has an inevitable consequence for parents' attitudes towards their living children. If parents can expect half of their children to die early in life, then we might expect them to withdraw from making the kind of deep emotional attachment that will result in unbearable grief when the inevitable happens.

Although controversial, the picture of medieval childhood presented by historians suggests that children were loved and indulged far less than the children of today. In fact, some scholars go so far as to suggest that the whole concept of childhood as a special time in which children are absolved of adult responsibilities, such as work, so that they can explore their environments and play together is essentially a romantic fiction contrived by English writers of the nineteenth century, such as Lewis Carroll, with the inspiration of French philosophers, such as Rousseau.[25]

In fourteenth-century England, there was a flourishing book industry with instructional manuals on every topic under the sun but almost nothing about how to care for children. Children were rarely depicted in fiction, and when they were, they tended to have brief unenviable roles, such as being left to die in a forest. The depiction of children in paintings and illustrations also suggests a lack of closeness and intimacy. For instance, the Christ child is often held stiffly away from the body of the mother, even when she is shown as being in the act of breast-feeding. This is not due to any prudery about expressing intimacy since people are shown making love and in their beds and baths. There is also a curious absence of children in otherwise ordinary scenes of daily life. It is probably not an exaggeration to say that adults were not very interested in children. They neither thought about them very much nor had particularly strong ties of affection to them. Yet, children were indulged in some ways, then as now. Mothers played with young children, and carefully washed and groomed them. Adults also enjoyed making toys for them. Children's toys of the period included dolls, doll carriages, balls, stilts, see-saws, and windmills, among other items still used by boys and girls.[26]

The impression is often created that children did not have a real childhood until the last century—that they were perceived as undersized adults.

This is probably not correct. What seems to be different is that childhood tended to end earlier. According to Barbara Tuchman, children who survived to the age of seven assumed the status of miniature adults and were expected to do useful work.[27]

Throughout the Western world, populations have passed through what is referred to as the "demographic shift." This means that far fewer children are being produced and far more of them are surviving. Underdeveloped nations, such as many of the states of Africa, still have the population structure of medieval England. There is a high birthrate, high infant and child mortality, and low life expectancy. In such societies, it is common for half of the population to be below the age of twenty-one years.[28]

For societies that have passed through the demographic shift to lower rates of reproduction, the conditions are ideal for very high levels of investment in children because very few children are born and their probability of survival to adulthood is very high. This makes it more likely that parents will form close emotional ties with children. In addition, the greater wealth of industrialized countries allows them to provide excellent nutrition, housing, intellectually stimulating toys, and educational systems for children, which allow them to acquire complex social and professional roles and grow up to be happy and successful individuals. These advantages have had a remarkable effect of increasing intelligence in some societies.[29]

Apart from the basic influences of offspring number and survival, the most potent societal influence on child socialization would appear to be the general willingness of men and women to cooperate in stable harmonious marriages for the purpose of raising children. Whereas few people have thought very much about the impact of reduced family size this century as a facilitator of child socialization, most have been concerned about the potentially harmful effects of marital instability.

While marital stability might seem like a moral issue to many readers, the perspective taken in this book is that how committed people feel in relation to marriage at a particular point in history is more determined by the marriage market. For this relatively new and largely underappreciated approach to marital stability, I am indebted to the work of Marcia Guttentag and Paul Secord. Guttentag died before she could complete her magnum opus, *Too Many Women: The Sex Ratio Question*, which was subsequently finished by Secord, her grieving husband.[30]

It is helpful to think of marriage as a market that operates according to the principles of supply and demand. This is not all that marriage is, of course, but it is the vital framework on which the contractual and emotional ingredients of marriage are suspended. The marriage market is measured in terms of the sex ratio, or ratio of marriageable men to marriageable women. In low-sex-ratio societies, there is a scarcity of marriageable men and an excess of marriageable women.

The key element of marriage, considered as a market, is that whichever sex is scarcer and more in demand tends to set the rules. Thus, the fewer women there are in the population, the higher the marriage market value of the average woman becomes. If many men are competing to marry her, a woman controls the market. She can expect to make a desirable match and marry a man who is not only of fairly high social status but also one who is kind, loving, generous, and likely to take seriously the responsibilities of raising children. The population sex ratio is therefore a crude index of parental investment. If there are too many women relative to men in the population, they will lack control over the marriage market and will have difficulty in attracting high-investing men. Such low-sex-ratio societies are characterized by hostility between the sexes and by marital instability.[31]

Guttentag and Secord organized their book around contrasts among societies and between castes that have high sex ratios and marital stability and those that have low sex ratios and unstable marriages. Low-sex-ratio societies not only have a good deal of hostility between the sexes but they also engender a basic lack of trust among individuals, which produces a high level of interpersonal violence and criminal behavior (a ramification that was not explored by Guttentag and Secord). Guttentag and Secord concluded that ancient Athens had a higher sex ratio than Sparta. Athenian women were valued largely as bearers of children, and respectable women were sequestered to protect their sexual reputations. Spartan women had more social power and much more freedom of movement. The Spartans were notorious as warriors and emphasized a culture of physical fitness that extended to women. In a scene that is remarkably reminiscent of modern health clubs, young men and young women exercised together, without any hint of sexual misconduct. (The only difference was that the Spartans exercised completely naked!) Writing after the end of the Spartan state, Aristotle was appalled by the power given to women, who were largely immune from legal restrictions and obligations, owned two-fifths of the land, and tended to dictate to their warrior husbands in the home. Aristotle was also shocked by the sexual liberties they took.

Apart from the greater liberation of women, it appears that Spartan society also resembled our own in that men lacked an interest in being married. Thus, laws were enacted that compelled men to marry, thereby fathering soldier-citizens to perpetuate the state. Those who failed to comply were turned into outcasts and became the object of ritual humiliation. One of the hallmarks of all low-sex-ratio societies is the undermining of marriage, which is often associated with an increase in personal liberty of women but is also associated with a variety of social problems, such as inadequate support of children and increased levels of criminal behavior.

Guttentag and Secord draw a distinction between two periods of European history: the early Middle Ages (c. A.D. 500–900), which had a high ratio of men to women, and the late Middle Ages (c. A.D. 1000–1500), when the sex ratio declined so sharply that in some European towns, according to tax records, there were only about 80 men per 100 women. In the earlier period women were greatly valued as mothers. Men who were married felt extremely fortunate since many men had no wives, and marriages were highly stable. In the later period, many women were left out in the musical chairs of the competition for desirable husbands. Many raised children alone, struggling to make ends meet in a work environment that was dominated by trade guilds, a form of early trade unions, which deliberately excluded women. This resulted in a spirited protest by female writers of the day, such as Catherine de Pizan, who rehearsed many of the protests that were subsequently to be heard from American feminist writers in the second half of the twentieth century, who were suffering the consequences of similar population trends.

The story of the difference between early and late medieval society is of great interest for its own sake, but it becomes more fascinating because a similar transition has occurred in America, although compressed into a single century, as the high sex ratios of the American frontier gave way to the low-sex-ratio urban society that is characteristic of today. The virtual adoration of motherhood that we find in American ladies' magazines and popular novels of earlier decades has given way to an egoistic search for self-fulfillment in all its forms—spiritual, occupational, and sexual.

Finally, Guttentag and Secord draw a distinction among different ethnic groups in the United States in terms of their sex ratios. This makes sense since most people are still highly likely to marry within their own ethnic group even when they are not strictly required to do so by their own traditions. In respect to marriage, America is still very far from being an ethnic melting pot.

Guttentag and Secord draw a distinction between the low-sex-ratio society of African Americans and the high sex ratios of American Jews. Most of the usual distinctions that would be predicted based on the pattern so far are also borne out in this contrast. Jewish marriages are exceptionally stable, and nonmarital reproduction is rare. African-American marriages are less stable, and most women cannot find desirable husbands and therefore raise children out of wedlock. African-American men are not only in short supply, but they are also less interested in marrying and providing for children. The cardinal distinction that can be drawn between these two groups is in terms of paternal investment in children. Jewish fathers make exceptionally high investments in their children and are therefore extremely preoccupied with their careers and businesses. African American men express less interest in being married and many do not have the kind of occupational success and stability that makes them desirable marriage partners.[32, 33]

The marriage-market factors militating against parental investment for African Americans are associated with a cycle of poverty and social problems. Throughout this book, I argue that such problems are not unique to any ethnic group. In fact, exactly the same dynamics that have resulted in increased rates of crime and nonmarital teen pregnancy for blacks have been at work everywhere because the sex ratio has been falling in the overall population this century, creating unprecedented increases in marital instability and the social problems arising from this.

IS GENETICS THE CAUSE OF SOCIAL PROBLEMS?

You would have to be living in a very deep cave to be unaware that social problems are not equally distributed among ethnic groups. A good rule of thumb is that more social problems are evident among recently arrived immigrant groups than among more settled populations. African Americans are a notable exception to this pattern, but their history is a great deal more complex than might at first appear, with different groups such as descendants of American slaves, "freed persons of color," and West Indians all having very different experiences in this country. Their complex history is discussed in Chapter 9 in terms of group differences in occupational attainment.[34]

Throughout this book I suggest that ethnic group differences in criminal activity, nonmarital reproduction, drug addiction, divorce rate, and so on are best interpreted in terms of differences in parental investment. In other words, social problems are more likely to show up among some groups than others because the children are raised in homes that provide them with lower parental investment. This conclusion is based on fairly compelling evidence that "racial" differences in social problems can be accounted for in terms of environmental factors having an impact on parental investment.

What if this conclusion is completely wrong? It is necessary to play devil's advocate and entertain the rather unappealing possibility that ethnic group differences have nothing to do with levels of parental nurturance but are entirely due to genetic differences as a handful of psychologists and sociologists have loudly proclaimed.

Proponents of the genetic view have assembled a large quantity of data that is superficially consistent with their theory but does not provide a decisive test of it. Without stealing all of my own thunder, I can reveal that the genetic hypothesis has a number of serious scientific problems. Most pertinent are the following:

- Genetic cartographers who study genetic markers around the globe find that race distinctions of the African versus European versus Asian types are not supported by the evidence. There is only one human race (biologically speaking) that derives from Africa.[35]

- Study of the very different outcomes for Chinese-American immigrants from different subgroups and African-American immigrants from different sub-

13

groups clearly shows that children whose parents inculcate a high need for achievement have better outcomes regardless of ethnicity.[36]

- There are very rapid changes in ethnic group differences over time that are not susceptible to genetic explanation but can be interpreted as due to changes in the social environment. For example, black-white differences in academic aptitude, according to the National Assessment of Educational Progress, were halved over a twenty-year period, something that could not happen if the differences were genetically determined.[37]

My objective is not to challenge the genetic determinist account of ethnic group differences but rather to examine the role parents play in determining group differences in child outcomes. How much does the environment created by parents influence the development of intelligence, economic success, sexual behavior, altruism, responsibility, and happiness of children? My central theme is that low parental investment predisposes children to develop all kinds of social problems, whereas high parental investment turns children into happy, altruistic, and productive people.

The effects of low parental investment may manifest themselves early in the form of exploitative attitudes toward other children coupled with aggressive and undisciplined behavior. This may culminate in a lack of ambition, criminal behavior, and unrestricted sexual expression leading to unplanned pregnancy in the teenage years.[38] Needless to say, children who do not have the advantage of high parental investment are not in a position to be ideal parents themselves, which is an important reason that social problems tend to run in vicious generational cycles. The next chapter presents the other side of the coin by describing what parents do to raise happy, productive, and law-abiding children. That is, it describes high parental investment.

Chapter 2

Higher Parental Investment and Its Outcomes

"Where did I go wrong? My daughter is only seventeen years old. Last week, she moved out of the house and went to live with her boyfriend. Now she has stopped going to school. Bad as all this is, I can cope. What really scares me is that the boyfriend makes his living dealing drugs." Many of us know a parent with this kind of horror story to tell.

Some parents feel unlucky. Despite their best efforts, their teenagers turn out to be delinquent, do terribly in school, have scary friends, and acquire police records. Some blame TV, others blame the poor examples given by seedy political and religious leaders, and most of all they blame peer pressure that encourages teens to have sex and use illegal drugs. It is ironic that at a time in history when families have never been more child-centered, the challenges to raising children well should seem so great.

Such horror stories can be avoided, however. Parents need to begin early, long before TV and peer pressure have a major impact on their children's lives. The human brain goes through sensitive periods when some aspects of character, personality, and emotional relationships are easier to change. Some of these windows of opportunity occur astonishingly early in life when children are very much under the influence of parents and well before the influence of peers becomes important. This makes good sense from an evolutionary perspective because parents are generally the most reliable, and unselfish, source of information about the environment.

Early is important. Developmental psychologist Peter Kaplan has found that babies at two to six months old are extremely sensitive to the quality of their mother's voice. This helps to explain the elaborate modulation of speech tempo, pitch, and rhythm that is baby talk. When the mother suffers from depression, her voice is flatter, less interesting, and less stimulating to the infant brain. The more depressed the mother is, the less likely the baby is to pay attention to her voice and to associate it with other events in the environment. This may contribute to the later emergence of learning difficulties and emotional problems that are characteristic of the children of depressed mothers.[1] Consider the following windows of opportunity in brain development (ages approximate):

- Emotional security in close relationships: first year.
- Intelligence: first two years.
- Social skills: first three years.
- Language skills: first five years.
- Impulse control (e.g., resisting a temptation to eat attractive candy): ages six to eight years.
- Formation of peer groups: ages six to ten years.[2]

Children do not become closely involved with peers until around the age of three years when they begin to play together cooperatively.[3] Stable peer groups emerge between the ages of six and ten years, when children become interested in playing games, like cops and robbers, which involve assuming roles and conforming to rules established by the group. Parents often blame peer influence for the behavior problems of their adolescents, but this may be getting things backwards. Children who receive a lot of sensitive attention from their parents in the first ten years of life are far less likely either to be associated with problematic youngsters or to cave in to peer influences with which they disagree. Of course, responsible parents can also decide whom their child associates with, just as they can decide what kind of TV programs the child watches. Admittedly, enforcing such decisions can be much more difficult in some circumstances, for example, if the parent is poor and cannot send the child to a good school.

A warm emotional connection between children and both parents is the best clue that the parents have made good use of the windows of opportunity early in their children's life. Children who are fortunate in having this close relationship with their parents are said to be securely attached. Security of attachment is evident by the age of one year, and it provides the emotional tone for our whole lives.

SECURITY OF ATTACHMENT

When you peel an onion, you find that it is a series of ever-smaller globes with nothing of consequence at the center. When you do an analogous thought experiment of peeling back the layers of time and experience that make up the personality of an individual, you find that there are two central layers that affect everything that follows. The first is the individual's early temperament, which is genetically determined. The second, which is influenced by temperament, is the baby's security of attachment, and this refers to his or her relationship with the principal parental figures in his or her life.

While security of attachment describes the infant's confidence that the mother is there when needed, it also describes a global attitude towards other people that can be observed in adults. For example, there is a fundamental difference between the characters played by Stan Laurel and Oliver Hardy that had nothing to do with Hardy being obese and Laurel being skinny. Although a bumbling incompetent, Hardy was unshakeably confident in his own abilities and believed that he could overcome practical problems and persuade other people to do his bidding. He was emotionally secure. The sad-eyed Laurel was gloomy, anxious, and highly sensitive to the many punishments and failures he experienced at the hands of others, not least of which was the abuse he suffered at the hands of Hardy. Laurel was emotionally insecure. Interestingly, in the real world, their lives followed the characters. The emotionally secure Hardy went on to have an emotionally stable marriage. Laurel had marital difficulties and, following his screen career, succumbed to alcoholism. We now know that this fundamental emotional difference between individuals is not just a question of genetics but reflects the treatment that infants receive from their parents.

The concept of security of attachment was introduced by developmental psychologist John Bowlby. It was refined by his student Mary Ainsworth, who developed a procedure for measuring security of attachment in a laboratory setting. This procedure is known as the Strange Situation Test, wherein the reactions of an infant to temporary separation from, and reunion with, the mother are observed. This allows the relationship between child and mother to be categorized as one of three types: securely attached, insecurely avoidant, and insecurely ambivalent.[4]

In the Strange Situation Test, the mother places the baby on the floor in the middle of some toys and then goes to sit at the far side of the room. Meanwhile, a strange woman arrives, converses with the mother for one minute, then attempts to engage the baby in play with a toy. While this is happening, the mother leaves unobtrusively. Then she changes places with the stranger. The baby is left alone and the stranger returns. Finally, the mother comes back into the room. Babies who want to interact with the mother when she returns are classified as securely attached. They have learned that the mother is a reliable source of comfort when they are distressed and seek the trusted security of her arms. Insecurely attached infants resist interaction with the mother when she returns. They have learned that the mother is not a reliable source of comfort when they are distressed. The insecure avoidant type ignores the mother when she returns. This baby is as easily comforted by a stranger as by the mother. The insecure ambivalent type simultaneously looks for and resists physical contact with the mother, perhaps crying to be picked up and squirming angrily to be let down. This is like the impossible restaurant customer ordering the soup only to send it back again. About two-thirds of American infants are classified as securely attached. Of the insecurely attached group, about twice as many are of the avoidant subtype as of the ambivalent subtype.[5]

Why are some babies securely attached and others not? There is some fairly compelling evidence that the attachment style of the infant is related to the behavior of the mother. Researchers who have observed the behavior of mothers of securely attached infants have discovered some telling differences between their behavior and that of mothers of insecurely attached infants. As early as the first three months of life, mothers of securely attached infants are sensitive in responding to the infant's needs. For example, if the baby cries, they respond quickly. When they pick the infant up, they behave affectionately. They are sensitive to the baby's desires and preferences. For instance, they tend to begin and end feeding sessions in response to signals from the baby. They pay attention to the infant's food preferences and will not offer apple juice if the infant happens to prefer orange juice. In summary, the interactions with the mother are largely positive from the infant's perspective. The infant can also feel that it is communicating its needs and that these needs are being responded to by the mother.[6]

It is interesting that in many of the preindustrial societies studied by anthropologists, infants are constantly held in the mother's arms, even sleeping with her in the same bed, and are often nursed on demand. Such conditions ought to promote secure attachment. By contrast, in modern child-rearing, infants sleep alone and spend much of their time physically separated from the mother. It is a testament to the adaptability of human infants that they can thrive under these very different conditions and still be securely attached to the mother. What matters is the responsiveness of the mother rather than constant physical contact.

The behavior of the mother is not the whole story, however. What the mother does can be strongly affected by the temperament of the infant, and possibly by how physically appealing the infant is (based on the finding that abused infants are more likely to lack cuteness, despite the fact that mothers may perceive their own infants as more attractive than others do).[7] From the very earliest age, some children are much more challenging

18

to parents, but it is a challenge that can generally be overcome, judging from what we know about irritable infants.

Human infants can be very puzzling, and frustrating, to their parents. They are apparently helpless and vastly dependent on the goodwill of those who care for them. On the other hand, they come with one powerful mechanism for controlling adults in their vicinity, namely a loud, obnoxious wail. This can be used to good effect when the infant is hungry or uncomfortable for any reason. It provides parents with a clue that something is wrong, and they must then run through a mental checklist of routine maintenance activities to infer what the cause of the problem is likely to be. When all needs are ministered to and the infant still cries, it probably wants to be reassured that a comforting adult is nearby.

All of this is normal and describes a simple but powerful technique used by infants to obtain the best care from their parents. I once read a serious scientific paper that argued that the infant was exhausting the parents thereby preventing them from having sex and thus delaying the birth of the next child, which would be competing for parental investment. This may not be a high point of scientific inference, but it does describe a scenario with which many parents of infants can connect.

So far, the aversive crying of the baby can be seen as adaptive. Like a customer, it rings the bell and receives prompt service. What happens when the customer keeps ringing the bell? The irritable infant is one that cries often for no apparent reason and cannot be consoled. The parents are like frustrated waiters who keep running to the table only to find that the customer needs nothing. Their response is either to try to ignore the irritating customer or to avoid him as much as possible.

This scenario describes the irritable infant who cries a great deal without obvious reason. Such babies used to be referred to as "colicky" on the assumption that the source of their discomfort was chronic gastrointestinal upset. Modern thinking leans more to the view that irritable infants are that way for temperamental reasons. They are highly sensitive to all kinds of unpleasant events and are generally anxious and fearful.

It is exceptionally difficult for mothers to know how to deal with irritable infants. In particular, they cannot decipher when the infant has a genuine need and when they are merely being difficult. As a result, the kind of sensitive responsiveness that is typical of the relationship between securely attached infants and their care givers is more difficult to establish. Mothers find it so difficult to deal with irritable infants that there is a tendency to become disengaged, which can make the irritability worse.

Even in the case of these difficult children, maternal behavior can prevail over biology. Irritable infants can be securely attached if their mothers are sensitively responsive to their needs. Furthermore, we now know from an experiment conducted in Holland that their secure attachment is caused by the mother's actions.[8] In this experiment, poor mothers of irritable newborns were trained in sensitive responsiveness to their infants. The training was carried out when babies were between the ages of six and nine months and consisted of three sessions. Initially, most of the mothers tended to ignore their babies. Mothers were trained to detect, interpret, and respond appropriately to infant signals. For example, when the infant averted its gaze, a signal that it was overstimulated, mothers learned to stop talking to it. They also learned to interpret the infant's response to their actions.

As a result of this brief training, infants of the trained mothers were twice as likely to be securely attached at the age of one year (68 percent versus 28 percent) as infants of the mothers who received no training. Security of attachment is clearly caused by what the mother does. When mothers are trained to be more sensitive to the needs of their infants, the relationship improves, which suggests a very economical intervention for reducing social and emotional problems by heading them off early in life.

Security of attachment is also affected by parental behavior in the real world outside the laboratory. Abused infants are much more likely to be insecurely attached to their mothers, for example. According to one review of many different studies with a total sample size of 829, only 28 percent of infants from all types of abusive and neglecting homes were securely attached compared to 69 percent of the normal control groups.[9] Given the poor quality of the relationship between abused infants and their mothers, it is no surprise to discover that such children grow up to be poor parents. A substantial proportion of abused children grow up to be abusive parents themselves. Estimates range from 25 percent to 35 percent, depending on how severe the abuse has to be before it is classified as such.[10] This suggests that the emotional foundations of parental behavior are laid very early in life.

Security of attachment is not just important for the welfare of infants but extends into many facets of adult life. Infants who are securely attached to their mothers grow up to be secure in their adult relationships. Security of attachment manifests itself in adult life as being comfortable with intimate relationships of love and friendship. Women who are classified as insecurely attached are likely to have trouble in maintaining long-term romantic attachments. They tend to have many different sexual partners and are more likely to have babies as teens. Insecurely attached men lack confidence and have difficulty in forming romantic relationships. Security of attachment has similar effects on same-sex friendships. Insecurely attached adults have conflictual friendships that do not last very long.[11, 12, 13]

The central role of early attachment to parents in respect to the ability to solve life's problems has recently begun to emerge from research in education, developmental psychology, social psychology, and psychopathology. According to Bowlby's original formulation, when a child is securely attached, she uses the mother as a safe haven from which she can venture out to explore her environment.[14] Anyone who has ever observed an infant monkey using contact with the mother as a source of security when it encounters something new or frightening will appreciate the intuitive appeal of this notion. It is as though the infant were attached to the mother by invisible elastic, venturing forth to explore, becoming spooked, and rebounding to the comforting zone of physical contact with the mother. Human toddlers also run excitedly away from the mother only to rush back to her arms in an endless yo-yo of courage and fear.

Researchers have focused on the consequences of secure attachment with the mother for social and cognitive development in childhood and later. Of course, children may also be securely attached to other adults, particularly the father. Children may be securely attached to their teachers, and this relationship apparently has similar consequences for social development as that with the mother[15] and may serve a protective function in the case of children who are insecurely attached to their mothers. The implications of attachment security for social development are rather clear and quite profound.

Researchers have typically measured security of attachment to the mother at the age range of twelve months to eighteen months and observed the interactions of the children six to eighteen months later. They have found that children who were securely attached as babies:

- obey their mothers more;
- cooperate more with female strangers;
- solve problems better at the age of two years;
- exhibit more complex and creative play;
- are more attractive to peers as playmates;
- are more likely to initiate play activities;
- are more sensitive to the needs and feelings of other children; and
- are good at negotiating fair settlements of disputes with friends without resorting to the use of coercion and force.

It is therefore no surprise to learn that they are much more popular with peers.[16]

While theorists from Erik Erikson to John Bowlby explain these effects of attachment security in different ways, all agree that the "model citizen" attributes seen in securely attached infants can be interpreted as due to a generalization of the relationship with mothers and other attachment figures to future social relationships. If the mother is sensitive to the child's needs, the child learns that people can be trusted. By the same token, if the child learns that it can elicit attention, nurturance, and support from its mother, it develops an expectation of good consequences from other social interactions, which might explain why securely attached infants are generally more outgoing in their dealings with peers.

Even though a child's security of attachment with the mother may change over time—for instance, if the mother is ill or if another child is born, particularly if the first is younger than two years old[17]—children who are identified as securely attached at the age of three tend also to be securely attached at the age of six. The problem behavior seen in insecurely attached three-year-olds is also observed in the same children at the age of six. By coloring all of the early social interactions of children, attachment security sets the stage for adult relationships. It also plays an important role in the moral development of children.

FROM ATTACHMENT TO SOCIALIZATION

Socialization starts out with the relationship of warmth and trust that exists between parents and securely attached infants. It culminates, after many conflicts and vicissitudes, in the emergence of a young adult who conforms to many of the core values and expected behaviors of the society in which he or she lives. This socialization process is a kind of persuasion in which children learn to do what is expected of them rather than what their impulses are telling them to do. High-investing parents strive for internalization of rules in which a child not only behaves in expected ways but does so because he or she wants to.

We live in an era in which many of the most important techniques of child training get brushed aside in the interests of a well-meaning but flawed liberalism. The baby boom generation in the United States has reacted against the authoritarianism that reigned for many of them in their parental homes in the 1950s and has moved to an opposite extreme of permissiveness. While allowing a child to do what it pleases may seem to be prochild, researchers who study different parenting styles have discovered that the outcomes of permissiveness are very much like the outcomes of parental neglect. Permissive parents produce children who tend to be self-centered and to have difficulty controlling their antisocial impulses and fitting in with the needs of a social group.[18]

Most children have little initial interest in picking up their toys after they have played with them and would never dream of making their own beds. If they are to obey such rules, two approaches are possible. Parents may either use the velvet glove or the iron fist. The iron fist approach is based on the concept of military discipline. In military training, everyone makes his own bed and polishes his own buttons because if he does not dire consequences are promised. Authoritarian discipline certainly works, but running one's home like a boot camp has problems. The most obvious is the emotional cost. While children obey authoritarian parents, they also tend to hate and fear them and to avoid their company as much as possible. Home life tends to be anxious and conflict-ridden—not a great deal of fun.

Perhaps the most important problem of military-style parenting is that it does not promote individuality. Just because children happen to obey rules does not mean that they like them, that they identify with them, or that they are deeply internalized. The test is how children of authoritarian parents behave when away from home. The moral effect of rigid external authority is like the effect of a plaster cast on muscles. Deprived of their authoritarian environment, the children are in a similarly vulnerable situation to the leg from which the rigid exoskeleton has been removed, revealing the atrophy and weakness of the muscle. They lack real moral fiber and have difficulty controlling their impulses.

Strong external authority may produce highly disciplined behavior, but it does so only in the presence of authority figures. Who could be more disciplined than a soldier? Yet, the presence of military personnel in towns throughout the ages has usually brought problems of alcoholism and prostitution, vices associated with weak control of impulses. Alcoholism is such a common problem among military personnel in the United States that many alcoholism researchers rely on Veterans Administration hospitals to acquire research subjects. The U.S. Army has recently acknowledged that spousal battery is a major problem for married personnel living in military housing. One study of ninety-four military families found that more than half (fifty-four) had problems of domestic violence.[19] It seems odd that men who are so disciplined in all of their actions on the parade ground should be so lacking in self-discipline in the company of their wives. External sources of discipline do not establish self-control and may actually weaken it.

High-investing parents strive for internalization of rules rather than obedience to authority. How is this done? One useful clue is provided by experiments of social psychologists in which children were forbidden from playing with an attractive toy. The investigators were interested in whether a mild prohibition or a forceful threat would have a greater effect in preventing the child from playing with the forbidden toy once the child believed itself to be alone. Children either were told that it was not a good idea to play with the toy or were threatened with punishment of losing tokens that could be cashed in for toys or candy. Interestingly, the mild request proved more effective at combating temptation. When a child controls its impulses without a strong external threat, it internalizes the prohibition, that is, it develops a belief that the attractive toy ought not to be played with. On the other hand, when strong sanctions are applied, the child will refrain from playing with the toy. However, when the experimenter leaves the room, the child has no reason to believe that the sanctions will be applied. In the absence of the threatened punishment, there is no good reason not to play with the toy, so the child succumbs to temptation. This elegant experiment reveals the more general principle that has been observed in the everyday world: that authoritarianism does not promote moral maturity any more than a leg can develop muscle strength when it is confined in a cast.[20]

Scholars working in the field of moral development have often used such "delay-of-gratification" experiments to study the development of impulse control in young children. In one such study children of different ages were told not to touch an attractive toy telephone. At eighteen months, children waited an average of only ten seconds before succumbing to temptation and playing with the toy. By the age of twenty-four months, they were much more successful at controlling their impulses, waiting an average of seventy seconds before giving in.[21] It is interesting that all of the children did give in, showing that at this age true impulse control is not possible.

There is some evidence that the glimmerings of self-control that emerge at around the age of two years are related to language development because children who had the most advanced language skills also delayed gratification the longest. Whereas younger children have difficulty in distracting themselves from thinking about an attractive, but forbidden, object, by the age of six to eight years, children can use deliberate distractions to help them overcome temptations. If presented with a piece of candy that they must refrain from eating in order to receive a whole bag of candy later, for example, they may put the candy out of view, or even cover their eyes, because they know that this will help them to resist the temptation. Older children of eleven to twelve years old may resort to more elaborate strategies using abstract ideas. For instance, they might resist temptation by making the candy unattractive, for example, by saying to themselves that it is made of artificial ingredients and tastes like toothpaste.[22]

The ability to control oneself, which is assessed in these laboratory tests, is considered by most developmental psychologists to be an important hurdle for two reasons. The first is that once this skill is mastered it is unlikely to be lost. Children who are good at self-control grow up to be morally mature adults. The second reason that early self-control is important is that, in general, children who can control their impulses are more likely to be intelligent, self-confident, happy, and socially skilled as adolescents. They also grow up to be occupationally successful.[23]

The development of self-control and the ability to internalize social rules of acceptable conduct are greatly influenced by the relationship of a child with its parents. Children who enjoy warm emotional relationships with their parents are better at learning to control their impulses. This is because their moral fiber has been strengthened by a sense of autonomy and responsibility. Parents also play a direct role in strengthening impulse control when they praise a child for not eating candy before dinner or not retaliating when provoked by a sibling. Researchers have found that when parents praise a young child (ages five and a half to nine and a half years) for being "patient" the child holds out longer in delay-of-gratification experiments.[24]

The velvet glove approach of highly involved parents strengthens moral fiber.

THE CHALLENGE FROM JUDITH HARRIS

In a recent best-selling book, Judith Rich Harris sets out to systematically devalue the role of parents in child development.[25] (She argues that peers are a much more important influence in social development.) In order to denigrate the role of mothers, Harris does not deny that how children are treated by their mothers produces a real difference in security of attachment. Instead she goes against the mainstream in developmental psychology by arguing that security of attachment has no important effect on the tone of a child's future relationships with other people apart from the mother.

What Harris has is a sincerely held opinion and a clever argument; what she lacks is supporting evidence. She begins with the argument that if Cinderella thought everyone was like her stepmother, she would never have gone to the ball. Actually, there is a very good adaptive reason to think that her future husband would be more like the stepmother than Prince Charming. The amount of sensitivity children experience from their mothers, and other people, during childhood is a good prediction of the degree of kindness and civility to be expected later in life. For children raised in extreme poverty, life is not a fairy tale. Everything about being poor tends to undermine parental investment, and it strikes right at the heart of the relationship with the mother by undermining secure attachment. An abusive mother is generally a good predictor of a stressful social environment in which an ideal marriage is unlikely.

Harris goes from a fairy tale to the evidence on monkeys. Harry Harlow conducted some astonishingly cruel experiments in which monkeys were raised apart from their mothers. The result was a complete deterioration of normal social behavior and the development of a syndrome that superficially resembles autism in human children (but is actually very different). The monkeys seem excessively fearful and often rock back and forth repetitively. They respond aggressively to social advances. Males are incapable of normal sexual behavior, and females cannot care for their infants. Harris leans heavily on the finding that some aspects of their social behavior improve when they are raised in peer groups. The finding that monkeys can scrape by without adult parental figures may be of limited relevance to the human species.

The sensitivity of such experiments can also be questioned. Just because the monkeys look normal to us, it does not mean that they could succeed in the difficult social competition faced by monkeys in the wild. Any problems might not be obvious in captivity or could be missed by the researchers because they did not know what to look for. Instructive here is the work on split brains, in which the two hemispheres of the brain were surgically separated. When this was done, human researchers could not find any difference between split-brain and normal monkeys. Amusingly, the *monkeys* could tell the difference. They preferred to interact with the split-brain individuals. We have no idea why.[26]

Since humans are not monkeys, Harris felt it necessary to use a sketchy anecdote retailed by Anna Freud (Sigmund's daughter) about six Holocaust children who were rescued from a concentration camp at the end of the war. At this time, the children, three boys and three girls, were between the ages of three and four. They were believed to have lost contact with their parents soon after birth and to have been raised by a succession of adults, all of whom perished. After the war, the children were brought to a nursery in England where they were studied by Anna Freud. She noted that while the children were extremely destructive of toys and very aggressive in their interactions with nursery staff, they were much more considerate towards each other, being willing, for example, to share food. It is hardly surprising that children raised in a concentration camp should have formed the impression that their custodians would be mean and threatening. Neither is it too surprising that they should have developed a culture of mutual aid. This is something that they could easily have acquired from their doomed "foster parents."

A far more telling kind of natural experiment is the situation of children raised in orphanages. In the past, these institutions discouraged nurturant relationships between occupants and staff both as a matter of policy and as a matter of economics since there were often thirty children for each staff member. When children are raised from birth in orphanages, they experience a variety of cognitive and emotional problems that are discussed in detail in the next chapter. The fact that these children were not "saved" by their relationships with peers constitutes a serious hole in Harris's argument, which is not mended by her claim that orphanages discourage the formation of friendships. Children who enter the orphanage at the age of four years have far less serious problems. This cannot be attributable to peer influences, which are much less important for preschoolers. What it is due to is the fact that they have had an opportunity to develop close relationships with parents or other adults during the crucial early years when the patterns of social relationships are being laid down in the brain.[27]

The relationship with the mother is not the only important relationship in a child's life, but it casts a rather long shadow. For instance, college students who recall secure attachment relationships in childhood are perceived by peers as less anxious and less hostile. They also experience lower levels of loneliness and personal distress in their daily lives. Furthermore, young adults who report insecure early attachments with their mothers form romantic relationships that have a similar quality.[28]

The sense of security and commitment that people have in relation to intimate others spills over into their attitudes towards study and work. Securely attached adults (identified by a reliable questionnaire) are committed to their professional goals leading to hard work and achievement.[29] These are two different facets of the mind set of people who are committed to high parental investment by establishing stable marital relationships and working hard at careers to establish the economic basis for a stable home. The American Dream, which revolves around contributing to the future of one's children, unites the economic and social aspects of high parental investment.

Generalizing from the research findings, criminologists and students of psychopathology have begun to speculate that since children who are insecurely attached have less self-control, do more poorly at school, are more aggressive, and are less altruistic, they would therefore be at greater risk for delinquency and involvement in serious criminal activities. Insecurely attached infants are less likely to go on to attain a high level of educational and occupational success. Since their intimate relationships are more likely to be exploitative and conflictual, they are less likely to develop satisfactory stable friendships or marriages. All of this suggests that they should be more likely to experience psychological stress in their lives leading to increased risk of anxiety and depression and other psychological problems and the decline in bodily health that goes along with this.

We know from the strongest kind of evidence, produced in an experiment on Dutch mothers, that sensitive maternal behavior produces securely attached infants. This provides a pattern for subsequent social relationships that tend to be of the "good citizen" variety. Not only are securely attached children more likely to be productive, outgoing members of their communities, but they also tend to be happier individuals, to have more favorable intimate relationships, and to be less vulnerable to psychiatric illness. While these conclusions are a logical extension of what we already know, most of the research connecting security of attachment of infants to adult outcomes has not been done because the necessary longitudinal studies extending from infancy to adulthood are extremely expensive to conduct and involve a tremendous commitment on the part of individual researchers.

The next chapter turns to a more detailed examination of the consequences of diminished parental investment so far as adult outcomes are concerned. This ranges from the mild effects of having siblings who compete for parental investment to the more profound consequences of being raised in an orphanage or by abusive parents.

Chapter 3

Lower Parental Investment and Social Problems

Parental investment can be reduced in many ways, such as by the birth of a sibling, the declining economic fortunes of parents, or parental divorce. It can also be reduced in more drastic ways, such as by extreme parental neglect and abuse or by being raised in an institution. Even minor reductions in parental investment can affect how children turn out as adults. Extreme neglect in early life can have devastating consequences because windows of opportunity for learning basic skills of social interaction are passed.

Parental investment varies along a broad continuum. If we are to assess how parenting affects the behavioral development of children, it is useful to consider how infants might turn out if completely deprived of all contact with their parents and other human beings. Even though such extreme deprivation may seem irrelevant to understanding the effects of abuse and neglect of a more ordinary kind, striking similarities can be found between the extreme case of feral children and that of children who are subjected to harsh and insensitive parenting. For example, the abnormality of sensory perception in the case of feral children has also been observed in the case of children raised in orphanages whose bodily needs were scrupulously satisfied but whose social needs were largely ignored. Interest in these problems was recently sparked by the adoption of Romanian children from very bad orphanages by American and Canadian familes. The problems of institutional children suggest that a lack of parental stimulation early in life interferes with normal brain development.

Abandonment of babies soon after birth has always been a fact of human existence. In some preindustrial societies, such as the Yanomamo of South America, when a mother produces twins, she abandons one, allowing it to die. The same extreme and brutal neglect is practiced in our own society, although it is thankfully rare. From time to time, one reads news stories of young mothers who leave their newborns in garbage dumpsters. A particularly wrenching recent example was the young mother who both gave birth and allegedly killed her infant in the bathroom at her high school prom.

In subsistence societies, abandoned infants have been known to survive in the wild. Difficult as this may be to believe, there are now more than fifty well-documented cases of such infants. It is interesting to tell their story because of the light it sheds not just on the devastating effects of parental neglect in early life but also on what can be accomplished by efforts at rehabilitation. Where rehabilitation fails, there are often irreversible effects of early parental deprivation.

When children survive alone in the wild, it is usually because they are nurtured by animals. A strange variety of animals have raised human infants. Host species have ranged from wolves, bears, and leopards to sheep, pigs, and gazelles to baboons and apes.[1] All of these feral children are completely nonverbal when discovered and most never manage to learn more than a few words, even when they have the benefit of sympathetic teachers. This implies that there is a sensitive period in early life during which children must be exposed to language if they are ever to communicate normally. Language is just a specific example of the general principle that stimulation by parents affects how the brain develops.

IS EARLY SOCIAL STIMULATION NECESSARY FOR SPEECH? THE GENIE STORY

The story of Genie, a social isolate in our own society, is often held up as an example of someone who managed to develop language in later life despite early social deprivation. Her case is worth discussing in some detail since it appears to challenge the notion that parental stimulation is necessary for normal development of the brain structures responsible for language. If this notion were true, then the important role of parents in early brain development could be called into question.

Genie spent twelve years of her childhood confined in a closet in Temple City in the San Gabriel Valley of California. Her listlessness and inability to walk at a normal age convinced her father that she was profoundly mentally retarded. When she was twenty months old, he decided to isolate her. It is important to remember that she did have relatively normal contact with her mother during the first twenty months when many critical events occur in relation to brain development, including the establishment of neural circuits for language.

The unfortunate child was confined in a tiny room, and her only contact was with her blind mother who hurriedly fed her a diet of cereal and baby food for the twelve years of her confinement, which ended in 1970 when the police removed her from her abusive home. She was kept harnessed to an infant's potty seat during the day. At night, she slept in a crib that was enclosed with wire mesh, confined in a tight sleeping bag, specially made by her father, that restricted her movements. There is controversy over whether her parents, or her older brother, ever spoke to her. Genie was punished for making noise because this annoyed her father. The claim that no one spoke to her was made by linguist Susan Curtiss, who published her doctoral dissertation on the abused child.[2] It was contradicted by Genie's mother.[3]

Curtiss evidently wished to see Genie as a wild child and actually calls her this in the title of her book. Referring to Genie as a wild child is misleading in several ways. First, she was held captive in a family home, rather than living in the wild. Second, even though she was given minimal exposure to other people, she was not entirely cut off from human society. According to her mother, she could hear neighbors come and go, and her love of classical music following liberation is attributable to having heard her neighbor receive classical music lessons on the piano. The view that she had some exposure to language is supported by the fact that when she was discovered, she could understand some twenty words, even though she could only pronounce around four: "stopit," "nomore," and a couple of shorter negatives. The "nomore" and "stopit" seem to have been addressed to herself, rather than to her abusive father.

Unlike most socially isolated children, Genie succeeded in learning to speak. She can express her needs and feelings and can understand much of what other people say to her. There are some interesting confusions, however. Genie has trouble in distinguishing between the meanings of sentences such as, "The boy hit the ball" and "The ball hit the boy." These object-agent relationships are mastered by normal children at around the age of two years. Genie's ability to learn (or relearn?) speech after she was liberated at the age of thirteen years is probably due to the fact that her brain had received sufficient verbal stimulation in the first twenty months. People who are socially isolated as adults, such as Alexander Selkirk, the real-life sailor who was the model for Daniel Defoe's novel *Robinson Crusoe*, may find that they begin to lose their ability to speak after a few years. Just because Genie could not speak when she was discovered does not mean that she never spoke. Her case history highlights the critical importance of early stimulation for normal brain development because she was not deprived of stimulation in early life.

It is suggestive that she is very good at language skills that are characteristic of children in the second year of life, which she was when she was confined—that is, learning new words and speaking simple sentences. She is not as good at the fine points of grammar, which children normally master in their own mysterious way between the ages of one and five. During this time, the child acts like a natural grammarian, imposing rules on what he or she says. We know this because the child makes some amusing errors that he or she refuses to correct. A three-year-old might say "The mouses wented away." These errors are referred to as "overgeneralization" because the child is overusing general rules of language. After he or she has mastered the general principles, a child learns the exceptions and so corrects his or her own mistakes. Even though children's brains have an inbuilt capacity to handle grammar, this can only occur if they have an opportunity to hear people speaking.

In Genie's case, it appears that she was deprived of language stimulation during the window of opportunity when the brain of a child naturally constructs its own grammar. For this reason, she will always have trouble with grammatical niceties that most normal two-year-olds have mastered.[4]

WORST-CASE SCENARIOS: FERAL CHILDREN

Feral children are a fascinating, although imperfect, natural experiment of how children would turn out if denied all social contact. They represent the lowest point of parental investment at which survival is still possible. They are an imperfect experiment because we have no way of knowing how the same children would turn out if they were raised in normal homes. Thus, it is possible that the infants were abandoned because they appeared abnormal, perhaps due to mental retardation or because they were sickly. Some of the accounts of true feral children make for harrowing reading because they remind us that much of what we think of as distinctively human is a product of unique nurturant experiences acting on our unique biology. When the necessary nurturant experiences get subtracted from the equation, children are no longer human in anything but a biological sense.

Genie's case history is unusual in the degree of neglect and abuse she suffered. This was so extreme that it undermined basic aspects of socialization, such as learning to speak. When this degree of social deprivation is experienced by children living alone in the outdoors, completely cut off from human contact, they are referred to as feral children or wild children, as in the case of Victor, the wild child of Aveyron. Victor was taken in by Jean Itard, a sympathetic young doctor who attempted to educate him. Itard's experiences are described in a book he wrote that formed the basis for an accurate movie portrayal of Victor, *L'Enfant Sauvage* (*The Wild Child*) by French art film director François Truffaut. Detailed case histories going back as far as the fourteenth century (the Hesse wolfchild) describe at least fifty such socially isolated children.[5]

Victor was a true wild child in the sense that he had little hope of ever being "civilized" to the extent of playing a normal role in society. For example, he had great difficulty with speech and succeeded in mastering only a few words. Children who have spent all of their first five years without human companionship may not speak at all.

From this perspective, it is clear that Genie does not qualify as a wild child, not just because she was kept in a small room rather than in a forest, but because she did have some human contact, however abusive, and because her early life was lived with a relatively normal level of social stimulation. In most of the critical circumstances, her life story is mirrored by that of Kaspar Hauser of Nuremberg.[6]

Hauser was apparently of royal blood and the victim of a struggle for succession to the throne. Abducted from his home at an early age, Hauser spent his childhood locked up in a dark stable. His food was delivered in a bowl slid beneath the door. Occasionally, he experienced a man standing behind him, inscribing letters on a board in front of him, apparently with the intention of teaching him to write. After he had been liberated, Hauser would spend days repeatedly writing his name or laboriously copying engravings from a book. Before releasing him, his captor, a game keeper named Frans Richter, evidently gave Hauser a crash course in motor skills from walking to talking to writing his name. The youth was abandoned in the streets of Nuremberg on May 26, 1828.

He was discovered tottering along Nuremberg's Unschlittplatz by a town resident who was resting in a chair outside his house around five o'clock in the afternoon. Dressed in a strange mixture of finery and old clothes, Hauser's pockets contained a tiny handkerchief on which his initials were embroidered. They also contained a rosary, some scribbled Catholic prayers, and a small package of gold dust. He carried a letter addressed to the local cavalry commander. The letter stated that Hauser wished to serve his king, but it was immediately apparent to the soldiers that he was not suitable for military service. They allowed him to sleep for one night on straw in the stables before depositing him in the police station. Hauser took up residence in a cell normally used for vagrants and became the object of local curiosity.

Although sixteen years old, Kaspar Hauser had the mind of a five-year-old and sometimes played with the local children. He cried often and seemed afraid of anything and everything. He had idiosyncratic likes and dislikes. When he saw a white horse, he would burst into delighted laughter, but he was terrified of black ones. During military parades, he was attracted to the bass drum, but the sound of music in the distance terrified him.

Hauser had very little language ability. It is true that he could utter a few words and had rote-learned a whole sentence in local dialect: "I want to be a soldier like my father." Otherwise, he had the same kind of grammatical problems experienced by Genie. His speech consisted mainly of a jumble of words and phrases without much appreciation for the basic rules of grammar.

In addition to his language problems, the social isolate had a number of strange cognitive deficits. He was insensitive to some sounds, such as the ticking of a watch and the tolling of a bell. His depth perception was very poor. He was extremely light sensitive. He had difficulty recognizing himself in a mirror and persisted in looking behind the reflective surface to see who was there. He confused his dreams with reality. All of these oddities suggest that sensory deprivation in early life permanently interferes with the ability of the brain to interpret sensory information.

True feral children are those who have been abandoned soon after birth and have survived in the wild, usually when they were adopted by another mammal species. Presumably, the foster mother responded to their cute infantile appearance, a propensity which is seen in many vertebrate species. Maternal behaviors are triggered by the rounded heads and flattened features of the young, as Austrian ethologist Konrad Lorenz first pointed out. While it may be difficult to believe that human children could possibly survive under these conditions, from a biological standpoint we are a lot tougher and more adaptable than most people realize. There are so many well-documented examples that it is unreasonable to deny that this occurs.

One of the most graphic and shocking accounts of feral children is the story, from India, of two children who were captured in a den with two wolf cubs in 1920. The two girls, Amala, about one and a half years old, and Kamala, about eight, were taken by the Reverend Singh to an orphanage he ran in Midnapore with his wife. Singh made a detailed record of their behavior and recorded their psychological development.[7]

What is so shocking about Amala and Kamala is that there was nothing recognizably human about their movements or demeanor. Everything they did was wolflike. They:

- walked on all fours;
- were nocturnal, coming to life at night and lounging around during the day;
- were light shy, seeking shade during the day;
- howled like wolves;
- slept for only four hours each day;
- lapped up liquids and ate in a crouching position;
- refused to eat anything except meat;
- panted, and protruded their tongues;
- snarled at people; and
- arched their backs menacingly when approached and turned their heads quickly from side to side to express vigilance.

In addition to these canine behaviors, which were presumably acquired by the practical requirements of life in a wolf pack, as well as by imitating their companions, the wolf children also had some unusual bodily adaptations. The skin on their hands, knees, and elbows was thickly calloused as a result of walking on all fours. Their lips were unusually thick and red, which reflected the fact that they ate using their mouths, rather than their hands, to secure food.

Since Amala, the younger child, died almost a year after being dug out of the wolves' den, her story, although it speaks volumes about the great behavioral and psychological flexibility of human children, tells us little about the equally interesting question of rehabilitation. Fortunately, Kamala survived for about nine years in the orphanage. Singh's journal provides a detailed record of the process by which her movements slowly became more human. After ten months, she was able to reach out her hand to take food. After fifteen months, she learned to kneel with her back straightened, and she quickly acquired the ability to walk on her knees. After eighteen months, she first pulled herself upright using a bench. A year passed before she could stand unaided. It was more than five years before she learned to walk, albeit with an unusual gait. The length of time necessary for learning to walk upright reflects the fact that the normal developmental window of opportunity for learning to walk, at around the age of eleven to twelve months in healthy children, had been passed.

Learning to speak was equally torturous. After three years of human companionship, she could speak only four words ("Mama," "yes," "no," and an expression signifying hunger or thirst). At the end of her life, following nine years of language experience, her vocabulary consisted of only around fifty words, which would be considered a mediocre performance for a normal two-year-old child. Kamala's slow progress in language learning is not indicative of low intelligence. When she is compared with other feral children, many of whom could not master any words, the opposite conclusion can be reached. She had simply not had language experience early enough in life when the brain is busily engaged in decoding sounds and constructing language.

Even though Kamala's motor and language development were much slower than those of a younger child, her social development was surprisingly good. This suggests either that she had not been abandoned at birth or that her attachment to the wolf mother had amounted to a satisfactory surrogate. While we may never have the answers to this and other questions about the origins of the children (including the extreme improbability of two children of such divergent ages winding up in the same wolf den), we do know that Kamala was devoted to her companion, Amala. When Amala died of nephritis, a kidney disease, Kamala cried for the first time. After the body had been removed, she refused to eat or drink for two days and sat crouched in a corner for a week. When she recovered from this depression, she continued to sniff around the house for her companion's scent for four days.

After her initial mistrust of human beings had been broken down, Kamala developed a strong attachment to Mrs. Singh and quickly became integrated into the daily life of the orphanage, performing chores such as collecting the eggs and watching the younger children. The first sign of taming was when Kamala would accept biscuits from the hand of Mrs. Singh. She then permitted Mrs. Singh to massage the muscles of her arms and legs in order to loosen up the joints and allow more normal posture and movement. Kamala soon developed a deep attachment to her new foster mother, getting upset when Mrs. Singh was away and greeting her with great joy when she returned.

Once the ice had been broken in this way, she became interested in other children of the orphanage and would play with them. She was affected by praise and tailored her activities to fit in with social expectations. For example, she never left the orphanage without first putting her dress on.

The story of Kamala has been of great interest to those who attempt to understand the vexed and complex question of human nature. It shows that unusual levels of neglect and deprivation can put a major dent in human potential. It also shows that many of the effects of early deprivation, however extreme, can be partially ameliorated by a sensitive, nurturing environment. Just how successful the rehabilitation can be depends not only on how skillful, loving, and determined the foster parent is, but on the raw material he or she has to work with. In other words, it is affected by brain development that is particularly sensitive to parental investment in the early years of life.

For example, it can be concluded that the speech difficulty of feral children is due to the fact that they do not hear language sounds early in life when the brain is most receptive to them. This point is underscored by the history of Victor of Aveyron who never learned to speak but nevertheless mastered written language under Itard's enlightened tutelage. He was not held back by lack of intelligence but by a brain that had not acquired sensitivity to the minor differences in speech sounds in the first year of life.

While accounts of feral children make fascinating reading, they usually do not allow us to draw reliable conclusions both because we cannot tell how the children would have turned out in a normal environment and because we do not know the circumstances of their earliest experiences, parentage, and abandonment. For this reason, it is better to examine the consequences of institutionalization to understand how children fare when they receive reduced parental investment compared to that available in most family homes.

CHILDREN IN ORPHANAGES

The vital role of parents in the normal psychological development of children is nowhere more clearly seen than in the case of infants raised in orphanages. Orphanages used to be run on the principle that young children have bodily needs but no social needs. Orphans usually received good nutrition and adequate bodily care but almost no social stimulation. In many cases the children suffered extreme social deprivation in the interests of maintaining a disease-free environment. In one institution, the site of a classic 1950s study by pediatricians Sally Provence and Rose Lipton, babies were kept in separate cubicles for the first eight months in order to reduce the risk of spreading infectious disease.[8] Their only opportunity for social contact of any kind came when they were fed or diapered. Feeding took place in the cribs by means of a propped-up bottle, after the style of water bottles for caged animals. The overworked attendant could not respond to an infant if it cried. There was virtually no opportunity for social interaction, and the infants received no verbal stimulation, were not held, and were not played with.

This particular institution (the identity of which was not revealed by the researchers) unwittingly created a real-world analogy with the maternal deprivation studies that Harry Harlow was about to conduct on monkeys.[9] For the first eight months, the infants were maintained like laboratory animals, kept in solitary confinement, adequately nourished, and protected from disease. The wider implications of institutional rearing practices were not lost on Provence and Lipton, who compared the psychological development of the orphans with a control group of children raised in ordinary homes.

During the first three or four months, no differences were seen. Thereafter, the institutionalized children showed devastating symptoms of maternal deprivation. The appalling consequences of social deprivation for infants are illustrated by a comparison between Teddy, an institutionalized infant, and Larry, a family-reared boy. Teddy was selected for detailed study because he showed the least severe developmental problems of all the institutionalized infants in the first year.

Why Teddy did so well in the first six months is something of a puzzle. The researchers feel that his early feeding problems offer a key. He would frequently lose contact with the nipple of the feeding bottle. When this happened, he would cry loudly. As a result, he tended to get more attention from the attendants than the other children did.

Teddy was a healthy infant who scored above average on one of two measures of behavioral development used—120 on the Viennese scale. He maintained this score, equivalent to that of Larry, the family-raised boy, up to the age of six months, the same age at which most of the other institutionalized children were showing marked developmental problems.

Thereafter, the scores of Larry march horizontally across the page, whereas those of Teddy show a steady decline. At the age of eighteen months, he was scoring around 65 on the scale compared to Larry's 125.

Verbal descriptions of the institutionalized infants at the age of one year, before the steepest decline for Teddy, are even more disheartening. The institutionalized infants:

- rarely turned to an adult for pleasure, comfort, or help;
- showed no signs of attachment to the attendants;
- could not speak any words;
- could not walk;
- had little interest in playing with toys;
- paid little attention, even to their own bodies;
- were apathetic and solemn, neither taking initiative to seek pleasure or avoid discomfort; and
- rocked excessively like autistic children and socially isolated monkeys.

The researchers also studied some of the children after they had been adopted out of the orphanage into families. Most showed quite dramatic improvements after they had received good maternal care and a stimulating family environment. Despite these improvements, they had lingering cognitive and social problems. These included difficulty in solving test problems and in learning. They had difficulty in forming close relationships and were reluctant to ask others for help. Their play was simplified and lacked evidence of the normal richness of a child's imagination. While their rehabilitation was remarkable, it was not complete. Evidently, windows of opportunity were passed in respect to brain development of intelligence and sociability because of the social and environmental deprivation of their first year.

Even though the recovery of the adopted children was not perfect, it is nevertheless of great importance because it demonstrated that there was nothing seriously wrong with the children to begin with. Interaction with the mother, even in the first year of life, is thus of critical importance in becoming an intelligent, sociable human being. Children who are deprived of such interaction quickly learn to be passive. There is a rapid loss of intelligence and sociability, which can be partially but not completely remediated in the second year of life, indicating a permanent loss of brain function. Children who are not intellectually stimulated by care givers quickly lose interest in their environment and even in themselves. There can be no more compelling evidence that children need their parents just as much as crops need rain.

My wife tells the story of elementary school children in a poor neighborhood in Birmingham, Alabama, who used to hang out in the local public library, to the great despair of the librarians, as they passed the dead time between the end of school and being picked up by their parents a few hours later. These kids drifted around the reading room in an uneasy mob, bored and unable to read or keep quiet. When my wife began reading to our son, she immediately acquired an audience of much older children who craved the attention of an adult. The children were so aggressive in their interruptions that my wife reluctantly stopped using the library. The combination of visible unhappiness and aggressively honing in on the attention of adults is also common among children who have lost ready access to a parent following parental separation. Children are designed by natural selection not only to need and want high levels of parental attention but to compete aggressively with other children, including siblings, to obtain it.

Studies of children living in group homes show clearly that peers are not a sufficient substitute for parental attention, as Judith Harris has claimed (see Chapter 2). Michael Rutter found in his study of Greek children in long-term residential care that these children are more demanding of teacher attention and more disruptive of classroom activities than children raised in two-parent homes. One might imagine that their social needs would get redirected to other children, but the opposite happened. The institutionalized children had problems interacting with other children that they did not know and, on the playground, mainly confined themselves to other children from the group home. Even their relationships with peers proved unsatisfactory. The institutionalized children did not trust each other very much. They fought often. They had much more difficulty confiding in each other than children raised in families.[10]

Children who are deprived of maternal attachment are far more difficult to socialize. This manifests itself later in life in terms of increased proneness to delinquency and drug use, heightened aggression, and a chilling indifference to others.[11] The best way of explaining these outcomes is to assume that normal social development relies upon the brain receiving certain kinds of social stimulation early in life to enable correct processing of social interactions. What makes this interpretation so compelling is that other primates, such as Harlow's monkeys, respond in similar ways to early maternal deprivation, suggesting that analogous mechanisms of social development have passed down the evolutionary tree from a common primate ancestor.

The whole question of the impact of early social deprivation has recently acquired new salience because of the adoption by Americans of hundreds of children raised in truly horrendous conditions in Romanian orphanages during the darkest days of the Communist regime. While most of the Romanian adoptees have had little opportunity for normal social development, many have adjusted surprisingly well to their new environments provided by the exceptionally nurturant individuals who have agreed to take them in. One of the most striking findings from studies of these children is evidence of problems not just with social adjustment, language skills, and intelligence, but with much more basic skills, such as the ability to feel pain, hear sounds, and guide movements using visual feedback.[12] These findings are reminiscent of the problems of social isolates, and they provide a chilling reminder of just how bad these orphanages were in terms of depriving children of social stimulation (since development of the brain and basic cognitive processes are dependent on receiving social stimulation[13]). Another implication is that a childhood environment characterized by such extremely low parental investment has profound consequences for brain development.

One of the strangest phenomena that crops up repeatedly in the accounts of feral children is the abnormality of their sensory perception, whether it is the insensitivity to pain of Victor of Aveyron, the deafness to some sounds of Kaspar Hauser, or the day-blindness of Amala and Kamala. From one perspective, this is not difficult to understand. If you spend most of your early life in complete darkness, it seems obvious that your ability to see in the dark should improve, if only due to practice and effort. However, experiments on visual development in cats, which are born with their eyes closed, have found that the way the mature visual system works is affected by the kind of light stimulation it receives. In one experiment, kittens were kept in complete darkness and allowed to see either only horizontal lines or only vertical lines for an hour each day. The cats were tested after their visual systems had matured by putting them into a test area in which there were many upright barriers that the cat had to weave through to get to an attractive snack. Cats that had seen only vertical lines did fine on this test. Those that had seen only horizontals blundered straight into each of the barriers as though they did not see them. It emerged that because they had not experienced stimulation from vertical lines during the critical period for visual development, the brain cells that normally register vertical lines stopped functioning. The principle of "use it or lose it" had made them blind to upright lines.[14] It seems likely that problems of sensory perception as well as problems of language development for socially deprived children are an example of the same principle in action.

Sensory problems are particularly troubling for socially isolated children because they are rooted in permanent brain changes and are therefore irreversible. Recent tests of the sensory capacities of children adopted out of Romanian orphanages revealed that the capacity of their brains to respond to most types of sensory stimulation is seriously impaired.[15] These problems suggest a lack of adequate sensory stimulation early in life. It is therefore hardly surprising that institutionalized children should score about ten points lower in IQ tests than other children.[16]

The brain responds to intellectual stimulation in much the same way that muscle responds to repeated exertion: it grows. This was first seen in experiments on rats. Rats that were kept in group cages, instead of the customary solitary confinement, and given varied toys to play with grew up to be more "intelligent." They were better able to learn a complex maze, which is the rodent equivalent of an IQ test. The enriched rats had measurable increases in brain growth, including better connections between cells (broader synapses). Their cerebral cortices were thicker and heavier, indicating that the more challenging environment had stimulated brain growth.[17] One optimistic sidelight from the study of enrichment effects on the brains of rodents is that enrichment can occur at any age, although the impact is much greater if it occurs early in life, possibly because the brain is more flexible for immature individuals. Nevertheless, there is no reason why the decline in intelligence produced by early exposure to an impoverished environment, such as that provided historically in many orphanages, cannot be at least partly corrected in later life.

The importance of early stimulation of the human brain is suggested by the fact that circumstances that reduce the quantity and quality of stimulation received by young children, whether this is due to institutionalization, poverty, having an inexperienced teenage mother, or having many siblings competing for parental attention, all produce a measurable reduction in IQ score. The role of social interaction and the opportunity to play with toys in promoting intelligence have been demonstrated very clearly in the case of Head Start programs. Although there has been a lot of controversy about how effective these programs are, it is now clear that if they are begun within the first two years of life, they do indeed cause reliable gains.[18] Head Start programs can be thought of as a form of supplementary parental investment. It is no surprise to learn that they have the greatest effects when parents are most fully involved.

ABUSE, NEGLECT, AND THE CYCLE OF VIOLENCE

If you consider that in the evolutionary past, infants always relied on constant care from their mothers, it is remarkable that children in modern environments who spend a lot of time separated from their mothers can turn out so well. In this respect, Israeli kibbutzim (or communes) and Western day-care arrangements can be considered a bold experiment. Infants raised in hunter-gatherer societies are constantly held by their mothers, sleep in contact with the mother's skin, and suckle on demand. These mothers are appalled when told that, in our society, children spend the night sleeping alone in their own beds in separate rooms.[19, 20]

In the final analysis, we are an extraordinarily flexible species. This does not mean that we turn out the same in different environments but rather that how we turn out is a reflection of the kind of treatment we have received at the hands of parents. While most social scientists use the language of pathology and refer to families as breaking down and socialization as having failed, it is more objective, and a lot more optimistic, to recognize that people vary in how helpful or antisocial their behavior is without necessarily being "sick." On the contrary, there are some contexts in which acting "nice" is interpreted as weakness and ruthlessly exploited.

By the same token, children tend to mirror certain aspects of how they are treated by parents. Clinical psychologists often refer to the cycle of violence in families, according to which people who come from abusive homes tend to become abusive parents. A less professional formulation is, "What goes around comes around." Children who are raised by harsh, abusive parental figures are different from the unfortunate children raised without parents in orphanages. Instead of being deprived of socializing experiences, they are actually provided with some very emphatic examples of what adults do. For example, they learn that social problems may be solved by the use of force. They also learn that since their fathers are physically stronger than their mothers, masculine will tends to prevail in family disputes. In addition, they learn that the social world of adults, from the family outward, is tough and competitive and that people are devious, mean, and unreliable.

Of course, these impressions of life from the perspective of an abusive home, whether it is in a poor urban neighborhood or a respectable suburb, are quite realistic. Children's brains have been designed by natural selection to keep them in efficient touch with the social environment in which they are raised. These attitudes can therefore be considered adaptive. They only come to seem like an illness when judged in terms of their bad social consequences. Such environments tend to undermine the potential of children to learn control over their impulses. They have difficulty grasping complex rules of expected behavior and wanting to follow them. In short, they do not learn those things that they need to know to succeed in the workforce, from speaking correctly and politely to self-discipline and the work ethic, and what they have learned makes it much more likely that their personal behavior and income-generation activities will get them in trouble with the law.

Harsh and inconsistent parenting actively teaches children that there are no consistent social rules. If you cannot predict when a parent will punish you, then it makes little sense to try pleasing the parent by obeying the rules. If there is little justice—your sister is always indulged despite her bad behavior and you are punished even when you are being good—then it makes sense to be constantly vigilant to protect your selfish interests. Reduced parental investment associated with abusive homes increases the risk of the child being delinquent, using illegal drugs, dropping out of high school, joining gangs, being unemployed, and becoming the parent of an unplanned child during the teen years (particularly for girls).[21]

One very important practical consequence of reduced parental investment is that children in some ways come to treat themselves like they have been treated by adults. If parents have been rather careless of the physical comfort and general well-being of children, the children grow up with a general lack of concern for their own safety and health. This manifests itself in a variety of risky behavior from careless driving to recklessness in picking a fight, to smoking, drinking alcohol, breaking laws, using illegal drugs, engaging in unprotected sex, and generally taking a cavalier attitude towards health by ignoring advice on healthy diet and lifestyle and avoiding regular medical checkups. A recent analysis of data from the National Longitudinal Study on Adolescent Health found that teenagers who felt strong emotional ties to their parents were less likely to engage in a variety of risky behaviors. They were less likely to have experienced emotional distress or to have had suicidal thoughts or attempted suicide. They were less likely to have engaged in violence. They became sexually active at a later age. They were less likely to smoke cigarettes, drink alcohol, or use marijuana. What ties all of these findings together is that children who are raised in circumstances of reduced parental investment behave as though they see the world as hostile and threatening. They protect their immediate interests by presenting a hard and cynical face to others. Instead of reflecting upon the potential negative consequences of their actions for themselves or for others, they pursue immediate pleasures and act in impulsive and thrill-seeking ways.[22]

When you study the relationship between childhood experiences and parental behavior, two superficially contradictory aspects of the cycle of violence stand out: First, children raised in violently conflictual homes are much more likely to be physically abusive parents. Second, people who are raised in abusive homes most often do not grow up to be abusive parents themselves. Approximately 30 percent of abused children become abusive parents. This means that the majority do not. Of course, the absence of abuse severe enough to come to the attention of authorities does not mean that interactions in the home are all sweetness and light.

There are so many obvious reasons why abused children should become abusive parents, it is difficult to know where to begin. Less obvious, but no less important, are the reasons that the cycle of violence and abuse gets interrupted. Developmental psychologists refer to this phenomenon as "resilience." Scholars studying resilience have found that resilient children always have a close relationship with at least one sympathetic adult, whether it is a neighbor or a teacher, who acts as a parental surrogate. One fascinating implication is that when children use their own social experiences as a kind of barometer for the civility of the world in which they live, they may be more influenced by the kindness of a relative stranger than they are by the abusive conduct of their own flesh and blood. This indicates that social programs of the big brother/big sister variety could be quite helpful to some individuals raised in abusive homes if the child is provided with a window onto an alternative social reality.[23]

Interpreted in an evolutionary context, this means that when there is the potential for going in two directions, children may prefer to move in the direction of high-investment parenting rather than following in the footsteps of abusive parents. This would explain why the majority of abused children do not mature into abusive parents. Most encounter alternative role models that they prefer to follow. It could be argued that where high parental investment is possible, it is a superior strategy since children are more likely to survive and to be successful in reproducing. Extreme neglect and abuse may cause a wide range of behavioral problems, emotional problems, and even health problems that make children less likely to survive and reproduce.

When children do not imitate their abusive parents, it seems as if they are swimming against a very strong current. Causes of the cycle of violence in families include:

- Genetics. An abusive parent transmits a genetic potential for impulsive aggression to children. If there is a tendency for impulsive people to marry, then children will receive a double dose of the genetic influence on domestic violence.

- Insecure attachment. As previously mentioned, abused infants are much less likely to be securely attached to their mothers (28 percent versus 69 percent). Boys with severe conduct problems (oppositional conduct disorder, or disobedience) are much more likely to be insecurely attached than normal (over 80 percent versus less than 30 percent[24]). Since security of attachment is largely a product of maternal behavior, this is compelling evidence of the importance of the early relationship with the mother in the cycle of violence.

- Social learning. Children acquire information about how people behave in intimate relationships by observing their parents. If parents tend to solve disputes in hostile and manipulative ways rather than through negotiation, then children would be expected to do the same. One reason that domestic violence occurs may be that children have not witnessed enough civility between parents to learn the lines that would be used in this particular role. They know only the script of hostile interactions. Consistent with this interpretation, it has been found that five-year-old boys who were physically harmed by parents are much more aggressive in their interactions with peers.[25]

- Poor social skills. Abusive homes are socially impoverishing in the sense that children have limited opportunity to learn the kind of social skills needed to resolve problems through discussion. Consistent with this view, it has been found that physically harmed children interpret social situations differently than others. They are less attentive to social cues. They are more likely to jump to the conclusion that another person is hostile towards them. They are also less likely to get other children to do what they want them to do.[26]

Since experiencing violence in the home can have important consequences for how children behave when they grow up, it is worth asking whether the thousands of incidents of aggression that children witness on TV are capable of producing similar effects. In other words, if people are designed by natural selection to become more violent when they grow up in a violent society, does watching television violence have similar effects? Is this a part of the child's reality, or does it fit cleanly into a mental compartment of make-believe that has no influence on the child's everyday behavior? Many commentators are impressed both by the sheer quantity of violent action in entertainment and by the extreme lack of realism in depicting its human consequences. Violence is often glamorized in TV shows directed at a young audience, and an essential part of this glamorization is that violent people are almost always rewarded for their aggression, rather than spending time in jail, which is the usual legal consequence of assault in the real world.

If children tend to learn and imitate the aggressive actions of their parents, then we might imagine that they would also repeat some of the appalling violence they see on TV. Do children who watch a lot of TV violence grow up with the same mind set as children who witness a great deal of aggression between real people in the real world? While the answer to this question may never be scientifically nailed down, a review of the technical literature indicates that children who view a lot of violence on TV may turn out to be more violent people as a result [27]:

- Viewing a violent video clip does make people temporarily more aggressive in experiments. For example, they are more willing to give high levels of electric shock in a simulation.

- When children are shown violent cartoons, they behave more aggressively on the playground.

- The rise of television in this country is correlated with rising rates of violent crime—particularly by juveniles. This may not seem too remarkable when you consider all of the other factors that go along with the rise of TV, including rising divorce rates, increased affluence, and so forth. Yet, none of these comparatively slow changes could explain why the introduction of television to towns where it had previously been unavailable was followed by an immediate increase in rates of violent crime.

- Children who watch a lot of violent TV grow up into more aggressive people who are more likely to be convicted of violent offenses.

Taken together, all these strands of evidence suggest that parents who allow unsupervised watching of TV are playing with fire. There is nothing intrinsically bad about TV, but the evidence clearly shows that children are strongly influenced by the content and transfer it to their everyday behavior. Moreover, excessive viewing of TV by children may be a symptom of neglectful parenting, and if such children are violent it might be due to lack of close relationships with parents and others as much as the television content.

If the argument pursued in this book—that what parents do really matters with respect to how their children turn out—has merit, then it should be possible to make a connection in the real world between low parental investment and social problems. One way of doing this is to look for a predictive relationship between changes in U.S. society that affect parenting and changes in social problems. Another is to examine the relationship between parents and children in the case of adolescents exhibiting delinquent behavior, such as use of illegal drugs.

PARENTAL INVESTMENT AND SOCIAL PROBLEMS

We have seen that the actions (and inaction) of parents are extremely important so far as conduct problems of children are concerned. While it is certainly true that some children are much more of a challenge to parents than others are, it is equally important to recognize that parents always matter a great deal in how their children turn out. This is obviously true of early childhood. It is less obvious, but still true, in the case of teenagers, even those who appear to reject their parents, succumb to dangerous peer influences, and develop adult-size social problems.

While most teens go through their period of adolescent revolt and come out of it looking very much like their parents, some do not. These are precisely the ones who do not have a close relationship with their parents. Parental influences are cumulative. Parents who have not provided their young children with order and discipline and find that they are getting into trouble as teens face an uphill battle.

It is during the teenage years that the influence of peers is most strongly felt. Even though parents often see peer influences as harmful to their children, in the sense of undermining parental authority, this is not necessarily true. Many teens can be quite conservative and respectable in their value system, which often mirrors that of their parents in important respects.[28]

When parents send their children to expensive private schools, they often choose a school that they know will endorse and strengthen their own value system. This is possible, in part, because they arrange for their children to mingle with peers who have parents who think much like they do. This process is even more obvious in the case of expensive private colleges in which the "product" being marketed is as much a value system and lifestyle as it is an education in any formal sense.

Parents who send their children to public schools may have more difficulty shielding their children from extensive contact with antisocial influences. Nevertheless, if they have been warm, sensitive parents who have instilled a strong sense of responsibility and discipline, their children should be well able to resist these influences.

Illegal drug use is one major concern to most parents. Whether teens smoke marijuana or use other illegal drugs is very much determined by what their friends are doing. In a study conducted in the 1970s, teens whose parents used illegal drugs were much more likely to smoke marijuana if their best friend did so (67 percent) than if the best friend was not a user (17 percent). If their parents did not do drugs but the best friend did, 56 percent of those teens smoked marijuana.[29] Of course these results are correlational. They suggest peer influence but do not prove it. One plausible alternative explanation is that best friends may smoke marijuana largely because it is freely available in their neighborhood.

Nevertheless, it is clear from these findings that marijuana use is much more connected with peer behavior than it is to parental example. These results certainly call into question the view that parents can be an important influence on the drug habits of their maturing children. Yet the findings mean very little outside of their context. During the period of the study, marijuana was grown outdoors and was not the frighteningly potent drug it is today, which is grown indoors under lights and sends thousands of teens to hospital emergency rooms with breathing problems each year. It is possible that most of the respondents who said that they had used marijuana experienced drug effects little more potent than they might have gotten from drinking a cup of coffee.

There is certainly peer pressure in such situations, but it does not necessarily have to be seen as bad. From a purely pharmacological point of view, marijuana used in the 1970s was a comparatively mild drug that had no serious after-effects. From an anthropological perspective, high school students sitting around smoking dope might as well have been participating in a genteel ceremony not all that different from an Indian tea ceremony. In their own minds, they were flouting the customs and laws of their society. In the process, they were establishing solidarity amongst themselves. They were fitting in rather than sticking out.

If peer pressure is to have really dangerous consequences, then peers have to be engaged in really dangerous activities. Smoking a more potent form of marijuana in higher concentrations would certainly qualify as dangerous today, but it did not in the early 1970s. Breaking the law might have been a problem, but the law was so widely flouted and so rarely enforced that few teenagers acquired criminal records from smoking pot with their friends.

One of the most astonishing aspects of teenagers' relations with their parents is that at the very time when they are revolting against parental authority, they are most in need of it. In that respect, they resemble the dynamics of parental interactions with toddlers who are learning to be somewhat independent but simultaneously crave parental attention and discipline. In viewing television discussions of high school students, I have always been struck by how authoritarian they are in their attitudes. For instance, when they are asked what a parent ought to do if a teen is disobedient and stays out late at night without permission, most insist that there should be unpleasant consequences. This is rather like the three-year-old scattering his breakfast cereal all over the table to see what happens.

When it comes to challenging parental authority, teens have plenty of new weapons in addition to untidiness, from drug use to sexual expression to poor school performance and frighteningly unsavory friends. In the case of illegal drug use, most parents are appalled to discover that their teenagers are using drugs, particularly if this goes along with declining school grades. Many feel that the situation is outside of their control. They feel victimized by the situation and develop a cold war mentality towards their teen. This is a grave mistake. If a teen is misbehaving, then becoming emotionally unavailable can make the problem worse. One ingenious study of the dynamics between parents and adolescent children, after the children had developed serious drug problems, found that relations between parents and children tended to be understandably strained. The researchers used a complex version of a statistical procedure known as path analysis to show that illegal drug use by adolescents (a) causes conflict with the parents and (b) is worsened by conflictual relationships with parents.[30] This shows that even though teens may prefer to follow the lead of their peers in experimenting with marijuana and other drugs, their patterns of drug use are very much affected by how they were raised. Children who have warm relationships with their parents are less likely to develop drug use patterns that interfere with their education, careers, health, and personal happiness.

In conclusion, it is clear that the amount and quality of parental investment received in childhood has important consequences for how children turn out. Children who are deprived of parental interaction in early life experience severe and irreversible problems with sensory perception and language development. These problems are seen in extreme form in feral children, who have survived without human contact, and, to a lesser degree, in children raised in orphanages under conditions of early social deprivation. They suggest abnormal brain development. The rationale for this is that a certain level of interaction with parents was always present in our ancestors who survived childhood, so that the developing brain today relies on parental stimulation as part of the natural environment to which it is adapted. Institutional children tend to have academic problems and to have difficulty forming close personal relationships. Their early behavior is oddly passive and asocial, reflecting their deprivation of social contact.

Children who have abusive parents also tend to have academic difficulties. They are more likely to form the impression that the world is hostile and threatening. They are more aggressive towards peers in childhood. When they grow up, they are more likely to be violent and to show up in problem statistics due to committing criminal acts, reproducing early, and having unstable marital relationships. They tend to be antisocial rather than asocial, reflecting exposure to harsh and aggressive models of adult behavior. Despite the strong pressures that produce cycles of violence and poverty across generations, children have a bias towards being influenced by highly nurturant individuals in their environment, which explains why some children can escape the cycles of family violence and poverty. Individuals receiving reduced parental investment are more likely to have anti-social attitudes and develop problem behavior. The next chapter explores this phenomenon in relation to parental divorce.

Chapter 4

Divorce and Parental Investment

Humans are mainly monogamous. Even though the overwhelming majority of the world's societies permit some kind of multiple marriage, this applies to a tiny proportion of individuals.[1] The distribution of monogamy among different animal species is interesting and instructive. Monogamy is exceedingly rare among mammals because the mother nourishes the young with milk from her own body and offspring have little to gain from the added care of fathers. Among birds, provisioning the young is extremely labor intensive and requires the cooperation of both parents. For example, parent swallows make literally hundreds of foraging trips each day to stuff the gaping throats of their fledglings. Without male support, the females would not be successful in raising healthy chicks who could make their own way in the world. About 90 percent of bird species are monogamous.

Monogamy in humans also reflects the fact that it requires a great deal of work to protect and feed a human infant. This point becomes very obvious in the case of surviving hunter-gatherer groups that constantly migrate to new camps in search of game animals. In the process, they must carry everything they own, in addition to their small children. The physical difficulty of this lifestyle means that it would be hard for a woman to raise children without male support.

Most monogamous birds cooperate for the length of a breeding season, but some, like swans, may mate for life. Recent research has established that adultery is not peculiar to humans: it has been found that some proportion of fledglings in the nests of ostensibly monogamous species have been fathered by males other than their mother's spouse. Unions that are not blessed with offspring tend to dissolve. According to data compiled by the United Nations, exactly the same is true of humans. For marriages with no children, the divorce rate across the world is 39 percent compared to 26 percent for couples with a single child, 19 percent for couples with two children, and only 3 percent for couples with four or more children.[2]

Even when marriages produce children, they can still break up over time. In the United States, a second divorce is most frequent after seven years of marriage, a phenomenon referred to as the "seven year itch." Evolutionists have speculated that this may be due to adaptive design. Seven years is long enough to raise a child to the stage where he or she is relatively independent of the parents. It is the bird equivalent of a breeding season.

When it comes to parental investment, it seems obvious that two parents must be better than one. (Yet this may not be true if the parents are constantly fighting with each other.) Divorce should generally cause a reduction in parental investment, and it would be expected that children of divorce should differ from children raised in the higher parental investment context of intact families. Looking at these differences thus provides a convenient entry point to the impact of parents on child socialization.

Divorce is a kind of natural experiment in which there are two groups, the children of divorce (as psychologists refer to them) and the children of intact two-parent families. Like any natural experiment, the conclusions that we draw must be guarded because the groups may not be the same to begin with. For example, it is possible that people who divorce tend to be unusually disagreeable and to have weak social skills for negotiating disputes. They may also be likely to spend a lot of time fighting. These differences are in the direction of reduced parental investment so that using divorce as an index of parental investment is justified.

A more troubling problem is that parents affect their children via genetics as well as by parental behavior. If children of divorce are more likely to divorce themselves, which they are,[3] it is difficult to determine if this is because they have developed disagreeable personalities for genetic reasons or because the experience of growing up in a conflictual home has taught them a mistrust of intimate relationships. The very great increase in rates of divorce over the past generation cannot be due to genetics, however, so it must be due either to socialization within families or to some other environmental influence.

Many of the social problems that elicit such concern today because of their strong tendency to increase over time are also strongly associated with parental divorce. These effects are far from trivial. Consider the following differences between children of divorce and other children[4]:

- Divorce raises the risk of school dropout by 150 percent for white children, 100 percent for Hispanics, and 76 percent for blacks.

- Children of divorce are more likely to divorce themselves (60 percent more likely for white women and 35 percent more likely for white men).

- Daughters of divorce are 50 percent more likely to become pregnant as teens.

- Children of divorce are 200 percent to 300 percent more likely to have emotional and behavioral problems and learning difficulties than those in intact families.

- Crime rates are about 50 percent higher among children of divorce. For children raised in poverty the risk of being a criminal can be elevated a great deal more by parental divorce.[5]

Of course, divorced and intact are not the only possibilities in respect to family structure. When divorced people remarry, they often acquire additional children and form blended families. Their effects on socialization are largely unknown, and they introduce all sorts of complications that have not been studied by psychologists. For example, when the biological father of a child in a blended family exercises his visitation rights, how does his relationship with the new couple affect the child? How does the relationship between resident father and biological father affect all the children? How does the presence of an unrelated man in the home affect the psychosexual development of daughters? These new and important questions are discussed in terms of the limited information available.

DIVORCE, CORRELATIONS, AND CAUSES

We live at a time of historically high divorce rates. In 1920, the annual divorce rate was 8 per 1,000 married women. By 1985, this had peaked at 21.7.[6] In other words, the risk of divorce for a married woman runs at over 2 percent per year, or 20 percent per decade. Population experts calculate that of the marriages being formed today, approximately half will end in divorce. Since some of these marriages are remarriages, substantially more than half of children will live in a home that has been affected by parental divorce. As a society, it can therefore be said that the United States has gone from being a society in which stable marriage was the statistical norm to being a society in which unstable marriage is the norm.

The instability of marriage has created a great deal of concern for potential ill effects on children and a great deal of misgivings on the part of divorcing parents about how the decision to split up affects the kids. Should parents be concerned? Should they stay together for the good of their children? Children of divorce do experience some disadvantages, but there is good reason to believe that they would have most of these problems even if the parents decided to stay together "for the sake of the children."

The problems of children of divorce are associated with reduced parental investment. Yet, divorce is as much a consequence of low parental investment as it is a cause. In practical terms, it is the conflict between parents in marriages that are doomed to failure that has the most profound impact on children. Severe parental discord may precede divorce by many years, and children are also caught in the crossfire of postdivorce conflict. From this perspective, the actual occasion when the parents formally separate does not necessarily have adverse consequences for children. To the extent that one of the antagonists is removed from the home, their quality of life may actually improve. For most families, however, parental divorce initiates a downward spiral of poverty, residential instability, and parental neglect. It is these indirect threats to parental investment, coupled with parental conflict, rather than the absence of one parent from the home, that is responsible for the emotional and academic problems of children of divorce.

Fighting parents contribute more than an unpleasant home environment to their children. They also pass on their "fighting" genes. If children of divorce are about 50 percent more likely to divorce than others, it should not be inferred that the only reason for this is that they have witnessed parental hostility. Genetics accounts for at least 50 percent of the risk of getting divorced.

When we study children of divorce, we find that fighting genes and fighting environments go together. From the perspective of this book, whether the differences are due to genetics or environment is not of critical importance since both tend to reduce parental investment. Just because we know that parents contribute a genetic risk of divorce, it does not follow that their behavior has no effect. Even though the one behavior/genetic study of divorce risk did not find an effect of shared family environment on propensity to divorce, such studies are quite unreliable. Large increases in American divorce rates during this century, such as the doubling of divorces between the 1960s and the 1970s, cannot possibly be due to genetics, and reflect changes in the social environment that are likely to occur via family interactions.

DIVORCE AND SOCIAL PROBLEMS

Given that it is often impossible to disentangle genetic and environmental influences in satisfactory ways, even though behavior geneticists may claim that they have done so, it is illuminating and practically important to examine how differences in the environments of divorced children predict differences in social and emotional problems. This is quite a complex issue, and it is only in the last five years that social scientists have begun to make sense of it.

Consider the case of the black American family, which has huge rates of single parenthood (about 75 percent of black families are headed by single mothers). At the same time, these families have severe academic problems, high unemployment rates, and crime rates that exceed the (already high) national averages by a factor of approximately four. (This scenario is taken up in more detail in a later chapter and is mentioned here for purely illustrative purposes.) One might imagine that the social problems of black families are caused by marital instability. An equally plausible perspective, however, is that the social problems result in marital instability. A black man who is uneducated and unemployed is not an attractive marriage prospect, however appealing he may otherwise be as an individual. The practical reality is that most black women cannot hope to marry black men, much as they might wish to do so. The scarcity of marriageable black men is a practical matter that is entirely independent of the wishes of African-American women. Moralistic interpretations are thus entirely beside the point; they do not help us to understand the problem in the least. Nonmarital reproduction is not a matter of wrong moral choices but a practical issue of limited marital opportunity.[7, 8, 9]

Does divorce cause social problems such as poor academic performance, increased teen pregnancy rate, or higher unemployment? It is difficult to answer this question without confronting differences in ethnic groups, parental education, and income (sometimes referred to as "nuisance variables"). One way of handling the differences is to control them statistically. This was done by sociologists Sara McLanahan and Gary Sandefur, who reported their results in a 1994 book entitled *Growing Up with a Single Parent*.[10] They used regression analysis to remove the effects of all of the nuisance variables except income. With race, parental education, number of siblings, and place of residence statistically controlled, they found that children living with only one biological parent were 6 percent more likely to drop out of high school, girls were 9 percent more likely to become pregnant as teens, and men were 11 percent more likely to be unemployed. When parental income was controlled, the risk of these social problems declined by approximately one half in each case. This means that reduced income in single-parent, compared to two-parent, homes accounts for half of the increased risks of school dropout, pregnancy, and unemployment. (The modest size of these differences may be due to removal of nuisance variables like ethnic group. As discussed below, the researchers may have thrown out the baby with the bathwater.)

McLanahan and Sandefur were interested in what accounted for the rest of the social problems. They knew that single-parent families tend to move frequently, which can be upsetting to children because they lose their friends and other forms of social support from acquaintanceships built up in the local community. When they included the number of moves experienced by a family in their analysis, they found that all of the differences between one-parent and two-parent homes in terms of high school dropout disappeared. In other words, academic problems of children in single-parent homes are explained by residential mobility as well as lower family income. Similarly, including residential mobility in the analysis explained about three-quarters of the differences between one-parent and two-parent families.

One might be excused for thinking that McLanahan and Sandefur had explained almost everything about the problem behaviors of children raised without their fathers. In fact, they have explained just about nothing. Imagine that you heard a politician deliver the following stump speech: "We have quite a problem with crime in this country. Teen births are also at a staggeringly high level. Moreover, half of the marriages being formed today are expected to dissolve. Fellow Americans, these are serious problems. I have come to you with a solution that will halve the problem of serious crime overnight. It will make a serious dent in teen pregnancies and produce a meaningful reduction in divorce rates for the first time this century. What is more, it will not cost a single penny. My solution is to ignore all of the social problems associated with being a racial minority. My technical people refer to it as regression analysis. Don't let the name confuse you, it's a progressive idea!" No sane voter would cast a ballot for this chump, but when the same thing is done and dressed up in an academic study, even clever social scientists go along for the ride. Race accounts for such a large chunk of differences in the way that children are raised that to remove it statistically and pretend that you have done your work is analogous to removing the baby along with the bathwater. When applied to segments of the U.S. population, the biological term of "race" is ill defined and probably meaningless. "Race" does include a welter of important variables that tend to reduce parental investment via environmental influences. They include:

- difficulty of black women finding a husband because of the low ratio of men to women and because of the small proportion of black men holding down steady jobs;
- poverty and residence in poor neighborhoods;
- drug use and addiction;
- poor prenatal nutrition and medical care, together with exposure to drugs, environmental toxins, and diseases, which predispose them to low birth weight and neurological problems;
- being a recipient of harsh parental discipline;
- being vulnerable to crimes of violence;
- knowing people who make their living from criminal enterprises and participation from an early age in criminal activities;
- being the child of a young, inexperienced mother who may not have been ready for the responsibilities of raising a child;

- attending atrocious public schools;
- spending a lot of unsupervised time hanging around with other youngsters; and
- possibly having more brothers and sisters.

If you exclude the role of all of these influences on social problems, you have clearly done nothing more than scratch the surface. This is true even if your primary interest, as in the case of McLanahan and Sandefur, is divorce. Thus, even though marriage rates of black women are much lower than those of the population as a whole, their divorce rate is higher. For example, in 1981, the divorce rate was 233 per 1,000 married blacks compared to 23 per 1,000 married white women.[11, 12] Hence, the effects of divorce are inextricably bound up with the effects of race. Since this whole question is taken up in much more detail in a later chapter, I will not pursue it here. My general point is that anything that undermines parental investment tends to increase social problems. Black Americans contribute disproportionately to social problem statistics because of influences in their lives that undermine parental investment. The same principle applies to the population as a whole. We know this because changes in the divorce rate and other population indices of reduced parental investment can be used to predict increases in social problems.

USING PARENTAL INVESTMENT TO PREDICT SOCIAL PROBLEMS

The most compelling evidence that the increased risk of social problems for children of divorce is not satisfactorily explainable in terms of parental genes is that there are pronounced changes over short periods of time in rates of crime and teen pregnancy. The changes are too rapid to be explained in terms of genetic changes in the population. For example, the rate of illegitimate births for white women in the United States almost doubled between 1940 and 1955 (moving from 3.6 to 7.9 per thousand).[13] Since this happened within a single generation, it is not even theoretically possible that any genetic propensity towards illegitimate birth (if such exists) could be responsible since no genetic change could have occurred in the gene pool of white Americans during such a short time.

What is causing such marked changes in American lifestyle? Many people believe that increases in crime rates and nonmarital teen pregnancies this century are attributable to a general moral decline that emanates from the decay of family values. The problem with this interpretation is not that it is necessarily wrong but rather that it is not particularly useful. When we see juvenile males committing horrendous crimes of violence and teenagers giving birth to large numbers of future criminals, it is very easy to say that today's youth have no morals because they are committing crimes in unprecedented numbers and producing children out of wedlock. Yet, this is not a real explanation. In fact, it is completely circular. The only reason that we infer lack of morality is the increases in social problem statistics. To say that teens are having babies because they lack sexual morality is equivalent to saying that they are having babies because they are having babies. Real explanations allow us to get beneath the surface and identify the prime movers that predict changes in social problems over time.

Divorce is just one of many factors that reduces parental investment, leading to increases in social problems. In the past, psychologists have tended to interpret the social problems of children of divorce in pathological terms because we tend to think of societies in which inexperienced teen mothers do a poor job of raising children and poorly socialized young men commit casual homicides as being "sick" societies. Talking about sickness has the same problem as referring to moral decay. Rather than directing our attention towards likely causes, it is an exercise in circular reasoning. To say young men commit apparently senseless homicides because they are sick is the same as saying that they are sick because they commit the crimes.

A much more promising approach is to assume that people respond in predictable ways to the kind of environment in which they are raised. Instead of thinking of human children as psychologically fragile and tending to fall apart at the whisper of trouble, it is far more realistic to accept that in the evolutionary past, there were a range of family environments that children weathered and that modern children are equipped to deal with a range of family environments. For example, some children had half a dozen siblings competing for limited food. Others had no siblings and never experienced starvation. The children in the first family would have been a lot more competitive and tough skinned, which is not to say that they did not care for each other. This kind of toughness can have some beneficial consequences in adult life. It helps people to stand up for themselves and to be independent-minded, tough, and competitive. The toughness produced by growing up in a reduced-parental-investment context, such as a large family, also predisposes people to lives of crime. We know this because across the countries of the world, children raised in larger families are more likely to commit serious crimes. It is better to think of crime as an unpleasant side effect of a functional mechanism of psychological development that facilitates survival under highly competitive conditions.[14]

Divorce is associated with increases in social problems because divorce occurs in homes that tend to have reduced parental investment both before and after the breakup of the parental marriage. It is only one of many possible reasons why children might grow up a little tough around the edges, and it is probably not the most important one. Others include poverty; ecological stress, which makes it difficult to eke out a steady living; large family size; high child mortality; and endemic hostility between the sexes.

If it is true that social problems are caused by reduced parental investment, then it should be possible to see a relationship between trends in parental behavior and trends in social problems. Such patterns have emerged loud and clear in the study of juvenile crime. For example, if children are left unsupervised during the day, we might expect the reduced attention from parental figures to show up in increased tendencies to commit crimes. In 1970, 37 percent of American households had children who lacked full-time parental supervision. By 1992, the number had shot up to 57 percent. During the same period, there was an approximate doubling of serious juvenile crimes, including homicides. The relationship between parental supervision and criminality is demonstrated with almost amusing clarity by looking at the time of day at which crimes are committed. Juvenile criminals are rather inactive during the day, when most juveniles attend school. Then there is a spurt in criminal activity around three o'clock when school lets out. Offense rates stay high until around seven in the evening, which is precisely the after-school period during which latchkey kids roam free.[15, 16]

When you look at the relationship between reduced parental supervision and crime, the connection between parental investment and social problems becomes very obvious. There are less obvious and more pervasive connections that can be studied by looking at the relationship between more general measures of reduced parental investment and changes in social problems from year to year.

Throughout history, it has been found that a relative scarcity of marriageable men not only undermines marriage and increases the number of extramarital affairs, but also produces an atmosphere of mutual hostility and mistrust between men and women. This sense of easy betrayal is well captured in the soap operas (not to mention talk shows) of our day and is present in the racy tales spun by English poet Geoffrey Chaucer in the fourteenth century, wherein all that was needed to produce an adulterous relationship was to allow the apprentice to be alone with his master's wife for a few moments.

The problems of black American women this century have also been mirrored in the rest of the population in which there has been a steep rise in nonmarital pregnancy, increasing divorce rates, and alarming increases in rates of serious crimes perpetrated by juveniles. All of these problems are indirectly related to a weak marriage market for women. Since a low ratio of men to women in the population destabilizes marriage and produces conflict between the sexes, it limits the ability of parents to invest in their children. The sex ratio can therefore be considered a population index of parental investment. When the sex ratio is high, women control the marriage market. Women generally do not engage in premarital sex. Marriage is stable, and parents are deeply committed to the joint goal of raising children.

Divorce rate and sex ratio are measures of parental investment that apply to the population as a whole. As divorce rate falls, and as sex ratio rises, parental investment increases and social problems should decline. Using the assumption that parental investment is most important in the first year of life, I tested the prediction that the number of juvenile arrests could be predicted by parental investment indicators at birth. They were. Lower sex ratios and higher divorce rates at the year of birth strongly predicted high rates of juvenile arrest and teen pregnancies. As the sex ratio declined, and as divorce increased, social problems became more prevalent. Advanced statistical techniques indicated that the marriage market was more important than divorce in predicting social problems. Part of the reason that divorce rates are correlated with social problems over time is that marriages are unstable at precisely those periods when women lose control over the marriage market.[17]

DO FATHERS MATTER?

Given the clear evidence that availability of marriageable men and the divorce rate are correlated with social problems, it may seem pointless to ask whether fathers matter. The big picture of societies having a scarcity of men tells us loud and clear that fathers do matter. In the United States, the shortage of marriageable men produces hostility between the sexes and a generally uncivil society with high crime rates and high rates of nonmarital teen pregnancy. The same pattern is seen across different civilizations and throughout recorded human history. A scarcity of husbands and fathers undermines marriage and family life and changes family life so as to reduce parental investment in children. Children raised in such societies become tough, unruly, egocentric, and undisciplined rather than civil, conscientious, and idealistic people. These effects are not only evident in comparisons of societies; they are also seen quite clearly in a comparison of children who are raised in the homes of single mothers, whether this arrangement is produced by nonmarital childbirth or by divorce.

In the presence of such unambiguous evidence concerning the important role played by fathers, psychologists have faced an embarrassing dearth of evidence about what it is that fathers do that is so important. As far as direct child care is concerned, most fathers do relatively little. In all societies, mothers are the primary care givers. Even though there is no reason why fathers cannot raise children, as a rule, this did not happen until the twentieth century with the granting of child custody to fathers by divorce courts. According to the research of anthropologists, there is no society in which fathers routinely carry out more than 50 percent of child care activities. The highest level of care is provided by low-status Ache men from Paraguay who compensate for lack of wealth by agreeing to help their wives look after children. Even though women in industrialized countries, such as the United States, Canada, Sweden, Norway, and Australia, are highly involved in the workforce, they still do most of the domestic work. This suggests a lack of social power for women, but it could also be that women are reluctant to give up their control over domestic matters.[18,19,20]

Even if men are beginning to assume more direct responsibility for their children, and other domestic work, than their fathers did, it is not clear that their child care activities are of any great importance in forestalling social problems in their adolescents. In fact, in the 1950s, which is often held out as an ideal period for raising children because the economy was good and sex ratios were high, many fathers saw very little of their children. They often spent long hours at work, returning to suburban homes after their children had gone to bed. No one ever suggested that these children were being deprived of their fathers, although the same claim is being made today when children are separated from their fathers to a perhaps equivalent extent by divorce.

We are thus on the horns of a dilemma, knowing that fathers matter but not having any very clear idea of what they do that makes a difference. In one of the most honest books in a publishing industry that has sprung up around the concept of father deprivation, David Popenoe, in *Life without Father*, asks the question about what fathers do that makes such a difference.[21] His answer is thoughtful, but it is not entirely satisfactory. The problem is a lack of clear evidence getting us from there to here. In other words, it is not clear that the activities of fathers actually do play a major role in child socialization. Popenoe lists the following possibilities:

- Fathers play an important economic role, and it was this role that tended to be emphasized in the 1950s to the exclusion of all others. Today, the economic role of fathers is less critical since women have careers. This traditional role has also been somewhat undermined by the government in countries such as Sweden, where the welfare state provides paid maternity leave with full health benefits. Such liberal policies undermine marriage and increase nonmarital pregnancy according to a cross-cultural study by the Guttmacher Institute.[22]

- Fathers serve as role models for responsible and nurturant behavior.

- Fathers are socially enriching because they interact differently with children than mothers do. For example, they play more boisterously with children and tend to demand more competence from them than mothers do.

- Fathers boost self-esteem, which may foster educational achievement and occupational ambitions, particularly for girls. This conclusion is certainly consistent with the literature on children of divorce, but it is not clear whether the presence of father in the home actually stimulates ambition or merely happens to coexist with it. For example, it is possible that it is parental conflict in homes that both undermines education and leads to divorce. One study that looked at the association between parental divorce and declining grades found that children of divorce only did worse than others if their parents fought a lot.

- Fathers are (or used to be) the disciplinarian of last resort. When all else failed, exasperated mothers could say, "Wait till your father gets home!" Of course, the implicit threat of corporal punishment administered by the father is less often used today. Corporal punishment has been outlawed in several European countries and is under attack in the United States. Despite these dents in the traditional disciplinary roles of fathers, it is probably true that solidarity between parents of difficult children helps them to weather the storm of rebellion better than a single parent could.

Plausible as each of these ideas is, there is really a shortage of hard evidence supporting them. What is more, the divorce literature suggests that the role of fathers following divorce is not of any great importance in predicting behavioral problems in the children. For example, there is no clear difference in outcomes between families in which the father makes regular visits to see the children and those in which he never visits, according to the results of McLanahan and Sandefur's nationally representative study.[23] Another of their embarrassing negative findings is that children who obtain a father substitute in the form of a stepfather are not protected from increased risk of social problems. Equally curious is the conclusion that a grandmother living in the home does not have a protective influence. Provided that the grandmother is not in poor health or an excessive drain on family finances, she would seem to be an additional source of emotional support and a sharer in the effort of child care, ensuring that children have less unsupervised time after school, for example. The lack of effect of grandmothers could well be a statistical artifact. Since black children are more likely to be cared for by their grandmothers, controlling for the effects of race could likely take out much of the effect of grandmothers. The lack of effect for visitation and stepfathers may result from inherent conflicts in these relationships, which have never been any secret.

The lack of beneficial consequences of visitation by the father following divorce is not such a deep mystery when one examines the frayed emotional environment in which such visits take place. Judith Wallerstein recounts the grim tale of Ellen, one of her research subjects, whom she studied during and after her parents' divorce.[24] Interviewed at the age of fourteen, Ellen was anxious to know when she could discontinue court-ordered visits with her father. She had to stay with her father two weekends each month and during summer vacation. Her problem was that she was very frightened of her father, who had a violent temper. Although he restricted himself to yelling at her when angry, she was frightened that he would hit her. Ellen was so tense about going to visit her father that before her weekend visits she developed psychosomatic skin rashes, which invariably disappeared on Sunday. She dreaded having to spend the summer at her father's house, cut off from the companionship of other children.

If the visits were so hard on this unfortunate girl, it seems astonishing that they should have been continued. Why were they? Apparently the child had become a postdivorce pawn in the end game of the parents. The lengths to which this battle of wits could go is illustrated by an incident in which Ellen had a fever. The mother called up the father to plead with him to let her stay at home in bed that weekend. Instead of agreeing, the father drove all the way to Ellen's home to verify that she really did have a fever. Ellen got out of bed to meet her father at his car. He admitted that she did indeed have a fever and conceded that she could stay at home. It is hard to imagine how parental visitations in such a poisoned atmosphere could be much good to anyone, particularly a helpless, vulnerable child buffeted between warring parents.

Searching for the effects of a father's absence or presence in the context of divorce is a bit like looking for the wood in a forest. It is all around you, and yet you cannot see it. Parental divorce is not associated with social problems because the father moves out of the home, depriving the children of his presence, but it is associated with adolescent problems because the marriage had been so conflictual that the parents could not cooperate to raise their children. Furthermore, conflict between the parents had painted a picture of hostility between the sexes. Children learned that one, or both, of their parents could not be trusted and formed a cynical impression of the nature of adult social relationships. In other words, regardless of the material prosperity or other favorable aspects of the parental home, they were exposed to a harsh psychological environment characteristic of reduced-parental-investment homes. Children raised in such an environment develop a self-protective shell of toughness and hostility, which puts them at risk for showing up in social problem statistics.

Parental investment is of critical importance in the early years of life. We know this from the study of attachment security, of intellectual enrichment, and of children raised at various ages in orphanages. The critical importance of the early years can also account for another odd paradox in the literature on fatherhood. It turns out that even though children who are separated from their fathers by divorce are at greatly increased risk of emotional and behavioral problems, the same is not true of children who are separated from their father by bereavement. While they may have a higher risk of being depressed, their limited research in this area finds little difference between them and children raised with two biological parents.[25]

The role played by fathers can only be understood when it is placed in the larger context of the marital relationship. This, in turn, can only be properly appreciated when it is placed in the context of the society. As we have seen, the relationship between the sexes is very much determined by the marriage market. When the sex ratio is high and marital opportunities for women are good, social problems such as teen pregnancy and juvenile crime decline. Relations between the sexes are good, and children reflect the civility they find in their homes back onto the communities in which they live by turning into happy and productive people.

Chapter 5

Sibling Competition as a Tragedy of the Commons

"Why can't you kids be nice to each other?" This despairing cry is heard in every household with more than one child. Parents often feel that their efforts to socialize children are directly counteracted by the dynamics between the children. The "tragedy of the commons" is a metaphor that helps us to understand why social relationships are not as harmonious as they might be. It is particularly useful in explaining why siblings so often compete fiercely rather than cooperating.

This metaphor was developed by Garret Hardin who noticed that some of humankind's most intractable problems involve a conflict of interest in which behaving badly has immediate gains but catastrophic long-term effects. He used the story of the destruction of common land, owned by a community, by overgrazing as a prototype or thought experiment. This system was widespread among medieval English villages and was also used by ranchers grazing publicly owned range lands in the American west.[1]

A commons system can work for centuries because wars, disease, and poaching keep the numbers of humans and grazing animals well below what the pasture can sustain. It is only when the number of grazing animals reaches the maximum number the pasture can support that the tragedy of the commons unfolds. At this point, there are so many animals on the pasture that adding any more will result in overgrazing. This causes soil erosion and weeds get the better of the fragile grassland ecology.

Hardin's critical insight in all of this is that such catastrophes are more or less inevitable. Each herdsman knows that it is not a good idea to overgraze the pasture because this would damage the grassland irreversibly. However, his gain in having an extra cow is his alone, whereas the damage to the fragile grassland ecology of putting out another grazing animal is shared out amongst all the other herders in the village.

The tragedy of the commons finds an exact analogy in the competition within families over parental investment. While siblings would all have a much more pleasant life if they were nice to each other, like the herdsmen, they are compelled to pursue their own selfish needs. Children are not competing over pasture, of course, but over parental investment. Sometimes the most effective way of obtaining parental attention is to cause trouble, perhaps by picking an unprovoked fight with a brother or sister. The problem is that this drives parents up the wall and generally reduces their responsiveness to offspring. In that sense, it might appear that young children needlessly cause erosion in the shared social environment of the home. As a direct effect of intense competition between them, children tend to reduce the value of the common resource over which they are fighting.

Since young children always want more parental investment than parents are willing to give, the family commons is perpetually on the brink of conflict. Young children are bottomless pits of attention-seeking. They want the complete slavish devotion of their mothers, and nothing less will satisfy them. If the mother decides to do something for herself, such as read a book or make a telephone call, this may unleash an emphatic protest. The toddler may turn up the volume to regain the mother's attention. This can be done literally, by making a lot of noise, or symbolically, by engaging in prohibited and dangerous activities.

Given that infants are in conflict with their own mothers over the desired level of parental investment, it is not surprising that, like selfish herdsmen, they should be in direct competition with each other. Competition between siblings is more intense when children are young and also intensifies if they are close in age. This conclusion can be drawn on intuitive grounds because we know that young infants are much more dependent on their parents for constant attention and care than children are when they can run around and play with their friends. It can also be drawn from evidence regarding direct competition over the affections of the mother. When two children are born closer together than eighteen months, the arrival of the second child can disrupt the relationship of secure attachment between the firstborn and the mother.[2] Since security of attachment has profound implications for adult relationships, we should keep in mind that when children compete for parental investment, the stakes can be very high.

The reason for the undermining of secure attachment in one of two young children is that they both have the same kinds of needs, which tend to be very demanding of a mother's time and effort. While sibling rivalry is inevitable when there are several young needy children, it is not inevitable that the household should resemble an environmental disaster. As Hardin pointed out, the solution to irrationally destructive competition of any kind cannot come from the competing parties themselves but must be imposed by an external authority whom the competing individuals respect. (In the case of the common pastures in England, the problem of overgrazing the common lands was solved by enclosure and private ownership.) If parents are effective in fulfilling their "governmental" role, then children can be induced to restrain their selfish tendencies and get along well together.

Conflict between siblings over parental investment is of great importance in determining how children turn out as adults. Even though it can be assumed that children's needs for parental investment will never be completely satisfied, how satisfied or dissatisfied a child feels is affected by comparisons with siblings. If Sibling A is seen to be favored, Sibling B tends to become disgruntled, and this can have permanent consequences in terms of promoting dislike of authority. Conversely, if Sibling A receives much worse treatment and is constantly scolded by parents, then Sibling B feels favored and is more likely to grow up into a happy person who respects authority.

COMPETITION AMONG SIBLINGS AND BIRTH ORDER EFFECTS

Conflict among siblings poses an evolutionary riddle. After all, siblings are just as closely related to each other as parents are to children. Why do children not have the same interest in providing for their siblings as their parents have in providing for them? This mystery was elucidated by Robert Trivers, who was the first biologist to provide a formal definition of parental investment. According to Trivers, parental investment is anything done by the parent for the offspring that increases its chances of survival while diminishing the parent's capacity to invest in other offspring (whether already in existence or not yet born).[3] This is an ingenious definition because it puts conflict between siblings right at the heart of parental investment. Not all social scientists would agree with this approach. For example, there may be some elasticity in parental effort. Parents with two children might conceivably work a lot harder and spend a lot more time caring for the children so that each receives the same high level of parental investment as the first would have if the second were not born. With the arrival of child number three, this hypothetical elasticity will obviously have reached its limit since two parents can hardly listen to the conversations of three children at the same time. Another clue to the inelasticity of parental effort is provided by the behavior of children themselves. Their aggressive antics suggest that they have been designed by natural selection to obtain the maximum benefits. Small children do not wait politely while their parents attend to the urgent need of a sibling, and they have no concept of parents themselves having needs of their own. A young child's own need always seems a great deal more urgent than a brother's or sister's.

Trivers was one of the first to formally recognize that the interests of parents and children are not the same. Parents with two children desire a fifty-fifty split of parental investment because this division helps them to guarantee the survival and success of both children. The children themselves do not. The rationale can be easily grasped by looking at the case of a firstborn child who is theoretically receiving 100 percent of parental effort. With the birth of a sibling, the share of parental investment plummets to 50 percent.

The mathematics of parental investment has some interesting implications that have not been fully pursued by psychologists. One is that the decline in parental investment with the birth of the second child is very much greater than that occasioned by later children. Treating the full pie of parental investment as equal to 100 percent, the birth of the second child decreases the share received by the first by 50 percent (100 percent–50 percent), whereas the birth of the third child decreases the share of parental investment going to the first two by only 17 percent (33 percent compared to 50 percent). Since there is the greatest conflict of interest between the first child and the second, it would be predicted that the level of hostility between the first and the second child would be greatest. Unfortunately there is no reliable evidence on this question.

Serious conflict between siblings in the animal world is both real and quite common. Occasionally, this escalates to the extent that siblings kill each other. This has provided the biggest ghoulish thrill in all of animal behavior, which is relished by Richard Dawkins in his early classic *The Selfish Gene*,[4] among others. Such deadly conflict is seen most often in birds where it evidently serves the function of family planning. First noted for eagles, which hatch two chicks but generally fledge only one, siblicide has recently been studied in cattle egrets and other species. The egrets are a particularly interesting example because they raise much larger clutches than eagles do and only kill off siblings during periods of food scarcity. By contrast, the older eaglet almost invariably batters its younger, weaker sibling to death while the parents stand by with astonishing indifference, in marked contrast to the reaction of human parents to fighting between siblings. When egret chicks are being well fed, they are drowsy and peaceful. When the food supply diminishes, they wake up in a bad mood and gang up on the smallest, weakest member of their group. Once a sibling is disposed of, the food supply improves and the egret chicks go back to sleep.[5]

What is fascinating about the egret story is that it is so simple. For egret chicks, the only really important currency of parental investment is food. Humans are in many ways the opposite. Food is usually quite unimportant unless it happens to be scarce. Human children are constantly alert, constantly vying with each other for parental love and attention. Egret chicks compete only for food, so they conflict with each other only when hungry. Human infants compete for parental affection, so they conflict with each other all of the time.

Competition over parental investment is one of the important influences that makes children in the same family different from each other. This conclusion has begun to emerge from recent discoveries in behavior genetics. Behavior geneticists have begun to move away from the view that parents matter only if they make children more alike. To the contrary, we are discovering that competition over parental investment, and how this competition is governed by parents, can push children to adopt different roles and behave in different ways.

BEHAVIOR GENETICS AND ITS PROBLEMS

One of the major weaknesses of behavior genetics is that it rarely studies the role of genetics in actual behavior, preferring instead to measure behavior indirectly using personality questionnaires.[6] The basic research strategy is to see whether family members will resemble each other on personality scales and to find out how much of this similarity is due to shared genes.

Studying siblings in the same family has several complications. Imagine that you are measuring sociability in two brothers, who are six and eight years old. Suppose that the older boy scores high on sociability and the younger one scores lower. Is this because of genetic differences, or does it merely reflect the fact that children become more sociable as they get older? Perhaps the difference has nothing to do with age as such. It may merely reflect the fact that firstborns receive more social stimulation from parents and therefore become more sociable. Nuisance variables such as age and birth order are referred to as confounding factors because they tend to confound, or hide, the true effect of the influence the scientist is studying—in this case, genetics. Behavior geneticists like to work with twins because they are the same age, have the same birth order, and are matched in a lot of other variables that could affect the outcome of the study. For example, they happen to share the same womb at the same time and are therefore exposed to a similar prenatal environment (even if it is not identical because location matters in the womb, as well as in real estate). Twins also conveniently come in two types, identical (who have exactly the same genes) and fraternal (who are no more closely related than ordinary siblings). This means that if individual differences in some trait are entirely caused by genes, then identical twins will be twice as similar as fraternal twins.

It turns out that whatever personality questionnaire is used, identical twins are a great deal more similar than fraternals. Even when the twins are separated at birth, as in the case of those of the Minnesota study of twins reared apart, a similar pattern emerges.[7] From such studies two important conclusions have been drawn. The first is that genetics accounts for around 50 percent of the differences between individuals for most personality traits. The second is that being raised in the same family does not make children more alike in personality.[8]

The results from studies of twins are backed up by other research designs. For instance, when children who have been adopted into a home are compared with the other children in the home, it is found that being raised in the same home accounts for only about 5 percent of total personality variation. Some scholars, including Judith Harris in *The Nurture Assumption*,[9] have used this finding to draw the conclusion that parents do not matter in how their children turn out. While this may seem a perfectly logical deduction, it is seriously flawed and flies in the face of much hard evidence proving that parental behavior does matter.

The problems are threefold: conceptual, technical, and evidentiary. The conceptual problem is in the assumption that parents do not matter unless they make children more alike. Students of family systems find that the relationships between a parent and different children can be very different and that this has consequences for how the children turn out. For example, if parents are often hostile towards a child, that child is more likely to experience depression and to behave in antisocial ways as an adolescent. Parents may be committed to fairness in the home, but they rarely treat their children the same because the children are temperamentally different, have different needs, and pose different challenges to parents. These differences in treatment lead to different outcomes independent of biological predispositions. There is a difference between personality and life course outcomes.

The technical problems of behavior genetic studies are many and are quite well known amongst psychologists. The most basic problems with concluding that the shared environment within families is of little importance have to do with (a) the limited environmental differences among respectable adoptive homes and (b) the use of questionnaires to study outcomes. No adoption board would place a child in the kind of low-parental investment home that is the nexus of our most serious social problems. Of course, these American homes may provide a much more nurturant environment than that available to children in the urban slums of underdeveloped countries. We cannot conclude that the family environment creates no personality similarities because the research has not looked at enough different kinds of families. If different parental investment is thought of as analogous to a medicine in a drug trial, we may have falsely concluded that the medicine does not work because we have not used a high enough dose.

Behavior geneticists have relied largely on self-report questionnaires. In these tests, people typically either agree or disagree with long lists of statements such as "I am glad that I am alive" (measuring depression, in the case of disagreement) and "I like to arrange flowers" (measuring femininity). Psychologists have been painfully aware for decades that these easy-to-use instruments have a tenuous connection with actual behavioral outcomes. Just because a person scores high on a measure of aggressiveness does not mean that he or she will be involved in bar-room brawls. Just because they score low on risk taking does not mean that they will not occasionally take foolish risks. Rather, the personality questionnaire assesses biological predisposition in these directions. Personality tests measure behavior at a second remove. They are easy to administer, but they do not tell us how people will turn out. The simplest solution to this problem is to look for genetic influences by studying actual behavior. When researchers study behavior as distinct from personality, they generally find that genetic influences are small or nonexistent.[10] The actual evidence collected by behavior geneticists does not permit us to draw the conclusion that parents do not matter.

It is always easy to pick holes in some field of research, but the most serious problem for the view that parents do not matter is evidentiary. It comes from incompatible findings. These derive from experimental studies in which parental behavior is deliberately modified to deal with children's conduct problems. Whether these studies are conducted with insecurely attached infants, preschool children, or older children, many show very beneficial effects that can be both large and long lasting even when the parental training is of modest duration. (See Chapter 10 for a more detailed discussion.) The fact that children in different societies are raised in systematically different ways and differ predictably in their adult behavior is also relevant evidence (see Chapter 9).

Experimental studies of interventions with parents of problem children not only provide evidence supporting the importance of parental behavior, but they allow us to conclude without any ambiguity that the differing outcomes are caused by differences in parental behavior. The causal conclusion can be drawn because the studies are actual experiments. An experiment is an ideally simplified situation in which groups differ only in the experimental treatment. If the groups differ at the end of the study, this must be due to their different treatment in the experiment. Of course, there is a great deal of other unambiguous evidence that parents do matter, from the effects of early social deprivation in orphanages, to enrichment in Head Start programs, to achievement beyond the IQ of Chinese Americans, which is assembled throughout this book.

It is quite clear that the shared family environment does make children resemble each other in behavior. Children in some families are much more likely to be industrious and achievement-motivated, whereas children in other families are much more likely to be delinquent. Of course, this does not mean that parents are going to get inside the brains of their children, so to speak, to modify the basic chemistry that is responsible for broad personality traits, such as extroversion and sensitivity to emotional upset. What parents can do is to modify how their chemistry affects behavior. For instance, the pioneering work of Jerome Kagan suggests that parents of shy children can help them to come out of their shell by gradually encouraging them to be more adventurous.[11]

Perhaps the greatest theoretical pitfall in interpreting the findings of modern behavior genetics is to assume that parents can only affect children by making them more similar. The studies show that growing up in the same home tends to make children develop into very different people. There are two very good reasons why parents might play a role in making children different. The first is that they treat children differently. The second is that even if they treat children the same, the children's perception of how they are treated (which has important consequences for behavioral development) may be very different. In other words, the assumption of Judith Harris and others that parents can only make siblings more alike is false. It is difficult to blame anyone for making this mistake because the whole landscape of what makes children of the same family so different from each other has only just begun to be mapped. According to at least one cutting-edge study of antisocial behavior and depression, what shows up in behavior genetics as the "nonshared" environment (or environmental effects which differ among siblings) may be largely explained by the fact that parents treat children differently.[12] Even if they didn't, the same treatment could produce a very different response in different children. These phenomena can only be understood within the context of a potentially destructive competition between siblings over parental investment. That is, they arise from the "tragedy of the commons" created by competitive interactions between siblings.

COMPETITION OVER PARENTAL INVESTMENT

Although there is little scientific information about the obvious fact that children in the same family spend a lot of time squabbling with each other, some of the findings of scientific studies make sense only if this conflict over parental investment occurs. As scientific observers, we are rather like astronomers inferring the Big Bang from the few straggling light waves entering our telescopes billions of light years later. What we are looking at are birth order effects on personality, criminal behavior, and political attitudes. Recently, developmental behavioral geneticists have begun to look at the different treatment of siblings by parents as a way of accounting for differences in depression and delinquency.

The study of personality differences as a function of birth order has a very checkered history. To give you the flavor of this frustrating field of inquiry, the authors of an early authoritative review of the literature, appropriately named Ernst and Angst,[13] concluded that there was nothing to it. Frank Sulloway reanalyzed their work and concluded that it was badly biased and wrong.[14] His work indicated reliable differences according to which firstborns were more competitive and jealous, and laterborns were more agreeable and open to new experiences. Later, Judith Harris reanalyzed Sulloway's reanalysis and found *him* to be biased and wrong.[15] One way of making sense of all of this is to conclude that birth order effects on personality, if they exist, are either too small or too complex to be reliably detected.

While personality differences due to birth order are generally quite small, birth order can lead to big differences in political behavior, which is the focus of much of Sulloway's original research based on biographies of prominent historical figures. Large effects have also been found for sex roles and for criminality. According to Sulloway's theory, firstborns are more likely to identify with parents, which makes them more leadership-oriented and more conservative in their political attitudes. Laterborns are more rebellious and more liberal.

Recent studies of contemporary political behavior do not, however, confirm the results from Sulloway's study of historical figures.[16] For example, there is no reliable evidence that firstborns today are more conservative or more likely to hold political office. The one exception is congresspeople, who are more likely to be firstborns, but this is attributable to the fact that congresspeople have college educations, and firstborns (particularly sons) are more likely to have received third-level education. Judith Harris makes the interesting point that birth order may have been more salient in the past when inheritance practices—such as primogeniture, or the passing of property to first sons—created a great deal of favoritism and jealousy within families and provided firstborn sons with a great deal of privilege and opportunity not shared by their younger brothers and sisters. If they were doing so well by the status quo, why wouldn't they be conservatives?

Judith Harris's re-analysis of Ernst and Angst[17] turned up at least one other interesting effect. She found that if the personality data were contributed by family members, 75 percent of the studies produced findings supportive of Sulloway's theory. If it was provided by the person themselves, only 22 percent supported the theory.[18] This means that even if birth order differences are illusory, family members believe that they exist.

Harris proposes two possible interpretations. The first is that since laterborns are actually younger, they will inevitably be seen by parents as less mature (and therefore less responsible and more rebellious). The second is derived from Ernst and Angst, who noticed this phenomenon and provided several possible explanations. It is that the firstborn personality is "parent-specific." That is, firstborns act like firstborns are supposed to do only in the family context. Outside the home, birth order differences are not seen. This view is consistent with the assumption that sibling behavior, at least in the home, is shaped in predictable ways by competition over parental investment.

When personality differences are detected, they are usually found in the comparison of firstborns with laterborns. In his review of the birth order literature, Sulloway found evidence that firstborns are more likely to fit the "goody-two-shoes" stereotype. They identify more with parental authority. This means that they tend to be more polite, civilized, and ambitious. By contrast, laterborns tended to be more rebellious—they were "born to rebel," according to the title of Sulloway's book.[19]

Sulloway found that laterborns in his database were much more receptive to new ideas. For instance, they were much more willing to accept innovations in science, such as Darwin's theory of evolution by natural selection. According to Sulloway's data, based on the biographies of historical figures, laterborns at the age of eighty are as receptive to new ideas as firstborns at the age of twenty. Sulloway also concluded that laterborns were more likely to be involved in political rebellions, such as the French Revolution in 1789. He argues that the over-representation of laterborns in the ranks of political rebellions arose from a constitutional dislike of authority that developed, along with other personality differences, from the interactions within families during early childhood.

Why might sibling interactions produce this pattern of personality differences? Sulloway sketches a theory that is loosely based on parental investment. He assumes that children are perpetually locked in a competition over parental affection. The firstborn succeeds in winning over the parents by identifying with them and acting "as good as gold." When the second child arrives, according to Sulloway, it cannot possibly beat its older rival at playing "goody-two-shoes," so it gravitates to a very different niche by being confrontational, fighting not only with the sibling but also rejecting the status quo, which revolves around an admiration society consisting of the parents and the first child.

This theory is interesting, but it is not well developed enough to be very convincing. For example, if the first child happened to be difficult, perhaps due to prolonged illness, does this mean that the second would occupy the vacant "goody-two-shoes" niche? Sulloway's account does not allow any clear prediction to be made because he does not explain in enough detail what it is that the children are competing over, or why.

On its face, the theory is also counterintuitive. When the second child is born, it comes into a world in which the first seems to have all the advantages, being older and therefore more competent in all aspects of development including movement and language and having already had an opportunity to become securely attached to the parents. Why would the second child now want to ruin its chances by behaving obnoxiously and causing grief to the parents? Perhaps obnoxious behavior is an effective tactic that a small child can use to win the attention of its parents. If parental attention is the fount from which parental love and all forms of parental investment must flow, then it probably makes sense for the younger child to do everything in its power to be noticed. While this idea is counterintuitive, it does capture the dynamics of problem behavior in children. For example, careful research in a classroom setting has shown that the bad behavior of children may be caused by the attention this gets them from the teacher. When the teacher ignores their bad behavior, it disappears. In all probability, what occurs in the classroom is a reflection of low parental investment received at home. The children are competing for the attention of the teacher as a mother-substitute.

Even if laterborn children tend to be more of a handful for their parents than the first child was, this does not mean that they are less loved. In fact, the opposite is true. In one study, 50 percent of parents with two children admitted that they preferred one child over the other. Of these, 86 percent said that they preferred their second child over the first.[20] This is an astonishingly clear result. It may be due to a parental adaptation designed to bias investment towards the younger, more vulnerable child, or it may reflect the effectiveness of tactics used by the second child to worm its way into the heart of the parents, or both. Interestingly, parents also reported more discipline problems with the secondborns, although this may reflect their immaturity. Results of this study are corroborated by observation of the interactions between mothers and their young children in two-child families. Mothers were more affectionate in their behavior toward secondborns than firstborns. The secondborn children also demonstrated more warmth and affection for the mother.[21]

While we know far less about the dynamics of family interactions in the early years than we ought to, the argument that these generate different behavioral profiles based on birth order is strongly supported by differences in risk of delinquency and criminality. Moreover, since children in larger families receive less parental investment, they would be expected to have more behavior problems. It has long been known that children in large families are at a higher risk for being delinquent. However, family size used to be greater for poor families, so that economic deprivation was suspected to play a role. Statistical control of family income found that delinquency is higher in larger families regardless of income.[22]

The effects of family size on delinquent behavior are fairly large. For instance, in one early study, conducted in 1950, when families were much bigger than they are today, being in a family larger than four increased the risk of delinquency by 27 percent compared to children in families of four or less.[23] For high-risk poor boys in 145 black families living in St. Louis, Missouri, whose two parents had been arrested, approximately half were delinquent if they lived in families of three or less children. If they lived in families of four or more children, all were delinquent. Similar findings applied to the girls, whose delinquency rates were less than half those of their brothers.[24]

The effects of family size are largely explainable in terms of birth order differences. A firstborn or only child as an adolescent is about 30 percent less likely to be delinquent (based on self-report questionnaires).[25] This finding can be explained in terms of the greater amount of interaction between parents and the first, or only, child, which may produce more identification with parental authority and increased willingness to obey authority. Moreover, in larger families, the laterborn children tend to get squeezed out of parental attention, making them more likely to be influenced by antisocial peer groups.

Birth order effects are highly complex and difficult to study. Researchers must not only deal with the many different types of families, so far as family size and age differences are concerned, but also have to take into account the sex of siblings. Boys tend to be much more delinquent than girls. How delinquent an adolescent is is not just a feature of their own gender, however, but of the gender of their siblings. Among three-child families, second- born boys with an older and a younger sister are much more delinquent than second-borns in all-boy families. Among two-child families, a girl having an older sister is more delinquent than any boy in a two-child family, even a second-born boy with an older brother.[26]

These findings indicate that there are strong contrast effects. That is, children are comparing themselves with siblings, or perhaps they are reacting to comparisons that the parents make. Analogous contrast effects have also been found for personality development. For example, one classic early study by Helen Koch (as reanalyzed by Orville Brim[27]) found that when boys are raised together, this tends to make them more masculine (at least to the extent of scoring high on measures of leadership, self-confidence, assertiveness, competitiveness, and aggression). Conversely, for boys with an older sister, scores on masculinity are as low as those of most girls. What is so interesting about this finding is that the effects go in two directions. The older sister makes boys highly feminine. At the same time, the younger boy makes the sister highly masculine. In fact, Brim concluded that birth order was two-thirds as important as sex itself in determining masculinity.

Frank Sulloway explains these phenomena by arguing that masculinity, as a status-enhancing tendency, is a strategy of firstborns as well as a strategy of men. A simpler interpretation is that the competitive tendencies of boys tend to exaggerate each other. Since the older brother of a boy will want to prevail over his younger sibling, this will enhance his aggressive and competitive tendencies. Having a younger sister would be less of a challenge in this respect and would call forth a lower level of masculinity. Exactly the same logic applies to an older sister dominating her siblings.

Since girls are generally more cooperative and less competitive, older sisters will generally tend to stimulate far less masculine, or competitive, responses in siblings.[28] Sex role development therefore involves a complex thicket of influences including one's own gender, gender of siblings, birth order, and the joint action of birth order with gender of self and siblings. It is hard to see how such phenomena can be understood without the assumption that children are actively competing over parental investment.

When interactions among siblings are responsible for differences in personality, they are referred to as contrast effects. Contrast effects may also be produced by interactions with parents. Parents may treat children very differently, without necessarily being conscious of any favoritism, and this may have major effects on tendencies towards delinquency and depression of adolescents. This conclusion was drawn from a study of pairs of siblings in which parental behavior was measured using videotapes of interactions between parents and children. The videotapes allowed parental behavior to be analyzed independently, ruling out the obvious biases to be expected from asking parents to describe their relationship with each child. The researchers found that the amount of depressive symptoms and antisocial behavior of teenagers was strongly related to the amount of hostility and rejection directed at them by parents. Even more important than the general atmosphere of hostility and negativity in the home was which child bore the brunt of the abuse. If parents are particularly hard on Child A, Child B is less likely to be moody and problematic.[29]

One problem about interpreting this study is that we do not really know, from the data, whether the hostility of the parents turns children into problem adolescents or whether difficult children bring out the worst in parents. Both are likely to be true. Without getting into the fine points of how important one causal direction is compared to the other, it is quite clear that children who are favored by parents have an advantage compared to those who are not. In other words, children who overgraze their parents' affection are starving out their brothers and sisters. The interactions between siblings in families are a real "tragedy of the commons" because the desire of children to be the apple of their parents' eye can be realized only at the expense of siblings. From the perspective of the child who gets cast as the dark sheep of the family, the love and affection shown to a more favored child must convince the less favored one that he or she has little possibility of improving the situation. If they can never be the "goody-two-shoes" character in the family play, then they might well give up trying to compete for parental affection through good behavior. Instead, their tactics might revolve around disruptive and antisocial activities that tend to punish the parents for their lack of emotional support. From their point of view, the commons of parental love must seem badly overgrazed.

One interesting implication of this study is that when parents are generally hostile and negative in their dealings with children, the children are better off if they do not have a sibling who fares much better, presumably because it sets a standard of comparison against which they judge their own treatment. Conversely, children who are generally treated with affection can benefit from the presence in the household of a badly behaved individual who is the subject of parental wrath and rejection. The authors of the study have christened this "sibling barricade." It is as though children were sheltering beneath their rejected sibling, feeling dry and warm as he or she endured the cold deluge of parental disapproval. The sibling barricade concept is important because it shows one way in which parents can influence personality development that is independent of an individual's own genes.[30]

If this logic is correct, then it is possible to make all sorts of predictions about interactions between siblings that will direct most readers to the familiar terrain of their own childhoods:

- Children in a family will be constantly comparing themselves with others to establish how they stand in respect to parental favor.

- Children will try to make themselves look good at the expense of their brothers and sisters. For example, if the siblings are fighting, it will always have been started by someone else.

- Children will be jealous of signs of parental affection shown to siblings.

- Children will actively undermine the positions of brothers and sisters by reporting on, and exaggerating, their misdeeds.

- Children will initiate fights with siblings without any obvious objective reason. The logic is that by doing so they can get the sibling into trouble, which may improve their own relative position in respect of parental favor, and hence parental investment. In the case of such spontaneous fights, favored children should most often be the victims and nonfavored children the initiators.

The logic of the barricade effect can easily be applied to birth order effects on criminal behavior. Since firstborns have a significant head start in currying their parents' love without the spoiling effects of competitive siblings, they are likely to retain their advantage into childhood. If the firstborn is well-behaved, later children will suffer an adverse comparison, particularly in view of the fact that their presence is associated with the emergence of a lot of conflict and trouble between siblings. Many parents may blame the second child for the trouble, possibly because they overlook the fact that it takes two to tangle. Aggressive disruptiveness is also a tactic that is more likely to be used by smaller children to obtain parental attention. For example, if they pick a fight with their older sibling, they can expect parents to rush to their side to help them out in an unequal match. If so, then antisocial tendencies may get reinforced from an early age, which would help to explain the strong birth order effects in delinquency.

WHY CHILDREN IN THE SAME FAMILY
ARE SO DIFFERENT

The whole question of what makes children who grow up in the same family so different from each other is an exciting frontier in developmental psychology.[31] We know that personality similarities can be attributed largely to genetics, which accounts for about half of the differences among individuals for most traits. On the other hand, probably less than 5 percent is explained in terms of the shared family environment, which comprises influences such as family wealth/poverty, religion, urban decay, parental alcoholism, parental divorce, government programs, TV violence (assuming the same programs are seen by siblings), exposure to environmental toxins, schools attended, and virtually every variable ever studied by sociologists. This is an astonishing and, to many, an appalling conclusion. Yet, if you accept that personality is biologically based, the conclusion is not all that remarkable. To say that parents have little effect on the biology of their children's brains should not be a revelation. Neither should it be confused with drawing the conclusion that parents can't affect how their children *behave*.

Studies of behavior find that children growing up in the same home, and people growing up in the same society, where they are exposed to similar parental practices, tend to be more alike. For example, in one study of the expression of aggressive behavior, elementary school children watched an inflated clown-like plastic doll being beaten up. Their aggressive behavior directed at the doll was then recorded. While this may seem like a game, it has been found to be a valid measure of aggressiveness in children that agrees with the evaluations of peers and teachers. Oddly, there was no effect of genetics, even though everyone knows that aggression, as a personality trait, is highly heritable. There is a world of difference between being biologically predisposed to doing something and actually doing it. It is precisely in this realm of impulse control that parental influence exerts its strongest effects.[32]

What makes children in the same family so different? Behavior geneticists have been puzzling over this conundrum for years and have not come up with any very satisfying answers. Of the possibilities that have been considered, some of the more obvious ones can be dismissed. They include:

- Birth order. Although siblings vary predictably in risk of delinquency and in masculinity, birth order influences are generally too small to account for much of the variation in adult outcomes.

- Peer influences. Siblings sit in different classrooms, have different teachers, and, to some extent, make different friends. While it is true that the peer group can affect whether teenagers smoke cigarettes and marijuana, this may simply be a question of drug availability in the neighborhood, as Judith Harris acknowledges.[33] Best friends are likely to belong to the same peer group (or groups). If these groups have access to cigarettes or marijuana, they are quite likely to smoke them. There is little evidence of any substantial, long-lasting personality or character change that is produced directly by peers independently of the effects of neighborhood environment. So far as attitudes and behavior are concerned, adults tend to resemble their parents to a frightening degree and bear little trace of the adolescent peer groups to which they briefly conformed.

If the usual suspects of siblings and peers are not solving the riddle, what conclusions are going to be drawn by the intrepid developmental psychologists of the future? The answer is *interactions*. Unfortunately, psychological development is more complex than the variables that we have assembled to account for it. We attempt to capture butterflies using strings when we need nets. An interaction is the combination of two variables, and it is like the crossing over of lines in a net.

Beginning with the premise that children compete for parental investment, some of the important interactions are beginning to emerge. For example, we know that in the study of the development of depression and antisocial tendencies, the amount of conflict and negativity displayed by parents predicts an increase in psychiatric symptoms in adolescents. The comparison between how a child is treated and how siblings are treated is what really counts, though. Children are designed by natural selection to be jealous of the amount of parental investment their siblings are receiving. Even in comparatively abusive homes, children who are treated better than siblings feel happier and are less likely to develop psychiatric problems, including conduct disorders. Children who are treated more harshly than others become disgruntled. They rebel against authority and develop antisocial attitudes and behavior. They also tend to be anxious and unhappy. This sets them up for serious psychiatric disorders, such as depression.[34]

One reason that parenting styles show up as comparatively weak predictors of adult personality is that these act in combination with other influences, such as birth order, sibling sex, and social status. For instance, an overpermissive parenting style is much less likely to result in criminal behavior for children from affluent households than it is for children living in urban slums where trading in illegal drugs is a primary source of income.

Parental behavior also acts in combination with a child's biological temperament. Some infants are born shy and fearful. Some parents may be highly protective of such infants and do everything to prevent them from being alarmed or overstimulated. Jerome Kagan, a leading researcher in the study of personality development, has found that parents tend to react against unreasonable fearfulness in their children by encouraging, or perhaps compelling, them to face their fears. Kagan finds that when parents teach infants to be more adventurous, they lose their shyness over time. It is quite unlikely that if the same parents had really reckless children they would encourage them to be even more thrill-seeking, resulting in avoidable injuries. Instead, they would tend to rein in their activities. In this case, parental behaviors are equivalent because children are encouraged to take the same low level of risk, but the consequences are opposite. In a behavior genetic study of the thrill-seeking personality trait, parental behavior would show up as having no effect whatever. In reality, parents can have a strong influence on how willing children are to assume risks but this can only be understood in terms of an interaction between the policies of the parents and the biology of the child.[35]

Children develop different personalities because of the complex social world of the family to which they must adapt. One adaptive challenge is posed by competitive siblings, whether they are older or younger. Siblings comprise a semiautonomous social system that serves their joint interests and, at the same time, allows them to compete amongst themselves for parental attention and favor. Competition over parental attention is illustrated by the way in which family dynamics affect IQ scores.

PARENTAL INVESTMENT AND INTELLIGENCE

In a study of poor mothers, conducted in Baltimore, researchers found that the birth of other children prior to the firstborn's fifth birthday had several deleterious effects.[36] Young children with sibling competitors scored lower on several behavioral measures. They had a greater likelihood of sadness and shyness, disobedience, and low academic preparedness (Preschool Inventory Score). Interestingly, the disruptive effects of a relatively short birth interval between the firstborn and secondborn are more prevalent for boys since girls could tolerate a birth interval as short as two years without any emotional or academic consequences.[37] These results can easily be accounted for in terms of sibling competition over parental investment. They also make some sense of the endless struggle among siblings over parental attention.

Small children often go to extraordinary lengths to obtain the attention of their mothers. This phenomenon can be seen in full force when the mother's attention is directed elsewhere, for example, if she is speaking on the phone. The child is likely to engage in sabotage by making lots of noise, by pulling at the telephone, or by asking pointless questions. If all this fails, the child may take the opportunity of obtaining prohibited foods or candy. He might then amuse himself by playing with breakable objects or even with sharp knives, or getting into other forms of mischief. Eventually the mother notices and ends the phone conversation to intervene.

Small children often misbehave in order to receive maternal attention. The arrival of subsequent infants clearly reduces the amount of attention the mother can give to each and may thereby increase the amount of naughty behavior exhibited by each child. Of course, new siblings also increase economic stresses within a child's home, particularly if the family is poor to begin with. It is very difficult to tease apart all of these influences, but they all fall under the rubric of reduced parental investment. As mentioned previously, reduced parental investment associated with large family size and with poverty go along with increased rates of criminal behavior all around the world according to the results of an extensive literature review by sociologist Lee Ellis at Minot State University.[38]

Increased family size is also associated with declining IQ scores. This decline still occurs when economic status of the parents is controlled. Although the addition of each new family member decreases the average IQ within the family by less than one IQ point,[39] the effect of family size is generally augmented by the effect of birth order. That is, firstborns tend to score higher than secondborns, who score higher than thirdborns, and so forth. These results are a logical conclusion when you consider how parental investment is diluted by the birth of more children into the family. If parents spoke to all five of their children as much as they spoke to the first, they would suffer from chronic sore throats!

These basic findings have been produced in at least five different countries, including the United States. The early findings are reviewed by Ernst and Angst in their book on birth order.[40] While Ernst and Angst found a very clear pattern of firstborns having higher IQs, for very large families (with more than five children) the birth order effect reverses. Firstborns in large families do systematically worse than laterborns. Ernst and Angst were so disgusted with this inconsistency that they concluded that there is no consistent effect of birth order at all. Yet there is a very simple possible explanation. Mothers who produced very large families tended to begin reproducing early in life—they were teen mothers. Teen mothers are inexperienced, and observational study suggests that they are both insensitive and inconsistent in their treatment of infants.[41]

In conclusion, the joint effects of family size and birth order on IQ scores make perfect sense if they are viewed from the perspective of competition over parental investment. Since children compete with each other over a limited amount of parental investment, the advantage of one is often to the detriment of another. Siblings, like herdsmen, may get along fine most of the time, but if a real conflict of interest emerges, family life becomes a tragedy of the commons.

Chapter 6

Money and Parental Investment

Life often seems unfair. Children of affluent parents tend to do well in school, whereas children of the poor are often academically disadvantaged. Yet, the real advantage of the children of professionals in respect to intellectual development is attributable more to love than to money. They do well in school principally because their parents have made a personal effort to interact with them in enriching ways. This provides important brain stimulation during critical early stages of development. Children who experience a warm relationship with their parents reflect this back on their future social interactions, including those with their own children.

PARENTAL INVESTMENT AND ECONOMIC COMPETITION

The long haul of human history has been an endless treadmill of reproduction, which has been balanced by forces of destruction, including disease, malnourishment, and warfare. The great tragedy of losing a child is relatively rare today in the West, due to effective techniques of controlling infectious diseases, but in earlier centuries it happened in virtually every family, wealthy as well as poor. Prior to the advantages of modern medicine, as many children died as reached maturity. Childbirth was extremely risky for the baby as well as the mother, and delicate infants often expired within a few weeks of birth. Those who survived infancy faced the many devastating illnesses of childhood, such as diphtheria and scarlet fever. Having survived to adolescence, they could be swept away by epidemics of infectious diseases such as influenza, bubonic plague, typhoid, or small-pox. The fact that so many children were born and so few survived meant that it would have been foolish for parents to become too closely attached to their children. Thus, evidence for intense parental grief at the loss of a child does not emerge in English diaries and other literary sources until late in the eighteenth century.[1]

Routine treatment of children in sixteenth- and early seventeenth-century England would be considered abusive today. According to historian Lawrence Stone:

There was the deliberate breaking of the young child's will, first by the harshest physical beating and later by overwhelming psychological pressures, which was thought to be the key to successful child-rearing in the sixteenth and seventeenth centuries. These four factors, the lack of a unique mother figure in the first few years of life [in the case of wealthy families that handed over infants to wet nurses], the constant loss of close relatives, siblings, parents, nurses and friends through premature death, the physical imprisonment of the infant in tight swaddling-clothes in early months, and the deliberate breaking of the child's will all contributed to a "psychic numbing."[2]

The consequence of this low-investment type of rearing was a society that was distinctly lacking in empathy, in which people

found it difficult to establish close emotional ties to any other person. Children were neglected, brutally treated, and even killed; adults treated each other with suspicion and hostility; affect was low and hard to find. To an anthropologist, there would be nothing very surprising about such a society, which closely resembles the Mundugumor in New Guinea in the twentieth century, as described by Margaret Mead.[3]

In the modern world, far fewer children are born. American women today produce an average of two children each, compared to an average number of five children per mother in 1900.[4] At the same time, the mortality rate for children is extremely low. In addition, there has been an unprecedented increase in incomes and monetary wealth, allowing, in theory at least, for very high levels of parental investment per child. In recent decades, however, unprecedented increases in social problem statistics suggest that parental investment has actually declined. There are two ways of resolving this paradox. The first is to recognize that despite the increase in wealth of the United States as a whole, many people have remained mired down in poverty, and conditions in poor families have never been worse than they are today because of a lack of opportunities for upward mobility in the form of well-paid blue collar jobs, the decline of two-parent families, and the encroachment of organized crime in poor neighborhoods.[5] The second is to argue that the demands of careers in dual-income families lead to some neglect of children, making them more vulnerable to social problems. This argument is politically incorrect, but there is some evidence supporting it (see Chapter 7).

POVERTY AND SOCIAL PROBLEMS

The United States has gone from a society of workers presided over by a rich elite of industrialists to a society that is more evenly divided between rich and poor classes. One convenient line of demarcation is whether people have a college education or not. The percentage of 18- to 24-year-olds enrolled in institutions of higher education has risen from 2.3 percent in 1900 to 51.1 percent in 1990, for example.[6] This indicates that the educated elite now comprises about half of the population, whereas at the beginning of the century it included only around a fiftieth. Since education is a vehicle of social mobility and strongly predicts income, it is no surprise to learn that the educated elite are also fast becoming the wealthy elite.

Conversely, children of the poor do less well at school and are more likely to get into trouble. Does being poor undermine parental investment, thereby causing academic failure and social problems? Does poverty cause people to drop out of school, abuse controlled substances, beat their lovers, abuse their children, deface public property, steal, lie, perpetrate confidence tricks, participate in prostitution, set fire to buildings, commit rape, run illegal gambling operations, commit homicide, and commit armed robbery? Sociologists have often drawn this conclusion.

Data on young people with police records show that about a quarter of middle-class adolescents get written up by police for some offense compared to about a half of working-class adolescents, indicating that being of lower socioeconomic status doubles the probability of having a police record.[7] Poverty is also associated with other social problems. Women who bear out-of-wedlock infants in their teenage years are much more likely to (a) be from poor families, (b) be from single-parent households, and (c) be doing badly in school. In other words, their current economic situation tends to be bleak, and their personal characteristics are predictive of future poverty for themselves and their children (see Chapter 8).

The association between poverty and drug addiction has been well known to historians, ever since the depiction of "Gin Lane" in a woodcut by William Hogarth, which showed poor women and children under the influence of this form of alcohol, which was extremely cheap in eighteenth-century London. The same association between addiction and poverty is found today. For instance, poor people are three times more likely to be alcoholic than are those in the middle class.[8] As Oscar Wilde said: "Work is the curse of the drinking classes." Poor people are more likely to suffer from high blood pressure and all other kinds of stress-related disorders, including serious mental disorders such as schizophrenia. Poverty is also a predictor of occupational and educational problems, including unemployment, school dropout, failure to pay bills on time, loan delinquency, and so forth.

Poverty goes along with increased risk of every social problem studied by sociologists. Why do these associations exist? The most obvious interpretation, that poverty causes social problems, can be easily dismissed. We have all heard of, or known, individuals who experienced the most grinding poverty all of their lives and never thought of beginning a criminal career in order to solve their economic problems. Furthermore, some of the poorest regions in the United States also have the lowest crime rates. This is true because crime is concentrated in urban areas, and some of the poorest regions are rural and therefore have lower crime rates.[9]

Just because poverty goes along with social problems, from violent crime to unwanted teen pregnancies, it does not mean that poverty causes these problems. Correlation is not the same as causation. One reasonable theory is that a host of social problems befall the economically underprivileged, not because they lack money but because they live in environments that undermine child socialization in the sense that children do not learn to control impulses and to have high career aspirations. For a variety of reasons, including the prevalence of organized crime, such difficult environments are much more likely to be found in large cities.

There is plenty of evidence that poor parents are likely to use a more insensitive, less nurturant parenting style that evokes a less civilized, more rebellious attitude in children. This difference manifests itself in superficial matters such as the use of slang in preference to formally correct language. It also shows up in behavioral problems including poor academic performance, delinquency, unrestricted early sexual activity, increased aggressiveness, and higher rates of arrest for criminal offenses.[10, 11] The fact that the tone and texture of parent-child relationships in poor homes are different from those in affluent homes shows up most clearly in a detailed study of the content of their conversations discussed later in this chapter.

Aggressiveness is associated with the reduced parental investment characteristic of poor homes. Aspects of low parental investment include lack of emotional warmth in parent-child relationships, inconsistent parental regulation of behavior, and greater use of corporal punishment. Harsh parenting can produce antisocial behavior in children who do not have a particular genetic predisposition for it.[12, 13, 14]

It is no accident that parents in some of the most economically depressed areas in the United States, inner-city slums, believe strongly in the value of corporal punishment and take a dim view of social workers' emphasis on understanding, communication, and the use of rewards rather than punishment. It is easy to decry such parenting practices as abusive if it were not for the fact that they have been practiced throughout history and are seen in all of the many violent societies studied by anthropologists. It is a mistake to assume that these children are being abused by dysfunctional, or evil, adults, or to describe them as "undersocialized." The point is that they are being socialized to take their place in the brutally violent society of the ghetto rather than to find gainful employment in higher status jobs.

Harsh socialization is associated with poor impulse control, weak self-discipline, and a lack of ambition. These qualities manifest themselves early in high school dropout, which is more likely for poor children. There are clear social class differences in academic conscientiousness. Children from higher social classes score much higher on need for achievement in the United States and in England.[15]

The greater risk of so many social problems among the poor can be explained in terms of reduced parental investment. This does not deny that biology also affects the risk of being delinquent. For instance, behavior geneticist David Rowe of the University of Arizona has shown that people who commit antisocial acts also are sexually active at an early age and that these tendencies are inherited together.[16] Unrestricted sexual activity is also connected in complex ways with academic underperformance.[17] The interesting thing about having a genetic predisposition for criminal behavior is that it is most likely to be expressed in an environment of reduced parental investment.

CAREERS AND REPRODUCTION

While teen pregnancy is seen as deviant and problematic today, in previous centuries, it was normative for women to begin their reproductive careers while still in their teens. Of course teenage mothers then were generally married, whereas today the majority are not. Teen pregnancy is seen as a problem today not only because the mother will be poor herself, but also because she is introducing her children and their descendants to a cycle of poverty with all of its difficulties for socialization and consequent social problems. This process begins when early reproduction interferes with education and career development.

The modern conflict between academic performance and sexual behavior revolves around limited time, energy, and money. It is difficult to raise children while simultaneously developing a career. Only about 13 to 17 percent of contemporary female college graduates succeed in combining a career and having children.[18] This conflict can be observed during the college years since women with poor grades tend to have active social lives while women with high grades generally have inactive social lives. From a practical perspective, some women often delay the birth of their first child for as much as ten years while they establish themselves in a profession.[19]

Education can be connected to parental investment in two different ways. First, parents who invest a great deal in each child tend to increase the probability that their children will be academically successful and develop careers. This works via direct effects of parental stimulation on intellectual development, and it operates more subtly by increasing the child's ambition and need for achievement. Second, education is a route to occupational success and the development of a career. In the past, this allowed men to make a higher investment in their children, largely by providing economic support for a stable home environment in which most of the actual child care was the direct responsibility of their wives. Today, careers allow both men and women to provide economic support for the care of their children. This means paying commercial providers for child care during much of the day. Whether putting children in day-care effectively reduces parental investment depends on the quality of care provided. Since wealthy parents have access to better day-care, their children are less likely to suffer adverse consequences of nonmaternal care.

Reduced parental investment goes along with poor academic performance, and this is clearly demonstrated in ethnic group differences in school grades (see Chapter 9). Further evidence comes from the finding that parental divorce is associated with reduced grades. This phenomenon can be observed at all levels of the educational system from elementary school[20] to high school[21] and beyond. The decline applies to both sexes and may be mediated by reactions to parental conflict both before and during the separation.[22, 23]

Teen pregnancy is also linked to poor academic performance. Data from the National Longitudinal Study of Youth strongly confirms this view: teenage girls in the bottom fifth for reading and math skills were almost five times as likely to become mothers in a two-year period than those in the top fifth (29 percent compared to 6 percent).[24] While much of this effect may be explainable in terms of economic status and ethnicity, the connection between an active sexual life and poor academic performance cuts across class and ancestry. In one study involving a population of young women with wealthy parents, it was found that merely asking one question about attitude toward casual sex predicted college grades eight times better than their ACT scores, which is rather astonishing when you consider that ACT scores were specifically designed to predict college grades. (Subjects rated their agreement to the item, "I can imagine myself being comfortable and enjoying 'casual' sex with different partners," using a seven-point scale.) By being sexually active, these young women were expressing a lack of interest in long-term occupational goals to the deep disgust of their wealthy parents, who were investing a lot of money in their education. Interestingly, the sexual attitudes of young men did not predict their academic performance. A likely interpretation of this is that men can operate in two modes simultaneously, both wanting to be sexually active and wanting to be academically successful, whereas young women tend to focus on one objective to the exclusion of the other.[25]

VERBAL DEVELOPMENT AND PARENTAL BEHAVIOR

Some of the most compelling evidence that poverty goes along with harsh, insensitive parenting comes from a study of language development. Since intelligence is highly heritable and intelligence predicts educational and occupational attainment, it is no surprise to learn that wealthy, successful parents tend to produce wealthy, successful children. To attribute this phenomenon purely to genetics, however, is to miss the complexity of the real world in which something that looks like genetic influence may be really environmental. Another reason that intelligent parents produce intelligent children is that they provide them with a lot of appropriate intellectual stimulation in the formative years.

The inextricable ties between genetic and environmental influences on child development are well illustrated in a small-scale but highly detailed study of interactions between parents and children from birth up to the age of three years. Betty Hart and Todd Risley of the University of Kansas studied parental behaviors and child outcomes for parents in different income classes.[26] Their subjects were thirteen children in professional homes, twenty-three in working-class homes, and only six in homes subsisting on welfare. While these numbers are too small to be statistically representative of the different economic groups, the conclusions they drew are so strikingly clear that no statistical inference is really necessary.

Intelligence test scores at the age of three revealed the expected pattern of economic gradation, although the group differences may have been exaggerated due to sampling error. The average IQ score for children of professional homes was 117, compared to 107 for working-class homes and 79 for welfare homes. Staggering as the magnitude of these differences were, what was really interesting about the study is the explanation it provides for the emergence of IQ differences as a function of parental behavior. They found that parental behavior was a stronger predictor of intelligence than parental income was. For example, when they looked at income differences within working class homes, these were unrelated to differences in intelligence or verbal development. Differences in parental behavior did matter, however.

These conclusions are nicely illustrated by the extensive information they collected on vocabulary development. There was a very strong relationship between parental stimulation and child outcomes. For instance, the vast majority of words recorded in the conversation of infants were also present in the speech of the parents (86 percent to 98 percent). (If you want your child to expound with Elizabethan eloquence, you had better pepper your ordinary conversation with long passages from Shakespeare!) This also suggests that what children say is surprisingly unaffected by television and other sources.

Another striking result was that the number of different words to which a child was exposed in conversations with parents varied greatly by social class. Professional parents used over 2,000 different words when talking to their three-year-olds, whereas welfare parents used less than 1,000. In each case, the child's vocabulary size was about half that of the parents (when talking to the child). The vocabulary of professional children averaged 1,116 words compared to 525 words for welfare children. Working-class children were intermediate with 749 words.

Not only did professional children receive more variety in terms of verbal stimulation from parents but they also received a greater quantity of stimulation. Professional parents directed an average of 487 words (or "utterances") at their child per hour compared to 176 for welfare parents. It is not surprising that children who received more conversation directed to them were more likely to speak themselves. Professional children produced an average of 310 utterances per hour compared to 168 for welfare children.

In summary, children in professional homes received almost three times as much verbal stimulation as those in welfare homes, and they responded by speaking twice as much and having twice as big a vocabulary. Children in working-class homes fell close to the middle in all these results. Looking at the substance of interactions between parents and children gives us a very clear insight into why, apart from their genes, children in professional homes should grow up to be more intelligent and to excel in school, providing them with an entry into lucrative professions. They do better because their brains receive the right kind of stimulation during critical periods in early development.

So far, the results clarify the relationship between poverty and intellectual development. It can be argued that welfare children are less intelligent than professional children partly because they receive less intellectual stimulation. This provides us with an environmental rationale for the association between poverty and low occupational attainment and hence for the cross-generational cycle of poverty. What does all this have to do with crime and other social problems?

Actually, the Hart and Risley study provides one of the most compelling pieces of evidence to date for the environmental nature of delinquency. Not content with a quantitative analysis of verbal development, they also scored the social comments of parents and children according to whether they were positive (i.e., affirmations) in tone or negative (i.e., prohibitions). As in just about every other measure, the tone of the remarks received by children in the home tended to be mirrored in their own utterances. If most of the conversation addressed to a child was positive, most of the child's own remarks had an affirmative tone, and if most of the comments addressed to the child were negative, they responded in kind. This is an interesting example of social learning in which the child not only acquires the vocabulary of the parents but also mirrors their interactional style.

None of this is very surprising, however. What is really astonishing is not just that the tone of parent-child interactions in welfare homes was more negative than that in professional homes, but that the difference was so huge. The average child in a professional household accumulated thirty-two affirmatives and five prohibitions per hour compared to five affirmatives and eleven prohibitions per hour for welfare children. In other words, the child growing up in a professional household was receiving six times as many positive reactions and only half as many negative reactions per hour. Stated another way, a child in a professional home was about twelve times as likely to receive a positive reaction as a child in a welfare home.

The emotional tone in professional homes was recorded as overwhelmingly positive whereas in the welfare homes it was predominantly negative. Once again, the working-class homes were intermediate, in the sense that positive feedback from parents was almost twice as likely as negative feedback. Another fascinating conclusion is that, even at the age of three years, children had already internalized the parental styles of their parents. The researchers were impressed that when they watched the children play at parenting their dolls, "we seemed to hear their parents speaking. We seemed to see the future of their own children" (177). If it assumed that parental behavior is influenced by genetics, then this is an eloquent example of the inextricable mingling of genetics and family environment in producing socioeconomic class differences in behavior. Whatever the genotype of the child or the parent, it is in the interactions between parent and child that the rubber really hits the road. Parental behavior is of overwhelming importance both for stimulating the developing brain and for providing children with a basic prototype for interpersonal relationships. If the relationship with a parent is characterized by warmth and consideration, children will learn to expect good things in their subsequent social interactions, whether these are with friends, lovers, educators, colleagues, business contacts, or government officials.

One of the themes that has been repeated throughout this book is that the imprint of family socialization experience is reflected back on all social interactions in later life. People who perceive their families as positive will tend to view the larger society in which they live in positive terms. They grow up to be more optimistic and more altruistic and to see the world as being a fairer place in which hard work is rewarded, and where it is possible for the individual to make a positive difference in their community. This mind set lends itself to self-confidence, ambition, and career commitment. If early experiences are negative and alienating, then children will see the larger social environment as hostile, threatening, and potentially exploitative. This mind set lends itself to low career aspiration, a lack of interpersonal trust, cynicism, antisocial behavior, and recklessness. A close relationship with parents is a protective factor in relation to risk-taking and delinquency. These differing pictures of the social environment picked up in the home go a long way towards explaining why social problems are so prevalent among the poor.

While the Hart and Risley study provides some very detailed and important data concerning the divergent experiences obtained by children in homes of different social classes and their intellectual outcomes, we cannot say if the varied types of parental stimulation really cause the different outcomes. Skeptics can always point to the likely role of genetics. People in the professional classes tend to score high on IQ tests and to transmit the genetic potential for intelligence to their children. What Hart and Risley observed could all have been due purely to genetics: the high IQ of the children; the stimulating conversation of their high-IQ parents; the warm tone of their interactions. All might be attributable to a genetic predisposition for intelligence and nurturance shared by parents and children.

In order to make a truly convincing case that intellectual stimulation from parents raises IQ, it is necessary to do an experiment in which one group of children receives enriched environmental stimulation, and their intelligence is compared to that of an equivalent group that received no special attention. Many such experiments have been done. They are called Head Start programs.

HEAD START PROGRAMS

Most people know the story of the hopes and disappointments of government-sponsored environmental enrichment programs for underprivileged children, which generally meant children living in inner-city slums. The early results were encouraging—substantial improvement in IQ scores following enrichment. The depressing part was when the enriched group was followed up in adolescence, the benefits had apparently been "washed out" by the diluting effects of their intellectually stunting environments.

Begun in 1965 as part of President Lyndon Johnson's War on Poverty, Head Start programs were based on a recognition that occupational success in our culture is related to academic success. Poor people are trapped in a cross-generational cycle of poverty because their environment holds them back in respect to academic achievement and occupational attainment. The lot of economically disadvantaged groups might thus be improved by helping them to achieve in school from an early age. Since poverty is associated with a lack of intellectually stimulating experiences, activities, and people, it stunts intellectual development. Therefore, artificially supplementing such experiences ought to promote intelligence and academic success. Funded by congressional mandate through Project Head Start, Head Start programs have varied in their design. They generally provide enriching experiences for young children by means of special teachers who involve the children in activities such as naming colors, building with blocks, and learning concepts such as "large" and "small." The teachers also showed parents how to engage their children in intellectually stimulating activities and encouraged them to read to their children. The thinking was that parents routinely provide this kind of stimulation for their children in prosperous homes.

The underlying logic for Head Start programs is entirely reasonable; they should work. After all, the basic principle of the influence of environmental stimulation on brain development had been verified in impeccable animal studies. Young rats that were kept in social groups, instead of the customary solitary confinement, and were given many different toys to play with when they were young became more intelligent. As adults, they performed better on the standard measure of rat intelligence—the ability to learn a complex maze. The enriched animals were more intelligent because they had measurable increases in brain growth, including better connections between cells (broader synapses). If it worked for rats, surely it ought to succeed with humans, distinguished as we are by unparalleled behavioral plasticity and learning ability.

There are several reasons why the early Head Start programs first seemed to work and then tended to fade out. One is that IQ scores of children can be strongly affected by their home environment. As they get older, the role of family environment tends to diminish and the role of genetics increases, as though more of the genes influencing intellectual ability are expressed over time, increasing their cumulative effects.[27]

Recent research by Craig T. Ramey and Sharon Ramey in Birmingham, Alabama, has shown that if an enrichment program is to have lasting benefits, it must be begun very early in life, preferably before the age of two years, when most of the Head Start programs were begun. At this age the brain is anatomically very similar to the brain of an adult, but cells are still busily establishing new connections. For this reason, the more different types of information a young child is exposed to, the greater its capacity to process such information in the future. Current thinking is that the earlier in life enrichment programs are begun, the greater their potential for substantial lasting effects, and some are now beginning as early as the age of three weeks. The lasting effects on IQ can be substantial (about half the group difference between blacks and the U.S. population in general).[28]

Even when the Head Start programs were conducted between the ages of 2 and 5 years, and despite the fact that IQ gains declined over time, they did produce lasting gains in academic performance and brought about the sort of changes that are predictable from the increased "parental" investment that is mimicked by a Head Start program. For example, in the case of one group of disadvantaged children who participated in special preschool programs beginning at the age of three, a follow-up when they were fifteen years old revealed that, on average, they had advanced more than a full grade ahead of their control group.[29] Their scores on tests of reading, arithmetic, and language usage were also higher. They were less likely to need remedial classes. The really interesting result was that they were more likely to hold after-school jobs and less likely to exhibit delinquent behavior. These effects were probably related to the greater self-confidence and better social skills observed for the enriched group. Given the theoretical orientation developed in this book, it is no surprise to learn that the beneficial effects of early Head Start programs were strongly related to the degree of "parental" involvement. If a child is three years old before he or she is provided with environmental stimulation, it is not going to have much of an effect on brain development or IQ scores because the brain is already too biologically mature. It can affect the inculcation of norms of hard work, discipline, and ambition, however, and can shift children in the direction of being productive citizens and away from antisocial behavior, consequences which are at least as important as boosting IQ.

Studies of parenting style have found that supportive parents who have clear performance expectations raise children who do better at school compared to children of permissive parents and children of authoritarian parents who set standards but do not provide much emotional support. This merely confirms the expectation that high parental investment homes foster achievement. What about the effect of parental style on intelligence? Studies of the home environment at the age of two have found that measures of maternal responsiveness, language stimulation, and encouragement of emotional maturity (Home Observation for Measurement of the Home Environment Inventory, or HOME score) predict IQ scores at the ages of three and four and a half years and first-grade achievement test scores.[30]

Of course, an association between parenting style and intelligence scores does not prove that parental behavior affects intelligence. To make this case, experiments are needed. Such experiments are very difficult to do for ethical reasons. However, the one such experiment that was done in Holland in the 1970s produced positive findings. The study involved 100 nine-month-olds and their mothers who were randomly assigned to 4 groups of 25 each.[31] One group of mothers was taught to be responsive to their infants. They were told not to direct their child too much but to give the child the opportunity to find things out for himself or herself. Another group of mothers was taught to initiate interactions frequently, which meant that they were directing the child's activities. A third group was taught to be both controlling and responsive. A fourth control group received no instructions at all.

When the mothers were studied interacting with their toddlers three months later, they were found to behave differently in accordance with whatever instructions they had received. Infants whose mothers were in the responsive group showed higher levels of exploratory behavior and preferred new to familiar playthings. They also learned more quickly to make a movement that controlled an interesting event. The results thus indicate that parental style can affect cognitive development in children and that it does so in a manner predicted by parental investment theory.

THE ECONOMICS OF PARENTAL INVESTMENT

It can be taken as a given that most parents want their children to be happy and successful. Yet reduced parental investment causes children to behave in ways that decrease their personal happiness and compromise their prospects for social and economic success in our society. Reduced parental investment is clearly a response to environmental conditions. The main environmental factors that reduce parental investment are large family size, poverty, and marital instability. Even though parental investment today is increased by affluence and small families, it is reduced by marital instability and the economic trend of both parents working most of the time outside the home.

In the United States today, one of the most important influences tending to increase parental investment is reduced family size. The sort of intensive stimulation that is typical of contemporary professional families would hardly be possible if they had more than two or three children. It would likely be physically impossible for professional parents to spend the same amount of time interacting with ten children as they could with one. Moreover, even if the parents were willing and able to provide the same amount of intellectual stimulation for their ten children as they had for the first, they wouldn't be able to do it since the social environment in large families is a "tragedy of the commons" (see Chapter 5) in which the selfish self-interest of each child works against the common good of the family. As a result of aggressive competition among siblings, parents in larger families spend a lot of time and energy in a peacekeeping role. Attempts to interact with one child might be jealously sabotaged by the others who resent parental attention being diverted away from them.

These tribulations are absent in the case of only children and greatly reduced for small families. If there are only two children, for example, a child has a reasonably good chance of obtaining the undivided attention of at least one of its parents at any time. If it seems that there is enough parental attention to go around, there is less reason for children to perform expertly obnoxious actions to gain parental attention. The recent convergence of family size for most ethnic groups on a norm of two children, compared to an average family size of five children at the beginning of the century,[32] tends to increase parental investment per child.

Despite the relatively larger family size in the 1950s compared to the present, this period stands out in the mind of many, particularly those who were raised then, as an ideal period of family stability in which there was stable sex role complementarity between men and women, and the raising of children was given considerable social importance. It was a period of great economic prosperity, which allowed families to prosper on a single income. Moreover, local communities were much safer for children to roam around, and neighbors tended to look out for the children of others. These conditions greatly eased the burdensome vigilance that is required of parents today and allowed the functions of socializing children to be distributed somewhat from the nuclear family to the local community.

During this golden era of the American family, marriage was highly stable and women identified strongly with their domestic roles. Few women with young children found it necessary to work outside the home. Family values also prevailed in regard to sexual behavior. Premarital intercourse was frowned upon, at least for women, and out-of-wedlock births were comparatively rare for white women. While this environment was ideal for raising children, it may not have been ideal in all respects. Intellectuals of the era found it materialistic, conformist, and stifling. After all, it was the era of McCarthyism.

As stated previously, the stability of the family in the 1950s and earlier is explainable in terms of a marriage market that favored women. The high ratio of men to women allowed women to pick and choose their marriage partners. Men who were economically unsuccessful had little prospect of marriage to desirable women. Restricting their sexual behavior helped young women to attract the most desirable bridegrooms. Sexual exclusiveness within marriage was desirable to men. When they returned to their suburban homes from their well-paid jobs, the last thing they wanted to discover was that their attractive young spouse had spent her day being sexually unfaithful.

Since the 1950s, there have been several trends that have tended to undermine the stability of marriages as child-raising entities. Most fundamental has been the declining sex ratio, which means that women lost their control over the marriage market. Since men now control the market, there has been a trend away from strict monogamy towards serial monogamy. This means that there is a high divorce rate coupled with a high remarriage rate for men, but not for women.[33]

Consistent with the findings for other low-sex-ratio societies, there has been a devaluation of women as brides and as mothers and increasing treatment of women as sex objects. The sense of devaluation and alienation felt by women under these conditions has produced a strong feminist back-lash, which has received more support from mainstream women than fem-inist movements of the past, such as that represented by the suffragette movement in England. As in the case of late-medieval feminist thinking, there has been a great deal of emphasis on women establishing independ-ent economic roles and participating in the workplace on an equal footing with men.[34]

Of course, being successful in a career has presented a rather harrowing conflict for many women since it interferes with their reproductive careers. While feminist tracts and womens' magazines of the 1980s, including *Cosmopolitan*, stressed that it was possible to have it all—career, marriage, and free-wheeling sexual expression—for most women it is not possible to have it all. According to data collected by Claudia Goldin for a National Bureau of Economic Research report published in 1995,[35] only 17 percent of women, at most, are able to both produce a child and have a career paying above the bottom quarter of the workforce by the time they are thirty-nine years old. These data suggest that for contemporary women, careers and reproduction present some tough conflicts. Thus, college women generally delay child-rearing for about ten years longer than women without a col-lege education, who can begin their families sooner by opting for a combi-nation of marriage and a low-paying job. This is a very great price to pay for a career, but most women who do it probably consider it worth the sacrifice because it allows them to provide better opportunities for their children than if they had opted for earlier reproduction.[36]

In the case of the heroic minority of women who do succeed in combin-ing reproduction and career by the age of thirty-nine, one encouraging note is that it is possible to have a career without necessarily compromising pa-rental investment. In fact, one study that measured parental activities of ca-reer women compared to homemakers found that women with careers spent more time interacting with their children and engaging them in activ-ities, such as sports, than the homemakers did. One way of interpreting this result is to say that career women are highly motivated people who want to excel in everything they do, including child care. Heroic though these ef-forts may be, they do not protect children from the increased probability of developing social problems, as discussed in the next chapter.

Given the 1950s as a reference point, it is rather puzzling why women be-gan postponing reproduction in favor of developing careers. Most com-mentators attribute the change to pure economics. Faced with stagnation or decline in real take-home wages, American families recruited wives as full time wage earners to supplement the dwindling paycheck provided by the husband. Families had every reason to feel the pinch. One startling statistic is that real household income rose only 2.5 percent between 1973 and 1994 (compared to a rise of 89 percent between 1952 and 1973),[37] despite the fact that more wives had jobs on the later date than the earlier one (58 percent compared to 41 percent).

Given the declining economic situation for workers, one possible response would have been to cut back on lifestyle, to sell the boat and the second car, live in a more modest home, and eschew the extravagance of owning a vacation home. Yet, during the 1970s and 1980s, Americans did the opposite, buying more boats and recreational vehicles and choosing to live in much more spacious homes. Thus, the average home size was around 1,500 square feet in 1970 compared to around 2,000 square feet in 1994, despite the fact that family size had declined.[38]

The paradox of increasing material wealth in the face of stagnant incomes can be easily explained. Family sizes declined, and with greatly reduced costs of child production (even allowing for the cost of commercial day-care), families ended up with more disposable wealth. It seems absurd that home size has increased even as family sizes have shrunk, at least if you consider a home as a child-raising facility. An alternative perspective is that the home is an investment, or store of wealth. The second perspective helps to explain why home size has increased as a function of disposable income.

Given that more wealth was available for purchasing luxury items in the 1970s and 1980s, it is arguable that parents could, in theory, have raised their normative family size from two to three, for example. Yet this was not a practical course of action for several reasons. For one thing, larger family size quickly invalidates the dual-earner strategy because the after-tax income of the lower wage is quickly eaten up by day-care costs and the cost of running a second vehicle for transportation to work. Second, the very high cost of raising children today means that having a third child could push family finances into the red. This is particularly true if parents are interested in facilitating their child's career by providing them with an expensive college education. The large, rather empty home can be an important means of financing a child's education since it provides the collateral for a substantial home equity loan.

Of course, large homes also make a statement about social status, and many of the other luxury goods for which Americans have avidly shopped in recent decades can be seen as making the same statement. Coupled with the willingness of parents to invest in expensive college educations for their children, these phenomena bespeak a competitive, materialistic culture. The increased number of college enrollments fits into this pattern because a college education used to be seen as a way of distancing oneself from the pack and beginning a lucrative career. Today, most young Americans attend some type of college, so that attending a prestigious university or having an exemplary academic record assumes increasing importance as young people compete for access to careers.[39]

In summary, the task of establishing one's children in the professions is one that calls for a very high level of economic investment. It appears that average families have the resources to do this for two children but not for three. As discussed in the next chapter, American women continue to do most of the work of caring for children while they have also assumed an important economic role in preparing their children to compete for entry into the professions. Their new-found economic responsibilities inevitably eat into their traditional child care responsibilities. The optimistic, and politically correct, view that maternal responsibilities are made good by increased efforts of fathers and by the use of professional day-care services does not square with the evidence of increased social problems among adolescents whose mothers work full time.

Chapter 7

Nine to Five: The Influence of Occupational Trends on Parental Investment

The twentieth century has seen two societal transformations that are of great importance for American families. The first is that there has been a mass movement of population from rural areas of the United States into cities, where these migrants came in to contact with immigrants from other countries. This resulted in an expansion of the number of people living in poverty in cities. With urban poverty comes the social problems and high crime rates that have dogged ethnic minorities such as the Irish, blacks, and Mexicans in U.S. cities. Needless to say, these conditions are disruptive of family life and undermine parental investment.[1] The second important transformation has been in gender roles. At the beginning of the century, a tiny minority of women worked for a living. The main professions open to respectable women were teaching and nursing.[2] Lower class women could choose between the drudgery of domestic service and working in a factory or store. Women's wages were much lower than those of men for equivalent work. Today, the majority of women work in well-paid jobs, generally earning wages equivalent to those of men for equivalent work. (The fact that, on average, women earn about 30 percent less than men can be largely explained in terms of occupational choice and hours worked.) Clearly, the fact that women spend much more time away from home must affect child care practices. One would expect that less time spent with the mother would result in lower parental investment, but this would be true only if day-care constituted a less nurturant and stimulating experience than that

provided in the home. In theory, it could be more like high parental investment than home care. Given the generally poor quality of many day-care
employees, who receive little or no training, are poorly paid, and often
have unsatisfactory personal histories, the opposite seems much more
likely. Moreover, the fact that most married women go to work bespeaks an
altered relationship between husbands and wives in which husbands bear
comparatively less responsibility for economic support of the family. It is
not unreasonable to expect that the reduced economic commitment of men
would be reflected in a reduced emotional commitment to marriage, and
there is plenty of evidence, including divorce statistics, to back this idea up.
Children of working mothers might thus be different from children of
homemakers. Furthermore, it would be predicted that reduced contact
with the mother would have more pronounced consequences during the
critical early years of life.

The scientific findings yield conflicting answers to this question. On
the one hand, children of working mothers are not very different from
children who have more extended contact with their mothers during the
day. On the other hand, when observing changes over time in the incidence of social problems, one finds that the more women there are at
work, the worse children fare. There are two possible explanations of this
riddle. The first is that working mothers are exceptionally highly motivated to protect the interests of their children, so that they more than compensate for time lost from child care. Conversely, it might be argued that
women who are content not to be employed, including welfare recipients
in the days before work requirements were introduced in many states,
may not be exceptionally warm or responsive mothers. The other is that
the strong increases over time in teen pregnancy rates, depression, and
crime are due to strong influences that affect all twenitieth-century families. All other factors being equal, separation from both parents for long
periods of the day can be expected to increase children's risk of developing social problems.

ATTACHMENT AND DAY-CARE: CONTROVERSIES AND FINDINGS

A child's secure attachment with the mother is the mark of high parental
investment in early life. We have seen that maternal deprivation has devastating consequences for early brain development in the case of institutional
children and that the developmental problems of orphans that are adopted
out of institutions into families quickly improve. Insecure attachment can
be caused by a lack of sensitive responsiveness on the part of the mother.
When mothers are trained to respond sensitively to the needs of their children, security of attachment increases. Similarly, when mothers were

trained to be responsive to infants, the IQ of the children was thereby boosted.

Conversely, all of the phenomena associated with low parental investment are conducive to insecure attachment. Poverty is associated with harsh and insensitive parenting, for example. Abusive parenting, in turn, is associated with a much greater likelihood of insecure attachment. If insecure attachment were only related to intelligence and academic success, the relationship between insecure infantile attachment and low academic performance would be of great enough concern. In reality, insecure attachment is predictive of all manner of antisocial behavior and personal problems, from oppositional conduct disorder and aggression, to delinquency and criminal behavior. There is also greater risk for cross-generational transmission of insensitive styles of parenting. This begins with increased risk of teen pregnancy and thereby incurs associated risks of low parental investment.[3, 4]

Given that a child's early relationship with the mother and other attachment figures is of such significance for later development, it is hardly surprising that concern has been raised about the consequences of prolonged daily separation between the mother and her preschool child when the mother goes to work. These concerns have come to the forefront in recent decades because of the unprecedented influx of women into the permanent labor force. The proportion of women over sixteen years old in steady employment rose from 35 percent in 1954 to 58 percent in 1992.[5]

Exactly the same concerns were raised earlier in the case of Israeli kibbutz women. The first kibbutzim were founded as a vehicle for promoting early settlement of the country by Zionists. They were organized around socialist principles, which meant that all members, regardless of gender, were expected to contribute to the welfare of the group through the sweat of their brow. Given that the main industry was agriculture, this could be interpreted literally.[6]

At the same time that mothers of young children labored in the fields, their child care needs were taken care of because children lived apart from their families in separate children's quarters and were taken care of by a woman or women who specialized in this work. Research on kibbutz children over several decades has produced mixed results. While it is possible for older children to be raised successfully apart from their parents, complete separation between mother and child during the first year of life is not a good idea.

In earlier times, the institution of the family was seen as somewhat of a threat to solidarity within the commune. It appears that this ideological focus, more than practical necessity, was behind the desire to raise infants apart from their parents. Parents thus visited their children after work but left them, even small babies, to stay overnight in the children's house where they were attended by a metapelet, or nurse.[7]

Complete nonparental care of infants and young children as the normative practice within a community is unheard of among the societies of the
world. Mothers in preindustrial societies are quite appalled by the notion of
infants being separated from their mothers for prolonged periods of the day
and night. Complete nonparental care in the kibbutz is thus a bold experiment.[8] Its results are of great significance for modern economies because
they are relevant to the fate of children of working mothers who spend much
of their waking time in day-care, out of contact with their mothers.

If you want to get a kibbutznik really upset, all you have to do is mention
the name Bruno Bettelheim. Bettelheim is the author of a book entitled *The
Children of the Dream*,[9] which is deeply resented not only because it is critical
of the kibbutz child-rearing system, but because it is felt to be unfairly critical. Bettelheim's book was impressionistic rather than a solid work of
scholarship. He believed that he had isolated a critical flaw in the kibbutz
rearing system, which could be observed in the young men and women
who had been raised there. There was no evidence of deep unhappiness or
disaffection, no antisocial acting out, no inappropriate sexual conduct.
Maybe this lack of normal adolescent revolt was a symptom of emotional
flatness. Bettelheim concluded that the young kibbutzniks were too bland.
They were incapable of feeling strong emotions, either positive or negative,
because their emotional sensibilities had not matured in the richer soil of a
family environment. This criticism was seen as unfair because what
Bettelheim chose to see as blandness would be interpreted by a more sympathetic observer as evidence of emotional stability, maturity, and restraint.
It can also be argued that Bettelheim's emphasis on individual expression
as a more important value than social restraint was a product of his own
cultural experience, which clouded his picture of the kibbutz rearing system.

Time has not been particularly kind to Bettelheim. The consensus today
is that the young kibbutzniks, who seem polite, poised, happy, and helpful,
really are content and prosocial and do not harbor the subtle flaw of emotional underdevelopment. Nevertheless, the controversy created by
Bettelheim was heated enough to stimulate the kibbutz movement to encourage psychological research into the consequences of their child-rearing
practices. Some of this work focused on the early relationship between the
child and the parents. It was inspired by John Bowlby's theory of attachment and the work of successors, including Mary Ainsworth, who devised
the Strange Situation Test, which allows children to be categorized into different attachment groups (secure, insecure avoidant, and insecure ambivalent). This work produced a bombshell. It was found that only 59 percent of
Kibbutz infants were securely attached, compared to 65 to 70 percent of Israeli children in other research. It quickly became clear that the difference
was specifically due to communal sleeping arrangements. Kibbutz infants
who had slept in their parents' house were just as likely to be securely at-

tached as infants raised in Israeli homes outside the kibbutz. When young infants wake up in the night and their mother is not present, they may be sensitive to this fact. Whatever the precise reason, it is clear that separation during the night can interfere with the relationship between mothers and infants, even though the effects are noticeable only for a small minority. Nevertheless, the kibbutz system has been anxious to ensure that children are given every opportunity for normal social development. In response to the research findings, they have brought back family sleeping arrangements.[10]

The parallels between the kibbutzim and day-care arrangements for working mothers in the United States and other developed nations are quite obvious. One implication is that if mothers have an opportunity to interact with their infant at home, there is no reason why the mother-child attachment should be undermined by nonmaternal care during the day when the mother works.

The findings from research on kibbutz children are generally quite reassuring for working mothers because they indicate that children can adapt to loss of their mothers during the day without adverse consequences. In some ways the kibbutz children have advantages in social development as compared to family-reared children. For instance, they develop unusually strong attachments to peers at an early age. They also acquire a strong sense of group identity and group loyalty. Their skills of social interaction are precocious compared to family-raised children.[11]

It is interesting that the social development of kibbutz children is advanced not only in relation to family-reared children but also in relation to children kept in Israeli day-cares. This is a testament to the unusually high quality of care offered in the kibbutzim. The main reason seems to be that the child care specialists, or metapelets, are hand-picked by the communities. They select only the best and most dedicated individuals for this work. Since day-care providers are standing in for parents, we might expect that their quasi-parental investment would have similar kinds of effects on children as the parents themselves. Since the metapelets are likely to be much more competent and dedicated than commercial day-care workers, it is hardly surprising that the kibbutz children are so socially advanced and well behaved. It is ironic that Bettelheim should have chosen to put such a perverse negative spin on this remarkable success in group child socialization.

Studies of the effects of day-care on American children have yielded some interesting differences from and similarities to the effects of kibbutz rearing. The main similarity is that children in both types of nonparental care tend to be more socially advanced. The important difference is that children in American day-cares tend to be more socially assertive and less sensitive to the feelings of others. Both the similarities and differences can be understood in terms of the competition among children for the care and attention of adults.

Children come into the world with a virtually inexhaustible craving for parental love and attention. In many subsistence societies, such as the !Kung of the Kalahari Desert, the infant is in constant physical contact with the mother both day and night and suckles on demand.[12] Obviously this ideal level of maternal investment, from the infant's perspective, is never approached in our society. The opposite extreme can be reached in some low-quality day-cares where a large number of infants and small children simultaneously compete for the attention of a single care giver who is also likely to be poorly paid, unmotivated, and untrained.

Even in the highest quality day-cares, workers may have too little time and energy to give all of the children the warmth and attention they crave. This sets up a competition over the "parental" investment provided by child care workers that is similar to the competition between siblings for the same reason, except that it is likely to be more intense because of the congregation of a larger number of children who are clumped in the same highly needy age bracket. Under these circumstances, children tend to vie with each other for attention. It is a sad fact that children who are loud and aggressive in their demands are most likely to be noticed first, and the attention they receive is likely to reinforce their strident behavior. These ideas can explain the findings that day-care children are both more socially assertive and more selfish than children raised at home.[13,14]

We know from the social experiment of the kibbutz that day-care arrangements need not threaten the happiness or well-being of children. Although the differences are unreliable enough to be controversial, some experts, such as Jay Belsky of Pennsylvania State University, have concluded, based on a review of the technical literature, that day-care children are less likely to be securely attached to their mothers.[15] This conclusion has produced some heated controversy. Nevertheless, it seems that insecure attachment in day-care children is more likely if children are placed in care in the first year of life and if the time spent exceeds twenty hours per week. This result is consistent with one aspect of the findings from the kibbutzim, namely, that the attachment relationship with the mother is most fragile in the first year of life. Needless to say, these results do not prove that day-care, in itself, causes insecure attachment. The real causes may lie elsewhere in the social environment. Thus, spending a lot of time in day-care in the first year of life is more likely to be associated with insecure attachment if parents are divorced and if the mother is relatively poor.[16]

WHY SOCIAL PROBLEMS INCREASE AS MORE WOMEN ENTER THE WORKFORCE

The evidence concerning day-care suggests that children are not harmed and may actually be socially enriched by nonmaternal care, at least if they happen to attend the kind of high-quality daycare in which research is conducted. Young children who get out of the house to meet caretakers and other children develop social skills as a result. While the relationship with the mother can be compromised, this may occur only in the first year of life.

On the face of it, it might appear that the services provided by a high-quality day-care can adequately duplicate the parental care provided by mothers in the home. Another interpretation is possible, however. It may be that the kind of mothers who place their children in good day-cares are exceptionally highly motivated to interact with their children after work. Psychologist Jack Demarest found, in an unpublished study, that working mothers actually spent more time in shared activities or interacting with their children than homemakers did. In other words, they compensated for the lack of shared time by an increase in the pace of shared activities.[17]

Once again, these highly motivated mothers may not be representative of the class of working mothers as a whole. Nevertheless, the correlation between devotion to a career and devotion to children should not be surprising. After all, whether people are consciously aware of it or not, the fundamental motivation behind developing a career is parental investment. This may not fit in with our individual attitudes toward careers, but it does fit in with larger societal trends.

For example, there is a great deal of cross-cultural variation in the economic contribution of women to raising children. In hunter-gatherer societies, women typically provide at least two-thirds of the food. In our own contemporary society, the economic contribution of men and women to families is more equal. At the turn of the century, almost no married women worked outside the home, so their husband played a critical role as breadwinners. Today, women's wages and salaries are much higher relative to men's than they used to be. This means that women who work, and develop careers, can make a major economic contribution to their households. They also play an important role in providing their children with a college education, which is essential for entry into the professions.

The career strivings of women today represent a general principle that can be observed at work in all societies at all times in their history. If it is possible to improve the economic circumstances of an individual and his or her family through work, then that individual will work hard. At the beginning of the twentieth century, married women found it difficult to work because of the demands of raising children. They had few occupational choices and were badly paid for their work. In 1900, a female factory worker toiled twelve hours a day, six days a week, and was paid around $30 per month, which was barely enough to buy food. If a woman chose her husband wisely, she did not need to work at all to support her children. Today, fertility can be regulated and families planned so that the conflicts between demands of careers and those of raising children are reduced.

Cross-cultural study reveals that people tend to be highly career-oriented if they live in a society in which it is possible to accumulate wealth so that the conditions of the next generation can be improved relative to those of the present one. These conditions applied to farmers in the Pearl River Delta who constituted the first wave of Chinese emigrants to the United States, but they did not apply to peasants who emigrated from Ireland at the same period because they had been oppressed by draconian legislation known as the Penal Laws, which prevented them from owning property (see Chapter 9).

If the accumulation of wealth and cross-cultural variation in career-mindedness can be interpreted in terms of parental investment, then Demarest's conclusion that career women make exceptionally devoted mothers should not be too surprising. Many strands of evidence lead to the conclusion that conscientiousness in work transfers to conscientiousness in child care. One is that people who are committed to forming permanent marital relationships are also likely to be deeply involved in their careers. Researchers refer to this phenomenon as security of adult attachment. In other words, if we can form a trusting relationship with our mothers and fathers as infants and young children, then we are capable of committing ourselves subsequently to both marriages and careers.[18, 19]

The notion of security of attachment to spouse and career helps us to see that, even on a deep emotional plane, there is not a conflict for women between career and family. In fact, developing a career can be seen as part of a more long-term commitment to raising children only when conditions are right. This view receives strong support from the evidence that poor academic performance is one of the strongest predictors of teenage childbearing. It is not simply the case that less intelligent young women are more likely to become pregnant because they do not use birth control. Once they become pregnant, they are more likely to bring their infant to term. On the other hand, young women having good career prospects who get pregnant are more likely to have an abortion, preferring to defer childbearing to a more auspicious time in their careers. In short, women who have little prospects of career or marriage have little to lose from having children early in life. Women who have good prospects of both career and marriage are able to raise children in more favorable circumstances if they postpone reproduction until after their careers have been established and they are married.[20, 21]

Since it can be argued that career women should make devoted mothers, we might expect that their children would turn out accordingly. That is, they should be competent, hard-working individuals who have satisfactory close relationships and do not add to problem statistics. To some extent this is obviously true. We know, for example, that living in poverty is one of the best predictors of every type of problem behavior. Successful women maintain affluent homes that, to some extent, shield their children from developing social problems.

Yet, when the same question is considered in terms of societal changes across time, a very different picture emerges. The more women that participate in the labor force, the higher the incidence of most serious social problems. There is nothing iffy about the strength of this relationship. For instance, Figure 1 shows that over the past four decades increases in juvenile crime[22] have increased steadily with the number of women in the workforce.[23] Apart from a period in the 1950s when the juvenile crime rate rose faster than female labor participation, the increases in juvenile crime and women's labor participation are in perfect lockstep. Incidentally, juvenile arrests are presented as a ratio of percentage of crimes committed by people fifteen to twenty-four years old to the percentage of the population fifteen to twenty-four years old. This number was multiplied by twenty to place the two lines on the same graph.

In Figure 2, it can be seen that the number of women entering the workforce increased at about the same rate as the divorce rate between 1948 and 1989[24] even though the divorce curve is S-shaped while the labor participation curve is a straight line. The correlation between the lines is highly statistically significant. Divorce rates are divorces per thousand population, which yields a lower number than a common alternative measure—divorces per thousand married women. The divorce rate was multiplied by ten to fit the two lines on the same graph.

If the relationship between female labor participation and divorce is attributable to a weak marriage market for women, then female labor participation would increase with declines in the sex ratio. This relationship is shown in Figure 3, which plots female labor and the sex ratio after they had been converted to standard scores. The population sex ratio was inverted so that both lines would run in the same direction and a rising line in the graph thus means a *decrease* in the sex ratio and a declining marriage market for women.

Strong as the relationships are between labor participation and divorce and juvenile crimes, respectively, they are dwarfed by the magnitude of the relationship between teen birthrates and female labor participation.[25] Figure 4 plots the relationship between nonmarital teen births and labor participation. This graph prompts two observations. First, both graphs rise in an almost-perfect straight line. Second, they rise at almost exactly the same pace. The underlying causes might be decreased supervision of adolescents, or teenage reproduction might be a response to diminished marital opportunity for young women, or both (see Chapter 8).

The very strong correlations between increases in women working and increases in social problems is open to a very simple interpretation, although one which is not necessarily correct. It could be that the absence of mothers from the home results in neglect of children, which, consistent

Figure 1
Female Labor Participation and Juvenile Arrest Ratio (×20)

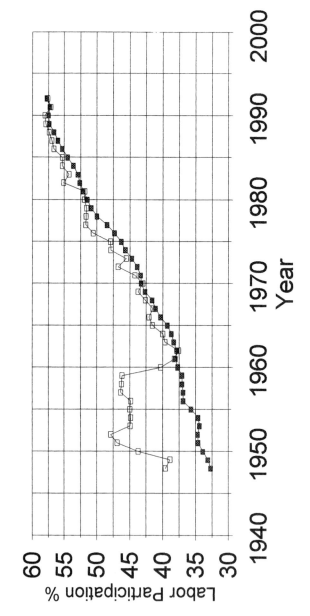

— F. labor — Arrests

There is a strong positive relationship between female labor participation and the proportion of juvenile arrests. An arrest ratio of 2 (=40 in the graph) means that juveniles (15–24 years) are twice as likely to be arrested as people of other ages. The relationship is weaker for the 1950s than for the other decades.

Figure 2
Female Labor Participation and Divorce Rate (×10)

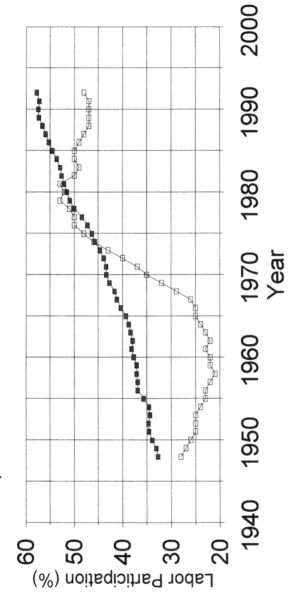

— ■ — F. labor — □ — Divorce

Female labor participation is significantly associated with marital instability. Both trends may reflect a weakened marriage market for women. While the trends are sometimes out of synchrony, the rate of increase over time has been similar.

Figure 3
Female Labor Participation and Sex Ratio (Inverted)

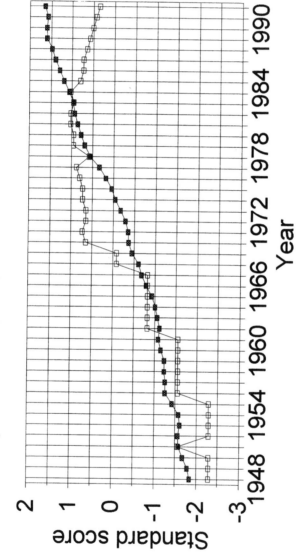

There is a strong relationship between decreases in the sex ratio (inverted scale) and increases in female labor participation. More women work when their marriage prospects are relatively bleak.

Figure 4
Female Labor Participation and Nonmarital Teen Birthrate (+20)

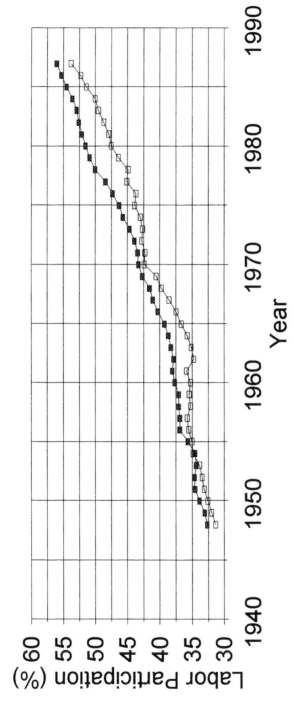

Increases in nonmarital teen birthrates are almost perfectly predicted by increased female labor participation.

113

with the evolutionary theory of socialization (see next chapter), makes them interpret the social environment as less nurturant and more hostile. When the going gets tough, the tough get going, and children who see their social environment as insensitive to them, or even hostile and threatening, tend to develop a protective shell of cynicism and manipulativeness. In short, they become more prone to delinquency and other social problems. An even simpler explanation that fits in with the same scenario is that working mothers are forced to leave their teenagers unsupervised more often, particularly in the afternoon. The number of "latchkey" kids has doubled in the past thirty years, and this phenomenon is seen by some as an important factor in the increased levels of violent crime among juveniles. Another interesting finding is that if women work full-time, their teenage sons have a 46 percent increase in the odds of early sexual intercourse. If they work part-time, providing less opportunity for teens to have sex at home, the odds of early intercourse are raised by just 26 percent.[26]

There are two alternative explanations. The first is what I call the "strangers in the train" theory. Two strangers end up on the subway train from Manhattan to Brooklyn. You might imagine that they had something in common, that they were going to similar destinations. In reality, one is going home to his apartment in Queens. The other is going to John F. Kennedy Airport to catch a flight for New Delhi, India. They will never see each other again. By analogy, it could be argued that just because the paths of female labor participation and teen birthrates are perfectly correlated for forty years, it does not mean that they have any intrinsic connection. In the jargon of statistics, the correlation is "spurious" or accidental. However, it seems unlikely, to say the least, that the proportion of women working should happen to be in lockstep with several different social problems over such a long period of time due to chance alone.

The other alternative explanation seems to have more merit. This takes the view that the reason labor participation and social problems are correlated is that all are caused by something else. In the jargon of psychology, we say that they are produced by a "third variable." What might this third variable be? One plausible candidate is that it is the deterioration of the marriage market for women, which (a) forces them into the labor market in larger numbers and (b) undermines parental investment resulting in increased rates of social problems in children. The most direct evidence for this third-variable argument is the fact that a declining marriage market for women is associated with the astronomic rise in social problems, which has been of such concern to social scientists who have observed it. One crude but useful index of the condition of the marriage market is the number of men per hundred women in the population—the population sex ratio. It is crude because it is insensitive to the fact that there are always more elderly women than there are elderly men because women live longer. The best measure of marriage market opportunity for women is the number of unmarried men per hundred unmarried women three years younger (since women tend to marry men who are approximately three years older than they are). While the population sex ratio ignores some of these subtleties, it is nevertheless quite good at indexing the condition of the marriage market at a particular year for the entire population.

If a declining marriage market for women is the third variable we are looking for, then the availability of men in the population should decline as social problems rise. In fact, there is a strong relationship between the population sex ratio and social problems such as teen birthrates, juvenile arrests, and divorce rates. Between the years 1948 and 1992, the sex ratio fell steadily[27] (see Figure 3) while these social problems rose. The correlations were all highly statistically significant. As the number of men relative to women in the population declined, the labor participation rate of women increased. This correlation is consistent with the argument that the sex ratio, and hence the marriage market, is the fundamental driver behind both the accelerated entry of women into the workforce and accelerating social problems.[28]

The most basic implication of the conclusion that social problems are related to marriage market conditions is that the explanation for alarming increases in juvenile crime and nonmarital teen births is to be found in broad historical trends that cut across such differences as whether a mother works outside the home full time or is a homemaker. Perhaps the most persuasive evidence for the explanation of trends in social problems in terms of deteriorating marriage market conditions causing social problems via reduced parental investment comes from the analysis of ethnic group differences. This topic is taken up in more detail in Chapter 9 wherein the much higher incidence of social problems among African Americans is related to a much worse marriage market for black women than even for whites.

Explaining the problems of today's adolescents in terms of demographics such as the population sex ratio may seem like an excuse. It may seem to release parents from their individual responsibility for how their children turn out. In that sense, it may seem little different from the hopeless hand-washing advocated by authors such as Judith Harris[29] who argue that how children turn out is determined mainly by genetics and by peer pressures, influences over which parents may have little or no control. Yet, it is very different.

Looking at the correlation between the sex ratio, or the proportion of women working, and social problems, one may feel there is a certain inevitability to teenagers becoming delinquent or getting pregnant. After all, they are merely responding to the domestic difficulties that arise when there is a lack of permanent commitment by men to their wives. Moreover, they are creatures of their time. It doesn't help when their sense of alienation and neglect is reinforced by the troubled or antisocial individuals they are likely to encounter in their schools and neighborhoods. Neither does it bode well when they are steeped in a teen culture of cynicism and violence in the form of music, video, and print media.

However, considering what is going on in the lives of individual children, there is no such inevitability. The fact is that despite influences to the contrary, most marriages are still highly stable over long periods of time. Despite the presence of antisocial cliques in high schools, most teenagers are well meaning and want to live law-abiding, productive lives. Moreover, despite the problems in families, schools, and communities, most teenagers do not deviate into serious delinquency. Why not? The answer is that children who have a good relationship with their parents, or even with an unrelated adult who fulfills a parental role, are at low risk for becoming delinquent. This is true whether parents live together or apart. It is also true whether mothers go to work during the day or stay at home.[30]

Chapter 8

Teen Mothers and Reduced Parental Investment

Before the Industrial Revolution, Western women focused most of their energies on the demanding task of child production and rearing. Their reproductive careers began early, and it was not unusual, or deviant, for women to become parents while still in their teens. How do we account for the fact that teen pregnancy was considered normal then whereas today it is deemed to be the very nexus of major social problems such as crime, drug abuse, violence, poor educational performance, low occupational attainment, and the cross-generational cycle of poverty?

THEN AND NOW: CHANGES IN THE REPRODUCTIVE ROLES OF WOMEN

There are many differences between the family environment of Europe in the eighteenth century and that in the twentieth century. Women today are physiologically capable of reproduction at much earlier ages than they were in the past. Thus, the average age of first menstruation, which signals maturity of the female reproductive system, has declined from over sixteen years a century ago to under thirteen years today. Possible causes of this change include improved nutrition and greater exposure to artificial lights. A good diet is obviously necessary for rapid growth and maturation. Animal experiments have clearly shown that female mammals mature more rapidly when they are exposed to high levels of artificial light.[1]

Even though women of the eighteenth century may have begun reproducing while still in their teens, they were no longer children. There is a big difference between the level of maturity of a nineteen-year-old and a fourteen-year-old, these being typical ages at which teens could be expected to reproduce in the eighteenth and late twentieth centuries, respectively, if they began having regular sexual intercourse at puberty.

Of course, teen mothers today are also much more likely to be unwed than would have been the case two centuries ago. This is partly because the age of sexual maturity and the onset of sexual intercourse are both advanced, while the age at first marriage is delayed. The typical American woman begins having sex at the age of seventeen[2] but does not marry until age twenty-three,[3] leaving a substantial window of time for nonmarital pregnancy to occur. Two centuries ago, there would have been little time between the onset of sexual intercourse and marriage, for most women, due to later sexual maturation and earlier marriage.

Since life expectancy was much lower in the earlier period, being approximately half of what it is today, there was no good reason for delaying reproduction. A common cause of mortality was infectious disease such as plague, smallpox, influenza, and typhoid. Children were more vulnerable than adults to these killers. This meant that a woman who survived her entire period of maximum fertility between her early twenties and her early forties might expect to bring about eight pregnancies to term, of which approximately four children would survive to adulthood. The reason that the number of pregnancies was not larger was that children were breast-fed for two to three years, and breast-feeding tends to suppress ovulation. Wealthy families farmed their children out to wet nurses, who were paid for their services. This allowed wealthy women to reproduce more rapidly. Since their children were better nourished, they had a better chance of surviving illnesses. The net result was that wealthy families often raised ten or more children to maturity.[4, 5]

Despite the horrific reproductive treadmill that was the lot of most women, teen pregnancy did not have the same negative connotations that it does today. This was not just because pregnant teens were likely to have been somewhat older when they began reproducing than is the case today, but because they enjoyed a great deal more social support. To begin with, they were highly likely to have been married to men who provided them with a stable form of economic support. They also had the support of an extended family when it came to child care. Manuals that instruct mothers on how to care for their infants are a relatively modern phenomenon,[6] probably not because people were indifferent about their infants, as some scholars think, but because the information was transmitted socially via oral tradition. Modern mothers often live in cities where they are cut off from a supportive network of family and stable friends. They often obtain basic information about how to care for infants from books. In the eighteenth century, it would have been virtually impossible for a new mother not to know several experienced mothers in her immediate circle of relatives and friends who would have been only too willing to share their child care expertise. Indeed it is improbable that young women would not have had direct experience in basic child care techniques such as how best to manage a fussy baby.

Sadly, modern urban teens who give birth may have no reliable source of information on how to care for, and manage, their infants. Not only do they not have a reliable family network, but they may not be motivated to read child care manuals.

While the stable family environment of the pre–Industrial Revolution era may seem enviable to some, this was not necessarily a golden age for children. Because child mortality was so high, it did not make a lot of sense for parents to form very deep emotional attachments to children. When children died, grief was a private matter, and it was considered poor taste to eulogize favorite children who had died since this honor was accorded only to those who had reached the status of adulthood. Parents were expected to swallow their grief and move on. The modern, more sentimental, approach to the death of children emerged in diaries written in the second half of the eighteenth century in England, such as that of James Boswell who describes his intense grief at the loss of his infant son.

Some of the routine aspects of child care used then strike us as odd, even as barbaric or abusive. Take the practice of swaddling. Infants were bound tightly in bandages, like miniature mummies. The point of this procedure was to calm the infant down so that it could be set in a corner while the mother carried out her domestic chores without being constantly interrupted by having to soothe a crying baby. Researchers have discovered that this immobilization is highly effective in slowing down the infant's heartbeat and breathing. Variants of the swaddling technique have been used in restraint devices that calm autistic children and in training wild horses. The horse is gentled by pouring grain all around it. The technique is so effective that wild mustangs, which once could only be tamed by elite horse trainers, can now be broken in a few hours.[7]

Swaddling is not popular today except in the management of newborns because it reflects a philosophy of child-rearing that is alien to us. The modern view is that infants should be stimulated because sensory information is essential for the development of the brain. Study of children in institutions demonstrates that stimulus deprivation can actually be harmful. However, it seems likely that infants who were immobilized by swaddling and other techniques, such as the Native American cradle board, actually received a more varied sensory world than did children who were in orphanages. They certainly received more social stimulation in the form of individual attention from their mothers and whatever friends and relatives they encountered. It is also possible that the current extreme preoccupation with providing brain stimulation is the result of concern about academic success, which would have been far less of an issue in societies in which most people made their living through manual work of some kind.

The nonstimulating perspective can be summed up in the phrase, "children should be seen but not heard." Most of us recognize that some quietness can be good for kids. For example, children learn best in a classroom where distracting noise is kept to a minimum. Nonetheless, the philosophy of minimizing adult interactions with children is 180 degrees removed from the current opinion that children need to be highly stimulated to promote cognitive development. It is a mass-production mentality compared to the modern perspective that no amount of trouble is too much when it comes to promoting optimal development of our children.

One reason for the change is that families today are in fact much smaller and child mortality is much lower, which facilitates greater levels of parental involvement with each child. Another is that modern life is a great deal more complex. Occupational success is predicated on doing well in school so that parents are more willing to provide the kind of stimulation to children that promotes intellectual development and future economic success. While parents can invest more in children, the bar has been raised regarding what is necessary for a child to succeed.

A large part of the reason that teen parenting is seen as problematic is that teen mothers are not considered equal to the task of raising children who can succeed in the very demanding society in which we live. Of course, raising a child also interferes with the mother's own education and career development, which means that the children of teen mothers are likely to be raised in poverty. At a time of rising expectations of women in their own careers, and as mothers are trying to support career-formation of their children, social support from extended families is declining.[8]

AN EVOLUTIONARY THEORY OF
CHILD SOCIALIZATION

We tend to think of child-rearing practices as good or bad. A more objective way of looking at it is that different child-rearing practices are endorsed by different societies and by the same society at different points in history. Why these practices vary across societies and across history is discussed in more detail in the next chapter. The central idea is that parental behavior is designed to produce locally successful children.

Despite the important influence of genetically based temperament in predicting personality and behavior of adults, children are quite flexible and respond in predictable ways to varied parental investment. The cornerstone of the evolutionary theory of child socialization proposed by Jay Belsky, Lawrence Steinberg, and Patricia Draper of Penn State University is that low parental investment is cyclical. That is, children who receive low parental investment are not only likely to have trouble fitting in with the requirements of their communities, so far as working for a living and obeying the law are concerned, they are also set up to be low-investing parents.[9]

This is a very simple theory, but it is also a very powerful one, in the sense that it can account for a great deal of what we know about the problems of poor people. For example, it provides a neat explanation for the cross-generational cycle of poverty, crime, teen pregnancy, drug abuse, and other social ills. This kind of theory is particularly helpful in accounting for changes in social problems within generations that cannot possibly be due to genetic change. It is an evolutionary theory because it emphasizes the fact that humans respond to their early environment in a manner that helps them to survive and reproduce. For example, if men are unlikely to invest in children, then it would be maladaptive for women to postpone reproduction until they find a desirable husband who is committed to helping raise their children. If a woman waited for this to happen, she would never have children. Women raised in a low-investing environment can maximize their reproductive success by beginning to have children early in life.

For this reason, a scarcity of men who are suitable marriage material is a strong predictor of nonmarital pregnancy across the nations of the world, across ethnic groups in the United States, and within ethnic groups across time.[10, 11] Wherever you look, young women who face a difficult marriage market are starting their reproductive life early outside of marriage. Fortunately, teen pregnancy no longer means that women will continue to produce children across their reproductive years, thereby committing a large segment of the population to grinding poverty. The widespread use of effective birth control techniques means that few young women in developed countries are likely to have large families.

According to Belsky and colleagues, low-investing parents direct harsh and inconsistent parenting practices towards children. This directs the social development of the children in such a way that they are predisposed to being low-investing parents. The central concept is that children who are raised by harsh and inconsistent parents grow up to see the world through jaundiced eyes. They learn that the world in which we live can be harsh and unfair and that it is foolish to trust the good intentions of other people. This generalized suspicion and cynicism make it difficult for children to comply with the wishes of others. They do not identify with the goals of education and tend to lack enthusiasm about devoting their lives to a career or idealistic cause of any kind. This mind set manifests itself in poor academic performance and a penchant for getting involved in delinquent activities, such as cutting school, underage drinking, and gang membership.

Together with adolescent rebellion, delinquency, and drug use, teenagers are likely to begin having uncommitted, and often unprotected, sexual intercourse. Sociologists who have studied the motivation for gang membership have found that young men in gangs are more likely to have sexual access to women. As one's status in a gang increases, sexual access to different young women increases. This is not a politically correct world, and women are treated as sex objects. For example, their initiation often takes the form of being sexually victimized by each of the male gang members.[12]

According to the evolutionary theory of socialization, young women who have been raised in a low-parental-investment situation are more willing to engage in casual sex. They tend to lack confidence in themselves and are willing to play the role of sex object. They also tend to be moody and are vulnerable to depression. An interesting biological rationale for this depression is provided by behavior geneticist Dean Hamer and P. Copeland in their popular book *Living with Our Genes*.[13] According to Hamer and Copeland, the biological basis for one type of depression, which has to do with the neurotransmitter serotonin, is also linked to having a high sex drive. For this reason one complaint of people taking antidepressant drugs, such as Prozac, is that when their depression lifts, they also lose interest in sex.

Being depressed may also be the result of an energy-conserving system. For example, many people are vulnerable to depression in the winter, when staying in a warm place to conserve energy makes adaptive sense. One of the features of depression is an unwillingness to move around. At a clinical extreme, sufferers from major depression have difficulty getting out of bed in the morning.

Another biological adaptation to low parental investment may be early onset of sexual maturity. This phenomenon is mediated by genetics as well as by the environment. Researchers have found that young women exposed to a psychologically stressful rearing environment tend to mature a few months earlier, which is the opposite of what is found for other primates.[14]

Early maturation has interesting consequences for energy storage. Girls who mature between the ages of nine and eleven have an average of 30 percent more body fat compared to those who mature between the ages of fourteen and seventeen. They also have shorter stature.[15] Since young women store body fat mainly around the breasts and hips, this means that early-maturing women are likely to be much more curvaceous in body build. That is, they tend to be stereotypically feminine. This means that they are seen as both more sexually attractive and less professionally competent.[16, 17]

While these biological mechanisms may not have any great importance in the modern developed world, in which there is little food scarcity and little shortage of body fat energy, they would have been more significant in the evolutionary past when reproduction constituted a major energetic challenge to women, and men evolved a preference for women whose body build indicated that they had sufficient stored body fat energy to meet the challenges of reproduction and breast-feeding. All of the facts fit into an interesting pattern that suggests that the behavioral and biological aspects of the response by young women to a low-investment family environment tend to prepare them for early reproduction.[18]

Psychological aspects of the response to low parental investment are more salient in the modern world. Children raised by harsh, insensitive parents are not only more delinquent in their behavior but also tend to be rather unhappy, which increases their vulnerability to clinical depression. In the case of parental divorce, it is probably not parental separation that weighs children down so much as the conflictual quality of the parental union to begin with. For instance, a study by Martin Seligman[19] found that there was a similar increase in depression for children whose parents fought compared to parents that were divorced or separated. When parents fight in front of the children, children naturally draw the conclusion that the parents are not very happy together and not very committed to each other. This probably creates a sense of insecurity in the child's own relationships with the parents.

Children in conflictual homes are more prone to depression because parental spats are unpleasant and because they have no control over these unpleasant and inescapable scenes. By analogy, it has been demonstrated that exposing laboratory animals to uncontrollable unpleasant events, such as receiving painful electric shocks, makes them behave as though they were depressed. Dogs whine miserably and give up trying to do anything to escape the shock. Another interesting aspect of the dogs' depression is that their inability to learn simple tasks, such as jumping over a barrier to avoid shock, is greatly impaired. The relevance of this for children of divorce is that in addition to increased risk for depression, they also have impaired capacity to learn in the classroom.[20, 21]

The lack of trust in interpersonal relationships that children see in their parental homes is often visited on the next generation where it shows up in all kinds of social and interpersonal problems from increased risk of delinquency to increased risk of teen pregnancy and divorce.[22] There are many possible explanations for this. One is the quality of the attachment relationship with the mother. Another is genetics. For example, the one study of heritability of divorce has estimated that genetics can account for half of the differences in divorce risk.[23] Rapid changes over time in social problem statistics cannot be due to genetics, however, and they are linked to population changes in parental investment, as discussed in Chapter 4.[24] Since population indicators of parental investment (such as divorce rate and the ratio of marriageable men to women) can explain rapidly occurring changes in social problems, the evolutionary theory of socialization is vindicated. Children receiving reduced parental investment are more likely to exhibit social problems because of their rearing experiences.

To summarize the argument thus far, reduced parental investment is associated with an increased risk of teen pregnancy and other social problems. This fits in with the evolutionary theory of socialization proposed by Jay Belsky and others, according to which low parental investment in the home of origin pushes young women (and men) in the direction of low-investment reproduction (as indexed by willingness to produce children early in life, outside of marriage).[25]

While teen pregnancies may often seem to be the accidental consequence of unprotected sex, this is a superficial reading of the situation. The decision to reproduce early in life may be made at an emotional rather than a rational or even conscious level. The underlying logic of such reproductive decisions is fairly compelling from an adaptationist perspective. That is, if there is no possible reproductive, or economic, advantage of waiting for marriage, women tend to reproduce early out of wedlock. On the other hand, if a woman has a good prospect of marrying and of establishing a career, then she should delay reproduction, since teen pregnancy tends to get in the way of each of these goals. Particularly revealing here is the response of such young women to accidental pregnancy in the United States. They are much more likely to terminate a pregnancy than are teenagers who are doing poorly at school.

THE VICIOUS CYCLE OF REDUCED PARENTAL INVESTMENT

Teen mothers are often blamed for the increased risk of social problems of their children. While the connection between early childbearing and social problems is certainly unmistakable, it is rather arbitrary to select only one phase in a cyclical pattern as being of critical importance. Teen motherhood is as much the result of low parental investment as it is the cause of it.[26] This point can be illustrated by the case of African-American women for whom nonmarital reproduction, often early in life, is a response to the great dearth of marriageable men and hence to an environment of reduced parental investment (see Chapter 9).

Much as we might want to explain social problems in terms of what is happening in the society in which people live, there is no question that individuals vary in how effective they are as parents, when "effectiveness" is narrowly defined in terms of producing the kind of adolescents that most of us see as desirable. We do not really know the extent to which individual differences in parental investment are explainable in terms of genetics. According to the results of studies of twins, we can say with confidence that many of the traits that might plausibly affect parental investment, including altruism, agreeableness, impulse-control, conscientiousness, traditionalism, ability to handle stress, risk avoidance, and desire for intimacy, are strongly correlated with genetics.[27]

Without denying the possibility of a role for genetic variation, we know that individual differences in parental investment are affected by how a person was treated by his or her own parents. There is a vicious cycle of low parental investment according to which children that have been treated insensitively or neglected by their parents are more likely to be low-investing parents themselves. While the importance of genetics in this cycle is usually difficult to evaluate, it is never the whole story. The most convincing evidence that parental behavior explains the cycle of parental investment is that interventions that are targeted at parents produce generalized changes in the social interactions of the children, which are extremely likely to affect how they will treat their own children. Evidence for environmental mediation of the cycle of parental investment includes the following:

- Teaching sensitive responsiveness to mothers of irritable infants produces a huge increase in security of attachment of infants to their mothers. Security of attachment has important consequences for our ability to form stable intimate relationships, such as those between husbands and wives and those between parents and children.[28]

- Interventions dealing with conduct disorders in elementary school children have been so effective that when the problem children are tested several years later, they are indistinguishable from a normal, untreated control group.[29]

- Head Start programs, even those that were begun too late to have much academic benefit, have been found to increase the interest of children in having a job and working towards a career, typical features of high-investing parents.[30]

- Observational study of children has shown that their ability to communicate effectively, as indexed by vocabulary size, sentence length, and so forth, is a function of the quality of speech directed at them by both parents. Clearly, communicative ability is a central facet of high-investing parents.[31]

- Experiments have shown that self-control in the context of delay-of-gratification tests is a skill that can be reinforced by parents. Self-control is also enhanced in the case of securely attached infants. Of course, security of attachment is also a product of the quality of parental interactions. It is a critical ingredient of consistent parental discipline. For instance, if a child's misbehavior is punished only when a parent loses his temper, then the child learns only one thing: Avoid Dad when he is in a lousy mood.[32]

- Parental investment not only is associated with language ability but also increases general intelligence, judging from the results of Head Start interventions begun early in life. Intelligent parents are better able to provide the sort of stimulating environment that facilitates academic success in children. We know that academic success is a negative predictor of all kinds of social problems from teen pregnancy to delinquency and criminal occupations.[33]

- Being able to perform well under pressure is an important asset for high-investing parents since there are times when even the best of children test the limits of parental patience. Research on the development of temperament has found that infants who are highly fearful can become much bolder if their parents encourage them to be more adventurous. This suggests that the ability to handle psychological stress is partly a function of parental behavior.[34]

Perhaps the most compelling evidence for the cycle of parental investment is to look at the childhood experiences of very dangerous criminals. Although many of them do not get married and have little interest in being involved in the care of children, it is obvious that they would be fathers from hell.[35] Here is an example of the kind of nightmare scenario in which a young woman named Lorina gave birth to several children while still in her teens and quickly lost all control over them in a gang-ridden, crime-infested urban neighborhood. Her third child, a boy, was born when she was only eighteen years old. Absorbed into gang culture, this boy quickly assembled a string of eight felonies, including arson, car theft, burglary, and armed robbery. He was charged with all of these offenses while still a child. Then, at the age of eleven, he went on a shooting rampage, permanently disabling one young boy and accidentally killing a fourteen-year-old girl. His criminal career was brought to a sudden end when he was executed by fellow gang members.[36]

This grim tale is only a little more grisly and extreme than thousands of others that we read about in the daily newspapers. It is all very well to argue that such sad stories are attributable to people being born with antisocial personalities. This may be true in many cases since a substantial segment of the prison population satisfies the diagnostic criteria for antisocial personality. At least half of people diagnosed as antisocial personalities have no criminal record, however. This means that antisocial personalities do not necessarily mature into active felons. Another way of putting it is to say that children with antisocial proclivities can be socialized to obey laws, even if they never have much empathy for the feelings of other people. If they are unfortunate enough to live in the kind of circumstances in which Lorina raised her children, there is little chance that they can avoid living destructive, unhappy lives and committing serious crimes.

THE PROBLEM WITH TEEN MOTHERS

Blaming teen mothers for the ills of our society may seem a little unfair. Most are probably doing the best they can for their children in very difficult circumstances. There are very few parents who do not love their children and want the best for them. In the case of teen mothers living in poverty, the dice are very much loaded against the children because of their environments. One of the most important environmental components is the quality of the care they receive from their mothers.

Teenage pregnancy is seen as a major problem in our society because it contributes to poverty. The central issue is that children of teen mothers do less well in school, which interferes with their ability to establish themselves in careers in the competitive skills-based economy in which we live. At the same time that they are doing poorly in school, they live in neighborhoods that expose them to the risk of joining street gangs and engaging in delinquent activities such as illegal drug use, vandalism, and having unprotected sex. When the teenage children of teen mothers become pregnant, the wheel comes full circle, making it highly probable that another generation will grow up in poverty and make its incremental contribution to social problem statistics.

Even if the influences outside the home are ignored, teen mothers tend to fit the profile of low-investing parents. Many are quite ill-informed about how to care for infants. This is partly a product of their lack of social integration, which may include having a poor relationship with their own mothers who would normally be an important source of information about child care. Teenagers often lack the emotional maturity to be good at managing their children. This is worsened in the case of individuals who feel that they have been deprived of parental affection themselves.

As mothers, teenagers tend to be insensitive to both the feelings and the needs of their babies and quite inconsistent in their actions. Judith Musick tells the story of one young mother she interviewed on a cold winter day. She noticed that the mother's child was not wearing a warm coat. When she asked the mother why, the teenager responded that *she* didn't feel cold. Such basic "thoughtless" insensitivity to the needs of young children is typical of immature mothers. They are more likely to use harsh physical punishment inappropriately. They also provide relatively low levels of stimulation in the sense of spending little time talking to their infants or exposing them to intellectually stimulating experiences in the form of toys and games. They are also less likely to read to small children or to provide informative answers to their questions.[37]

These problems are clearly articulated by Judith Musick in her book *Young, Poor, and Pregnant* (references omitted):

The available data indicate that teens are more likely to use physical punishment with their infants, especially when they fail to meet developmental expectation and display more hostile (and childlike) behaviors such as teasing and pinching. Adolescents spend less time talking to their infants than do adult mothers. This may be evidence of their greater self-absorption, not only their apathy, or lack of knowledge about the importance of talking to young children. Whatever its cause, the fact that they vocalize less and offer less stimulation in general to their infants may be key factors in these children's later depressed cognitive functioning.[38]

The fact that teen mothers produce children who do badly at school is no surprise because young women who become pregnant often do so following a dismal academic performance of their own. According to data from the National Longitudinal Study of Youth, teens in the bottom fifth of their high school class in reading and math skills are approximately five times as likely to become teen mothers as those in the top fifth (29 percent vs. 6 percent).[39] The low academic performance of the children is apparently not due to genetics, however, since few differences are seen in infancy between children of teens and children of older mothers. Delays in cognitive development are seen in the preschool years, which resembles the pattern for children reared in orphanages and suggests that having a very young mother is intellectually impoverishing. Children of teen mothers exhibit a variety of other behavioral problems from an early age. These include increased aggression and more problems of impulse control. In adolescence, there is an increased risk of grade failure, delinquency, early sexual activity, and teenage pregnancy for girls and a greater likelihood of imprisonment for crimes in the case of boys.[40]

In addition to low levels of intellectual stimulation, teen mothers are less likely to provide the kind of emotional support that may be equally important to young children in facilitating their exploration of the environment. According to Musick, teen mothers often feel deprived of the love of their own mothers and therefore are unable to give it to their offspring.[41] Along with low levels of empathy goes a relative lack of insight into the motives of infants:

Many adolescents give the appearance of having little tolerance for their children's developmentally-appropriate demands or attempts to explore or assert themselves. They tend to speak very critically and negatively to their children, handle them roughly, and terrorize them one moment and smother them with kisses the next. They spank and slap babies when they cry or spit up or spill food; attributing willful naughtiness even to very young infants—"He's just trying to get me!" These responses seem insensitive and inappropriately unconnected to who their children are and what they need. These same sorts of interactional problems have been observed in older, troubled mothers by clinical investigators.[42]

The kinds of parental practices that Musick describes for teen mothers are obviously not specific to teen mothers. They are typical of low parental investment, regardless of the age of the mother.

In addition to low occupational attainment, children of teen mothers are set up for all manner of personal and social problems that go along with low parental investment. These disadvantages are immediately apparent to people who make hiring decisions. Children who are raised in poverty almost inevitably attend the worst public schools. This means that they tend to communicate using slang and have trouble managing formal English, which is essential for job interviews for good jobs. Emotional insecurity also makes it difficult for them to behave in businesslike ways when dealing with colleagues and customers. Needless to say, they are unlikely to make sensitive and emotionally mature parents.

LIGHT AT THE END OF THE TUNNEL?

When you review social problem statistics from the 1950s to the 1980s, there are many dismal trends such as skyrocketing crime rates, teen pregnancy rates, divorce rates, and increasing numbers of children raised without fathers in abject poverty. According to the theory developed in this book, these trends can be explained largely in terms of poor marital opportunities for women. The data are strongly supportive of this argument since there is a strong relationship between the proportion of unmarried women to men and social problems. During periods when there are more women than men, family ties are weakened and there is reduced parental investment in children. This is partly due to lack of positive investment, attributable to being raised in poverty, or having insufficient attention, emotional support, and intellectual enrichment from sympathetic adults. Of equal importance is the negative effect on parental investment of an atmosphere of hostility and suspicion between parents, which is typical of unstable marriages.

As Marcia Guttentag and Paul Secord pointed out in their influential book, *Too Many Women: The Sex Ratio Question*,[43] the oversupply of American women is partly due to the baby boom phenomenon, a phase of concentrated post–World War II baby production. Since women typically marry men who are about two and a half years older than they are, the women of the baby boom generation did not have enough potential husbands. The group (or cohort) they were choosing among had been born around three years earlier when there was a trough in the birthrate, right in the middle of World War II. Many delayed the age of their first marriage, which only prolonged the imbalance.

Some idea of the size of this problem can be gleaned by looking at the ratio of men to women at the ages of twenty to twenty-four, which includes the peak ages of marriage for both sexes. In 1958, there were approximately 102 white men for every 100 white women. By 1968, this had fallen to exactly 93 men per 100 women. For blacks, the corresponding numbers fell from 98 to 91. If you look only at unmarried people, the gap is even wider.[44] For whites, but not for blacks, the sex ratio reached parity for twenty to twenty-four-year-olds in 1976 and has remained relatively high. This is probably the fundamental reason that social problems, including teen pregnancy, which had shown an astonishingly rapid increase during the 1960s, 1970s, and 1980s, have turned a corner and are beginning to decline.[45, 46]

There is light at the end of the tunnel. Population trends predict a decrease in teen pregnancy and in the social problems that go along with reduced parental investment. As the marriage market for women improves, marriages will become more stable. As men become more committed to marriage, relations between the sexes will improve. Children raised in harmonious homes will be less likely to show up in social problem statistics. When they grow up, they will become sensitive and committed parents. Needless to say, this upbeat scenario does not apply to all segments of the population. It does not apply to those who are trapped in the cycle of poverty. The next chapter examines the role of parental investment in accounting for ethnic differences in social problems in the United States.

Chapter 9

Group Differences in Child Socialization

The question of racial differences in the United States is so emotionally charged and so shrouded in the history of slavery and segregation that it is difficult to examine objectively. Academic explanations for the vulnerability of African Americans to social problems have not been very satisfactory as science. Advocates of a biological determinist view have generally put forth clearer arguments and have assembled a mountain of scientific evidence. However, none of the evidence is in the least convincing unless you happened to be a biological determinist to begin with.

The contrary view, environmental determinism based on a history of prejudice and injustice, is the received opinion in academic circles. When black Americans have three times as many illegitimate babies or commit several times as many crimes as the rest of the population, they are simply responding to societal conditions. What is it about the social environment? The answer is a familiar litany: poverty, bad schools, lack of economic opportunity, drug addictions, poor prenatal health care, racial prejudice, and so on.

Representative of this approach is an explanation, by sociologists, for the extremely high divorce rate among African Americans: "Racial differences in divorce may derive from African Americans' history of restricted opportunity, a sense of resignation, and ultimately a strategy of adapting to a bleak situation. . . . It is more than a statistical accident that the segment of society most vulnerable to many types of difficulties is also more prone to divorce."[1] Divorce is therefore part of a nexus of social problems that have been produced by a pattern of prejudice and discrimination extending back in history.

The same kind of interpretation is often applied to other social problems as well. For example, in their textbook on delinquency, LaMar Empey and Mark Stafford apply a similar rationale for ethnic group differences in criminal behavior: "Why are arrest rates higher for black than white juveniles? Arrest data imply that centuries of exclusion from the benefits of American life have profoundly affected the lives of young black people."[2]

Just how tenuous explanations of social problems in terms of prejudice may become is illustrated by an account of African-American divorce that connects divorce rates to prejudice in the workplace. Excessive scrutiny of black workers and the energy required for "contriving a 'white' personality" constitute occupational stressors that "deplete psychological resources for marital communication, conjugal cooperation, and conflict management."[3] While it is certainly possible that trouble in the workplace may spill over to domestic life, the scientific logic for this argument as an explanation for group differences in divorce rate seems diffuse and far-fetched. It begins with a hypothetical, or unmeasured, work discrimination that is supposed to cause (hypothetical) stress, leading to depleted (hypothetical) psychological resources, which produce a (hypothetical) deterioration of relations between the sexes, thereby facilitating marital dissolution. Individually and collectively, these connections may not be wrong, but they are extremely inelegant and would be difficult to test.

Such environmentalist explanations may appear quite reasonable, but they have several weaknesses when considered as science. The most fundamental one is that they are not really explanations at all. It is not obvious why prejudice or the adverse conditions that are assumed to go along with it would make a young woman want to become pregnant outside of marriage. Neither is it clear why prejudice would make someone commit a crime except in the vague sense that social stressors might contribute to unhappiness and alienation. The critical weakness of prejudice explanations for group differences in social problems is that they do not help us to understand why the majority of African Americans do not become criminals or flunk out of school even though they are victims of the same racial prejudice as individuals who do.

Prejudice explanations for social problems are extraordinarily resistant to contrary evidence. Thus the poor academic performance of African Americans is often attributed to prejudice and discrimination despite the fact that some of the ethnic groups who have been most discriminated against this century, such as the Jews and the Japanese, actually score well above average on many academic tests.[4] Moreover, successful interventions that are designed to improve academic performance of black students, such as P. Uri Treisman's mathematics workshop at Berkeley, generally do so without directly addressing issues of prejudice, although they do attempt to increase academic involvement, which is supposedly reduced due to racial stereotypes.[5] In other words, black youths are disinclined to work towards academic goals because they do not believe they can succeed.

To say that the academic problems of black Americans are caused by prejudice may seem like a convenient shorthand, but if the causal steps have not been filled in, it can be scientifically perilous. Instead of dealing in causal explanations, we may get involved in a circular labeling exercise. The circularity of the labeling exercise can be seen by looking at how easy it is to shift from forward to reverse arguments. For instance, many commentators invoke the concept of a prejudiced society to explain why African Americans obtain so few advanced college degrees, have poor prenatal care, have high rates of criminal incarceration, have high rates of poverty, and so on. How do we know that American society is prejudiced? It is prejudiced because African Americans have high rates of poverty, have poor prenatal care, obtain relatively few Ph.D.s, and so on. Invoking prejudice is a form of shorthand for saying that African Americans have many social problems. This gives us very little idea of why they do, except to imply that the causes are to be found in the reprehensible, unfair, and oppressive behavior of whites rather than in the behavior of blacks.

In short, the prejudice argument involves apportioning blame rather than identifying scientific causes. Clearly, if you are not establishing real causes for social problems, you are not in a good situation to generate solutions. In this respect, the prejudice perspective resembles its mirror-image opposite, the genetic determinist explanation for group differences in social problems. The main difference is that the genetic determinist explains social problems in terms of defective genotypes whereas the environmentalist explains them in terms of defects in the political system.

THE VITAL ALTERNATIVES: PREJUDICE AND GENETICS

"Are you more interested in the Cadillac or the Lincoln?" A salesman at work gives you a limited set of alternatives and tries to trick you into verbally committing yourself to one. The trick is called the vital alternatives.

The vital alternatives also affect the intellectual decisions of scholars, including their interpretation of group differences in social problems. When presented with two theories that seem the opposite of each other, one tends to prefer one or the other instead of entertaining the other logical alternative, that both are wrong. Most scholars have fallen into the trap of assuming that either the prejudice explanation or the genetic determinist explanation of group differences has to be correct. Not only are both approaches flawed, but they actually share many of the same fundamental weaknesses, such as circular reasoning.

The problem with saying that the increased risk of social problems for African Americans is due to prejudice is that it is not clear how we get from the fact of prejudice to the fact of increased risk of some social problem, such as teen pregnancy. The causal steps need to be filled in. For instance, if prejudice against African Americans meant that qualified individuals did not get jobs (and there is currently little evidence for this)[6] and if unemployment reduced marriage rates, thereby increasing nonmarital pregnancy, then it could be argued that prejudice plays a role in causing increased rates of teen pregnancy. As it is, nonmarital birthrates can be satisfactorily explained in terms of the marriage market and the fact that large numbers of black women are not marrying black men, and introducing prejudice as an explanation tends to obfuscate rather than to clarify the issue (see Chapter 8).

In short, the prejudice argument apportions blame for social problems rather than providing a clear and useful explanation for why they occur. In this respect, it resembles its mirror-image opposite—the racial genetic explanation for group differences in social problems.[7] The genetic determinist position, however, blames the individual for the social problems rather than assigning blame to another powerful social group that controls the environment. According to the genetic determinist view, social problems are attributable to inferior genes. Thus, if people do badly in school, it is because they have genes for low intelligence.[8, 9] The parental investment approach to social problems described in this book is intended to be nonmoralistic, although it might be naive to imagine that all readers will interpret it in this way.

Even though the genetic determinist explanation for group differences in social problems may seem much more rooted in the hard sciences than the prejudice explanation, this appearance is deceiving. For example, Philippe Rushton amassed quite a lot of data concerning behavioral and biological differences as a function of racial adaptations to conditions in Asia or Europe, as compared to Africa, which, as all scientists agree, is the cradle of humanity. Some of these biological differences are fairly uncontroversial. For instance, it appears that Chinese infants are less active and less responsive to stimulation immediately after birth than are European infants.[10] The map of genetic disorders and metabolic peculiarities also shows regional variations. Cystic fibrosis is most prevalent in Africa, lactose intolerance is most prevalent in Asia, and so on.

The view that natural selection should create genetic differences for different geographically segregated populations is eminently reasonable and is actually supported by the work of geneticists who study the frequency of different gene types (or alleles) around the globe, whether these code for diseases like sickle-cell anemia or metabolic differences such as lactose intolerance.[11]

Even though a single-gene condition, such as phenylketonuria (PKU), can cause mental retardation if it is not detected and treated through dietary management, it is a large jump from such single-gene phenomena to the genetic explanation of intelligence in healthy individuals because intelligence is affected by so many different genes. According to Philippe Rushton, northern climates are more intellectually demanding than the Africa of our ancestors. This view is based on the untested assumption that it requires more intelligence to hunt cooperatively and to store food for the winter than it does to make one's living near the equator, where fruit drops off the tree into your hand. This may seem plausible until one looks at the lifestyle of existing equatorial peoples. Many live in a state of perpetual warfare. I think I would rather get together with my friends and plot the downfall of a polar bear, the most dangerous animal on the ice, rather than participating in the constant web of political intrigue that determines the alliances, and hostilities, of warlike tribes. Surely it takes more intelligence to defend yourself against attack from intelligent fellow humans, than it does to cooperatively hunt down a polar bear.[12]

The climatic theory for racial differentiation of intelligence and social complexity also encounters a very large rock of contrary evidence since the most complex societies, city cultures, emerged not in chilly northern climes but in balmy Mediterranean climates. The first cities developed around intensive agriculture of the type made possible by irrigating the alluvial soil of river deltas. This was so productive that it allowed for large numbers of people to live in the same region. This, in turn, ushered in the first complex centralized governments. High levels of social organization did not develop as a response to cold climates following the exodus of early Europeans and Asians from Africa, as Richard Lynn and Philippe Rushton argue. In fact, some of the earliest cities emerged in Africa itself, on the banks of the Nile.

Rushton finds a variety of evidence suggesting that the social problems of black Americans are attributable to their African ancestry. His argument is that populations of African extraction always manifest the same symptoms of high criminality and low educational, occupational, and cultural achievement, compared to Asians and Europeans. The main weakness of this argument is that it is only correlational. If African ancestry tends to go along with social problems, this does not have to mean that African ancestry caused the problems. One plausible alternative is that Europeans and Asians have enjoyed centuries of living in well-regulated centralized states, having the benefit of surplus material wealth, public education, and so forth. Rushton concedes that this may be so but argues that the differences in level of civilization are themselves genetically determined. We have now come full circle. Genes are supposed to cause social problems leading to low levels of civilization. Now we find that genes cause low levels of civilization that result in social problems!

The seductiveness of the fallacy behind Rushton's thinking is nicely illustrated by another ethnic group, the Hispanics, who share many of the social problems, such as high crime rates and high teen pregnancy, that are experienced by African Americans. It would be very easy to conclude that the social problems of Hispanics are attributable to their genes. The only problem is that there is no "Hispanic" race because there is no distinct Hispanic ancestry. The term is a fictive category dreamed up by U.S. statisticians to avoid miscategorizing certain ethnic groups, such as Mexican Americans, by calling them "nonwhite" or "black." "Hispanic" could be loosely defined as anyone whose female ancestor was impregnated by a man from Spain or Portugal. The point is that the category includes people of all geographical extractions, encompassing Europeans, Asians, Native Americans, and Africans. The only thing we can say about them with any certainty is that whatever differences exist between them and "white" Americans cannot be due to genetics because there is no legitimate distinction to be drawn between whites and Hispanics, unless it is that Hispanics have more genetic variation than whites.

Perhaps the most fundamental problem with Rushton's genetic determinist theory of group differences is the assumption that, in a genetic sense, there really are three super races of human beings corresponding with the splitting off of early Africans into a European and an Asian line. As far as geneticists are concerned, the concept of racial diversity—which seems so compelling on the surface when you look at traits such as pale skin and long noses, which are adaptations to a cold climate—crumbles when you look below the surface at actual gene types.

Scientists such as Luigi Cavalli-Sforza who study changes in gene frequencies as a function of geographical location have found that the genetic variability within sub-Saharan Africa is virtually representative of the genetic possibilities of the entire species. There is almost as much genetic variability in this one region as there is in the rest of the world's population combined. The reason that there is so much genetic variability in Africa is that people have lived there for so long, cumulating a large number of mutations in their gene pools. Since Africans are so variable in their genotypes, it makes no biological sense to put them into a single category or to distinguish between Africans and others on the basis of genetics. There are not three genetically distinct races. There is only one. Beneath the skin, we are all genetic Africans.[13]

The genetic explanation and the prejudice explanation are fairly rigidly deterministic. That is, they assume that people cannot rise above their genes or above their environment. If some black people could live perfectly happy and productive lives, the prejudice position would be unsatisfactory because it does not account for the critical environmental differences that allow some individuals to succeed in spite of political adversity. Obviously, it *is* unsatisfactory on this basis. Individual differences in outcome for African-American children can only be explained in terms of family differences and, more specifically, in terms of parental investment.

The fact that most poor black children avoid serious social problems is a real problem for theories that seek to explain group differences in social problems in terms of either biology or racial discrimination. In one interesting study of the role played by social capital in differentiating between developmental outcomes of young people who are at risk of developing social problems, sociologist Frank Furstenberg followed the children of poor black teenage mothers living in Baltimore in the 1960s.[14] The great majority of these mothers were poor. When the children were studied at the age of twenty, in 1987, most had avoided serious social problems. High school graduates constituted 63 percent of the total while 65 percent of the women had avoided becoming teen mothers, 65 percent of the men had avoided serious criminal activity, and 78 percent had robust mental health. Furstenberg obtained information about a wide range of different kinds of social capital and investigated which of these predicted favorable developmental outcomes. The most important factor in avoiding teen pregnancy was the mother having a close friend who was seen on a weekly basis. This doubled the chances of daughters remaining childless in the teen years. Another important variable was the quality of schools attended. The logic for this may be that good schools help teenage girls to develop career aspirations that make them more likely to postpone reproduction. Interestingly, girls who were more involved with their extended families were more likely to become pregnant as teens. This may be due to the important supportive role played by grandmothers in the care of children.

The only important predictor of young men avoiding criminal activity was the presence of a strong help network outside the family. It is interesting that a strong help network quadrupled the chances of these men being enrolled in college and doubled the chances of them being in the labor force, which suggests that criminal activity is related to inability to exploit career opportunities. Furstenberg did not produce any evidence that the presence of the biological father in the home reduces the probability of either teen pregnancy or criminal involvement. These results are anomalous and conflict with a large body of evidence showing that single parenthood is a major predictor of social problems for the population as a whole. The presence of the biological father in the home multiplied the chances of high school graduation by eight and almost quadrupled the chances of being in the labor force (effects which were not produced by the long-term presence of stepfathers).

Furstenberg found that whether or not children graduated from high school—a useful predictor of subsequent occupational success—was related not just to the presence of the biological father but to other variables reflecting the emotional security of the mother, such as support from friends and from the woman's own mother and having someone to turn to in emergencies. Moreover, if the world of the child and the mother were closely integrated as indexed by the mother being familiar with the child's friends, the child was significantly more likely to graduate from high school. Educational success for black children born in poverty is thus very much a matter of the emotional tone of their home life. Specifically, if there is evidence of emotional closeness in relationships within the family, children are more likely to be educationally, and hence economically, successful. Since a great deal of variation in outcomes for poor African-American children can be explained in terms of family variables, people who look to political change as a means of ameliorating social problems in the black community are likely to be disappointed. This is not to deny that prejudice and discrimination exist and have hurtful consequences for African Americans and other ethnic groups. It is merely to argue that prejudice and discrimination can only contribute to social problems if they reduce parental investment in children.

Moreover, if entire groups of black people could do much better in their occupations than their biological heritage would predict, then the genetic determinist view would be false. This information is less obvious, but in the history of African immigration to the United States, two different subgroups, the freed slaves and the West Indians, evidently were at least as economically successful as the white population. The fundamental reason for these subgroup differences is different inculcation of achievement motivation in families. Moreover, a parental investment approach helps to explain why individuals like Clarence Page and Colin Powell can rise to the top in difficult professions despite experiencing racial discrimination.

Society-level explanations for group differences in the United States are incomplete, and actually quite vacuous, unless they can show how the societal phenomenon (be it prejudice, welfare, or low funding for some schools) affects the socialization of children so as to produce the difference in their behavior that is being explained. In short, differences between different ethnic groups in social problems is largely, or completely, explainable in terms of different parenting practices. If so, then group differences provide some of the most compelling evidence that parents matter in how their children turn out.

ADAPTIVE VARIATION IN CHILD-REARING IN DIFFERENT SOCIETIES

Different societies and social groups see different adult traits as desirable. In the United States, for example, extroversion is clearly valued. Some businesses promise that their employees will be friendly and outgoing (extrovert qualities). When introverts are hired, they find themselves greeting complete strangers with broad smiles—something they would never do on the street where they live. If friendliness is valued and required in businesses, it is likely that commercially advanced nations promote extroversion. While confidence and self-assertiveness are valued traits in the United States, many non-Western societies see these as disruptive and undesirable. In these cultures, children are encouraged to fit in with their communities rather than to compete and stand out.

Valued personality traits in a community reflect the way that the community makes a living. In traditional farming communities, hard work and responsibility are required as the soil is prepared for a crop that may not materialize for several months, or years. Individual initiative is not valued because tinkering around with crop rotation schedules can result in disastrous failures. On the other hand, in hunting communities, economic success is largely determined by individual skill and initiative. In such societies, men who are autonomous and self-reliant are admired. If child-rearing practices matter a great deal in how children turn out, then there should be a match between how children are raised in different cultures and what is expected of them as adults. In other words, child-rearing practices should have adaptive value. Children would thus be raised in ways that promote their economic success in their own society and ecology but not in others.[15] In support of this view, researchers have found that obedience and responsibility are much more strongly stressed in child-rearing practices of agricultural communities. Hunting societies teach children to be independent and self-reliant. Formal tests have also shown that people from agricultural communities are actually more conformist than hunter-gatherers.[16]

The adaptive theory of child training was investigated by anthropologist Bobbi Low at the University of Michigan using the Human Relations Area Files Database, a compendium that faithfully represents what is known about all of the world's preindustrial societies. She found that parents emphasize exactly those traits that their children need to fit in and succeed. For example, girls were taught to be obedient in societies in which men controlled property and women had little political power. Modesty and restraint were emphasized in the training of girls in societies in which chastity was highly valued in brides. These values were not emphasized in the raising of girls in societies where women had more economic and political power and were less economically dependent on husbands.[17]

The training of boys was also heavily influenced by factors related to reproductive success. For example, obedience to authority was emphasized in stratified societies in which young men could rise in social status by deferring to their elders. She also found that men in polygamous societies, where wealth increases the number of wives a man may keep, are trained to work hard. Moreover, this was true only of those societies in which a man's wealth could be substantially increased by individual effort. It did not apply in polygamous societies having a rigid class system in which most of the wealth was inherited instead of being built up throughout the life of the individual.[18]

Child-rearing practices are thus modified by the reproductive system and the property inheritance system in ways that help individuals to succeed in the differing social environments in which they find themselves. Different societies require different traits of people to promote their economic success. These desirable traits are stressed in the training of children. The consequence is that adults tend to have the valued traits. While the range of variation in personality types is probably similar in different cultures, we find that the whole group tends to be pushed in a particular direction for some traits.

The notion of child-rearing practices adapting to promote economic success in the local ecology also applies to advanced societies. For example, differences in need for achievement and ambition among different groups in the modern United States are partly explainable in terms of the local ecologies in which their ancestors developed. This view has been developed by political scientist James Flynn to account for the different levels of academic success and prosperity of different ethnic groups in America.[19]

EXPLAINING GROUP DIFFERENCES IN IQ AND ACHIEVEMENT

The evidence that an early rearing environment affects intelligence, and even brain development, is now fairly copious and quite compelling. While Head Start programs designed to boost the IQ of children raised in poverty have been a disappointment to many, most were begun too late in life to have substantial and lasting effects on IQ scores. The work of the Rameys in Birmingham, Alabama, has demonstrated that if enrichment programs are to have practically significant results, they should begin in the first year of life.[20] Of course, this does not mean that later intellectual stimulation by parents is unimportant, but merely that it does not produce permanent change in the information processing capabilities of the brain. Of course, all of the specific cognitive skills to which a child directs its intelligence can be enhanced by parental stimulation. Thus, a child who receives much verbal stimulation from parents after the age of two years will have an increased vocabulary size, more precise pronunciation, and better communication skills although its score on verbal IQ may not change.

Other evidence for the influence of early parental stimulation on the information processing capability of the young brain includes the specific sensory defects, slowness of behavioral development, and low IQ produced by harsh and insensitive parenting, by institutional rearing, and by social isolation in early life (see Chapter 3). These phenomena reflect the fact that in the evolutionary past, infants spent virtually all of their time in close contact with their mothers. The development of the brain has thus become closely adapted to an environment in which social stimulation is available and is compromised in the case of extreme environmental impoverishment, such as that associated with institutional rearing.

After the critical period for brain development in respect to intelligence has passed, parents cannot boost the IQ that their children will have as adults. Interestingly, they can boost IQ scores obtained during childhood. That is why some Head Start programs have often been such a heartbreaking disappointment. After raising IQ scores of children during childhood, researchers saw these gains from enrichment being gradually eaten up over time, until, by the late teens, they had disappeared.

Recent work by behavior geneticists has found that the influence of the family environment on IQ wanes steadily during childhood, while the effect of genes increases. The heritability of IQ measured in adulthood is around 55 percent, whereas the heritability of IQ for midchildhood is only 30 percent. Between childhood and adulthood, the influence of the shared environment on IQ wanes from around 30 percent to 5 percent. This means that IQ scores can be boosted by enrichment during childhood, but the increases diminish as genetic influences assert themselves.[21] No one has satisfactorily explained these patterns, but a plausible hypothesis is that as children age, there is a cumulative effect due to the expression of a larger number of genes. Another complementary interpretation is that as young adults get liberated from the parental home, their natural proclivities get expressed. Hence, the George Costanzas of the world, who are inherently intellectually lazy, will stop reading school textbooks and assigned novels and will confine themselves mainly to reading the *TV Guide*. Over time, there will be a corresponding atrophy in the information processing capability of their brains.

Even though the influence of parents on measurable intelligence following the first two years is limited, parents can still have an enormous effect on how their children turn out in terms of occupational success. This may seem counterintuitive. After all, the main reason that IQ is measured, beginning with the pioneer Alfred Binet, is to predict how well children will do in school. In Binet's case, he was solving the problem of which children could benefit from a French public school education. The French government evidently did not want to make public education compulsory for children who would not benefit from it.[22] Today, we are primarily interested in IQ as a predictor of college performance. A related consideration is that some occupations are stratified on the basis of intelligence. For instance if you tested all of the doctors in your local hospital, it is highly unlikely that any of them would score below 115. Tests such as the SAT, which is used to screen college applicants, are technically "aptitude" tests but behave very much like IQ tests in terms of their ability to predict college grade point average (GPA). This is partly why medical schools, for example, only admit people who are highly intelligent.

Even though intelligence tests and aptitude tests do predict college performance, they do so imperfectly. On average, they explain less than 25 percent of differences in college GPA.[23] Parents cannot affect that 25 percent of the variance, but they can, and do, express their effects in the other 75 percent of the variance. This phenomenon is strikingly illustrated by the story of ethnic differences in academic success and occupational achievement in the United States.

The fact that Chinese Americans and Japanese Americans are overrepresented in the professions has often been attributed to biological determinism. They are supposedly more successful than most other ethnic groups because they have higher IQs by virtue of a biological advantage. This view runs into two major problems. The first is that there may be no IQ difference between Asian Americans and European Americans. The second is that although IQ score is generally a good predictor of occupational success for different ethnic groups, there are some groups that do much better than their IQ scores would predict.[24]

The controversy over IQ differences between Asians and Europeans is complicated by the fact that while Asians score higher on tests of visuospatial IQ, they score lower on verbal ability. In the case of new immigrants from Asia, there is a large difference between nonverbal and verbal IQ of around 12 to 14 points (where 100 is the average and 15 the standard deviation). It has been suggested by Irish psychologist Richard Lynn that the superiority in visuospatial skill may represent an adaptation to living in cold conditions. Lynn sees the advantage in spatial processing as coming at the cost of reduced verbal ability. This evolutionary theory is not supported by the evidence that in the United States the gap between verbal and spatial ability for Asians declines steadily over time. In 1965, for example, an authoritative government report on ethnic differences in ability, the Coleman Report, found that this gap had narrowed to less than 4 points. This strongly suggests an environmental, rather than a biological, interpretation for the original difference. In other words, there is something about being raised in Asian countries that promotes visuospatial ability at the expense of verbal ability. Conversely, there is something about being raised in the United States that promotes verbal IQ at the expense of visuospatial ability. One possible explanation is that American children are generally encouraged to be more extroverted. According to James Flynn, the 1 to 5 point advantage in overall IQ for Chinese people living in China disappears when they are raised in the same environment as Europeans in postwar America.[25]

While we normally think of IQ scores as predicting achievement, it is also possible to do the opposite kind of prediction. By examining the occupational attainment of a particular ethnic group, one can predict what their average IQ should be. When James Flynn performed this kind of reverse prediction, he found that Japanese Americans were achieving at a level that suggested an average IQ of about 110. If this were not startling enough, he found that Chinese Americans were achieving at a level that suggested an average IQ of 120. Stated another way, Chinese Americans with an average IQ of 100 are producing occupational achievements equivalent to European Americans with an IQ of 120.

These enormous differences between potential for achievement, as indexed by IQ score, and actual achievement of different ethnic groups provides convincing evidence for the important role played by families and communities in fostering occupational success. Everything we know about the historical differences among different immigrant groups in America suggests that community influences are played out indirectly via effects on child-rearing practices. This history provides one more example of the adaptive fit between how children are raised in families and how they make their living in communities.

Chinese migrants originated mainly in the Pearl River Delta where they made their living from intensive agricultural practices such as rice production, which has endured for over 4,000 years at this location. The fertile land allows two rice crops and one dry crop to be produced each year. Intensive horticulture produces large quantities of fruit, tea, and mulberry trees on which silkworms are raised. Livestock includes pigs, chickens, buffalo, and farm fish. In this ecology, hard work is very important and people who are diligent succeed in accumulating capital and rising in social status. Conformity and obedience to authority help young men to learn traditional agricultural practices and to inherit land and money.[26]

When peasant migrants from the Pearl River Delta arrived in America, their immigration beginning in earnest around the middle of the nineteenth century, they brought with them, and transmitted to their children, an intense focus on hard work and achievement. Observers have been impressed by the speed at which the immigrants worked and the length of the hours they were prepared to put in. They also saved money that was earmarked for their children's education.

Chinese-American households have been described as educationally efficient. This means that children are expected to study at home and are provided with an environment that is conducive to study. Parents may not be involved in the details of their children's work, but they transmit an expectation that the work will be done and that it will be done well. It has been noted that the tone of Chinese households is considerably more authoritarian than is true of most American households. For example, there is more emphasis on respect for elders and living up to their expectations. There is also more emphasis on living up to criteria of academic performance and less emphasis on self-expression, feelings, individuality, and self-gratification. Some of the implications for classroom discipline are spelled out in Chapter 11.

Chinese-American children are strongly motivated to achieve excellence in school, and their academic achievements set the stage for advancement into professions. James Flynn points out that they are quite selective in the professions they enter. For example, they are overrepresented in technical and academic fields, and underrepresented in the ranks of lawyers. It is not altogether clear why this kind of selectiveness exists, but one consequence may be that there is a certain streamlining of the process by which occupational success is achieved. If you have a number of relatives and friends who are accountants, for example, it is much easier for you to understand how to go about becoming an accountant.

A fascinating footnote to the ecological interpretation of achievement motivation in the case of Chinese immigrants is provided by evidence that the Sze Yap people who inhabited the edge of the Pearl River Delta region, where the soil was less fertile and agriculture less intense, apparently have had lower levels of achievement motivation and have been less economically successful than other Chinese Americans. This is just one more example of the principle derived from Low's cross-cultural study that parental training serves to bring out in children qualities that favor their economic success in a particular ecological situation. As far as the Sze Yap were concerned, the rather poor land made it difficult to accumulate surplus wealth. Since extremely hard work was unlikely to be rewarded by social success, it was not inculcated.

Like the Chinese immigrants, the Irish have come to the United States from rural communities. In contrast to the Chinese, however, they have come from a background in which individual effort was neither rewarded nor encouraged. As tenant farmers, they had no incentive to improve their holdings since this would have resulted in rent increases. Moreover, repressive legislation enacted in the English Parliament, known as the Penal Laws, prohibited Irish people from owning property, conducting commerce, or even obtaining an education.

Eking out a living on small holdings, their lives were organized around simple subsistence activities, such as planting potatoes. This gave them considerable amounts of leisure time, which they relieved with music, dance, and storytelling. Their idleness was also relieved by alcohol, in the form of illegal homemade whiskey (or poteen). Alcoholism continued to be a major problem among Irish Americans, whereas Chinese Americans have always had a very low rate of alcoholism, true to their traditional emphasis on hard work, moderation, and self-control. This contrasts with the romantic individualism and Dionysian excess and exuberance that the Irish brought with them.

While the collective social status of the Irish in the United States at the beginning of this century was lower than that of African Americans, it has slowly risen to the point that they have reached the middle of the American distributions for income and occupational status. They have not experienced the meteoric rise in social status of the Chinese, who began from the same lowly status as unskilled laborers. This raises two interesting questions. First, why did the Irish manage to do so much better than African Americans? Second, why did they not achieve the same occupational success as the Chinese?

To answer the second question first, it seems clear that the Irish Americans were not exclusively focused on making money. They enjoyed a rich social life spent hanging out in bars, attending sporting events such as street boxing matches, and engaging in political discussions. As James Flynn points out, they may not have been all that successful economically, but many had a very good time.

It seems clear that this level of hedonism is bound to interfere with upward mobility. Moreover, Irish Americans have never been particularly focused on amassing large fortunes, preferring secure civil service jobs with limited horizons to the more difficult and more rewarding professions and businesses. This relative lack of ambition can easily be explained in terms of a background in Ireland in which social mobility was practically impossible and therefore neither valued nor inculcated in families.

It is interesting that the Irish have managed to rise from the ghetto despite considerable stigma. Around the beginning of the twentieth century, their standing was close to the bottom of the ethnic totem pole. Immigrants seeking employment in cities were greeted by signs that read, "No Irish need apply" and even "Colored man preferred, no Irish need apply." During this period, Irish Americans were associated with life in slums, and their situation seemed as bad, or worse, than the plight of African Americans living in today's inner-city slums.

Some of the points of analogy are striking. The Irish were noted for street fighting. They were deeply involved in organized crime. Irish draft riots killed ten times as many people as the civil rights protests of the 1960s. Alcoholism was a more serious problem for them than the combination of alcohol and other drug addictions is for African Americans today. Under these conditions, marriages were highly unstable, with as many as half of Irish-American families experiencing marital disruption. During this period, the movement of one Irish family into a respectable neighborhood was sufficient to motivate the other residents to move out.

Given all of these problems, it is remarkable that they ever managed to pull themselves up out of the gutter. One important trump card that they brought with them was a history of political activism associated with the stirrings of nationalism in Ireland under the leadership of Daniel O'Connell. O'Connell had presided over the first populist political protest movement in the modern world, which sought to obtain religious liberty and fostered a nationalist identity.

These political interests, skills, and experiences were used to develop the political machines within the Democratic party, which ran cities like New York and Boston. After gaining control over local government, the Irish proceeded to take full advantage of their situation through extensive patronage and corruption. For example, they gave themselves most of the best civil service jobs, asserted direct control over neighborhoods by taking most of the police jobs, and gained safe jobs as municipal workers. In addition, they obtained construction contracts and proceeded to hire large numbers of unskilled Irish workers, many of them fresh off immigrant boats. The net effect of machine politics was that the Irish were raised out of poverty. The infusion of money into Irish homes created a more stable environment for families. The slum Irish became the suburban "lace-curtain" Irish. Irish families became interested in education as a vehicle of upward mobility. This process was greatly facilitated by the Catholic Church, which provided schools that were better than public ones.

The story of occupational achievement by blacks in America is more complex than that of any other ethnic group. This history indicates that contrary to the genetic determinist position, there is no inherent reason why African Americans should not be as economically successful as other groups. From the earliest period of slavery, they have encountered political and demographic pressures that have tended to undermine parental investment.[27]

Our perception of African Americans today is very much influenced by what we know about the history of slavery in the South. Many plantation slaves remained to work the land as share-croppers following their legal emancipation from slavery in 1865. Then, around 1900, they began to flood into large American cities. By 1970, approximately 80 percent of African Americans lived in cities. In 1965, Daniel Moynihan detected an alarming trend in the increase of homes headed by single black mothers. He recognized that father absence was a strong predictor of all kinds of social problems, including crime, teen pregnancy, low educational performance and occupational attainment, and the cycle of poverty.[28] Although Senator Moynihan was criticized for blaming the African-American family for being the root of all American social problems and for using terms like "pathological" and "dysfunctional" in reference to black families,[29] his report can be seen today as an astonishingly accurate piece of sociological prophecy. Since his report, there has been a steady increase in nonmarital births and marital instability, to the point that about 75 percent of black children are being raised in single-mother homes. Over 60 percent of these families are living below the poverty line.[30] At the same time, there has been a staggering increase in the number of black men incarcerated in prisons. In 1985, 3.5 percent of African-American men were locked up in state and federal prisons and local jails. By 1995, this figure had leaped to 6.9 percent.[31] In 1994, there were more black men in jails than white men even though blacks constitute only around one-eighth of the population and there are far more black women than men. African-American men are overrepresented in the prison population, compared to white men, by a factor of around 10.

The image of unskilled black cotton plantation workers migrating to American cities and living in urban slums and having frightening social problems does not do justice to the complexity of African-American history. It is true that the descendants of liberated southern slaves did not always fare well in American cities. However, there were two other groups of African immigrants who were much more successful and about whom we hear much less.

The first were those who had succeeded in liberating themselves from slavery, the "free persons of color." Descendants of freed slaves had a much more favorable upbringing so far as inculcating achievement was concerned. As free persons, their ancestors had opportunities to acquire skills and to found businesses. Many taught themselves to read and write. They also arrived early in towns and cities, which provided them with educational opportunities not available to plantation workers in the South. It is hardly surprising that the families of freed slaves flourished under these conditions or that they transmitted ambition and need for achievement to their children.[32]

The descendants of freed slaves were effectively swamped by the arrival of hordes of southern plantation workers, who dragged down their neighborhoods and schools and discouraged white customers from visiting their places of business. Despite this merging of the two groups, in 1950 it was still possible to make a distinction on the basis of achievement. At this time, only about 12 percent of American blacks traced their ancestry to freed slaves. Nevertheless, 60 percent of black professionals living in Washington, D.C., had a paternal ancestor who was a free person of color. About 80 percent of American blacks who received a Ph.D. were descended from free persons.[33]

Just as interesting is the second group, West Indian blacks who are descended from nineteenth-century slaves. The West Indians settled mainly in the New York metropolitan area and were initially distinguishable from the larger black population. Even though their ancestors were slaves, the conditions of slavery in the West Indies were different in some important ways from the lot of cotton-plantation slaves in the American South. Since the white population was very small, amounting to no more than 10 percent of the population, it fell into the niche of a pampered elite. This meant that a great many different kinds of occupations were open to West Indians. They mastered trade skills and grew their own food. They were permitted to sell whatever surplus food they grew, which was a powerful incentive to good husbandry. In many ways, their situation was closer to that of the freed slaves in the American North than it was to the cotton-plantation slaves who were unskilled and had no reason to believe that their lot could be improved by hard work or ambition.

The conclusion to the West Indian thread of African American history is that the children of these immigrants prospered. According to the 1970 census, they had a family income above the national median, equal to the New York City median and 95 percent of the income of whites living in that city. This shows that contrary to the genetic determinist camp, there is no inherent reason why African Americans cannot achieve at the same level as other ethnic groups. This is an important piece of evidence, since it is often pointed out that freed slaves had a higher proportion of European ancestry than plantation blacks and their educational and occupational achievements are attributed to "European genes." It turns out that the West Indians have a higher proportion of African ancestry than southern blacks descended from plantation slaves.[34, 35]

Contrary to the genetic determinist view, it is clear that the social problems of African Americans today may be entirely of environmental origin. However, the most important environmental influences are within the family, contrary to the prejudice perspective. The social status of African Americans as a group is similar to that of the Irish at the turn of the century. This certainly raises the possibility that their circumstances can improve, although most of the trends in the past few decades have been far from encouraging, particularly the astronomical rise in criminal activity as indexed by incarceration rates. This is attributable, in part, to reduced parental investment associated with the decline in the two-parent African-American family.

If nonmarital reproduction has become the statistical norm for African-American women, it does not mean they do not want to marry[36] but reflects the unavailability of suitable marriage partners. When black women marry, it is almost always to black men. This may be due to a general principle in mate selection according to which husbands and wives tend to resemble each other in interests and background as well as appearance.[37] It may also be connected to the racial segregation of neighborhoods, which restricts meeting opportunities for black-white couples. Whatever the reasons, in practice, this means that a woman's marriage opportunities are restricted in the first instance by the number of black men in the population.

In 1980, at the peak reproductive ages for women of twenty to forty-four years, there were only about eighty-six black men for every hundred women of that same age bracket, the others having perished from illness, murder, suicide, and the Vietnam war. Of the survivors, about 2 percent were locked up in prisons, leaving 84 percent available. Of these, 30 percent were not participating in the labor force, leaving 54 percent. Deducting 8 percent who worked for a living but were currently unemployed left only forty-six African-American men in steady work for every hundred women.[38, 39] While many of these numbers are unreliable (because the census does not reach a large chunk of the underclass) and change considerably from year to year, they paint a compelling picture of extremely restricted marital opportunity for black women. Women cannot marry if there are no suitable marriage partners available. Moreover, the percentage of suitable marriage partners subtracted from 100 is a good rough estimate of the percentage of black women reproducing outside marriage.

The demographic information suggests that single parenthood is often a practical choice rather than a moral one. Even though African-American women are more likely to produce children outside of wedlock, they endorse family values as strongly as whites. Given the choice between having children outside marriage or not having them at all, many select the first option.

There has been a great deal of demonization of single mothers because the association between father absence during childhood and social problems of delinquency and teen pregnancy are so strong. According to the perspective taken in this book, it is more reasonable to see single motherhood as a symptom rather than the cause of low parental investment. There is nothing wrong with single motherhood in itself except that it is likely to occur in an environment of reduced parental investment, which is caused by (a) a scarcity of men able and willing to commit themselves to raising children, (b) the increased likelihood that the children are raised in poverty, and (c) a nexus of environmental factors including poor prenatal health care and exposure to environmental pollution, including noise and neurotoxins, bad schools, troublesome neighbors, inadequate nutrition, crime victimization, limited role models, delinquent companions, inadequate after-school supervision, and all the drawbacks of life for the working poor. My point is that it is rather unreasonable to blame single mothers for the social problems of their children given the number of environmental factors beyond their control that reduce parental investment in their children.

The prevalence of social problems in African-American families is sometimes interpreted as being due to biological "racial" differences in propensity to be violent or to reproduce early in life. A careful analysis of patterns of social problems over time clearly falsifies this view in several ways. First, the stark patterns of ethnic group difference that are evident today shrink steadily when compared with the past. For example, in 1993, the rate of illegitimate births for white Americans stood at 36 per 1,000 single women, the same as it had been for African Americans in 1940, and the rate for whites has subsequently risen.[40, 41] This clearly invalidates a biological determinist explanation for the differences. Perhaps even more impressive is the fact that most of the differences in nonmarital births between races and within races over time can be fully accounted for by the same environmental changes. From this perspective, much of what is said about "race" in this country is a myth. Just as there was no inherent reason why Africans could

149

not be successful in America, so there are no inherent differences between ethnic groups in their proneness to social problems.

NONMARITAL BIRTHS AND THE CAUSES OF BLACK-WHITE DIFFERENCES

The general view that differences in social problems between African Americans and the rest of the population rest on inherited biological differences is, of course, a very old chestnut that has been thoroughly roasted by the academic community. Scientific racism not only was at the center of political ideology in this country for many decades but also found its way into the projects of early scientific psychologists, culminating in the army intelligence test fiasco, which purported to find not only that more than half of the draft, and hence half of the U.S. population, was feeble-minded but also that the more a subject looked and sounded like the testers, the more intelligent he was.[42]

These embarrassing mistakes have sensitized American academics to the perils of biological determinist accounts of ethnic group differences in social problems. Nevertheless, the mainstream environmental determinist position (the "prejudice" school of thought) has not been particularly successful in explaining how differences in the social environment get translated into group differences in social problems.

This weakness of the environmental camp has allowed a certain amount of support to return for the genetic determinist position. For example, many respectable academic journals are publishing papers that purport to test the genetic explanation for ethnic group differences in IQ scores and social problems. It is risky to speculate about why journal editors are now much more sympathetic to genetic accounts of group differences than they were twenty years ago. One reason may be that, due to the work of modern behavior geneticists, strong biological influences have been established for all kinds of personality dimensions measured in paper-and-pencil tests.[43] Since ethnic group differences are quite large and extremely persistent over time, many academics are evidently scratching their heads and saying, "If it is not genetics, what *can* it be?"

The historical inability of social scientists to decompose ethnic group differences into environmental causes has apparently lent support to the view that ethnic groups are essentially different. Ethnic group has such powerful predictive value that just about every social problem studied is affected by it. Environmentalists assume that "race" goes along with a slew of contextual factors including family structure, income, nutrition, health care, education, discrimination, residence, and so forth. It is therefore customary to treat ethnic group as a nuisance variable. By entering "race" into their regression analyses, sociologists remove its effects in a statistical sense. This allows them to study what they are really interested in with the confusing (or "confounding") effects of race simplified out of existence.

This is an expedient solution to a technical problem for researchers, but it has a downside. First, if it is repeatedly established that there are large effects of "race" on social problems, and the environmental causes of these differences are not identified, then the impression is, however unwittingly fostered, that African Americans are different from other Americans. (The reason why "race" almost always refers to African Americans in this country is due to the questionable practice of government statisticians and researchers of collecting data in "black" and "white" categories.) In other words, if statistical differences as a function of race are repeatedly reported, they start to seem intrinsically real. They are reified. Second, the statistical maneuver of "removing," or controlling, group differences virtually guarantees that they will never be explained. If people want to believe that these differences are due to biology, the term "race," a biological term, is not going to stop them.

It is wrong to treat ethnic group as a hold-all category because if you do, you can never learn why these group differences exist in the first place. A more defensible approach is to split up the sample by ethnic group and to see whether the same conclusions can be drawn for different groups. For example, when studying crime rates, one could ask (a) whether predictors such as parental divorce and unemployment are associated with increases in criminality for whites as well as blacks and (b) whether these influences are equally important for both groups.

Another approach is to deliberately set out to break apart ethnic group differences into their environmental causes. Such research can be extremely revealing. For example, one recent study found that most of the black/white differences in IQ scores can be explained in terms of family variables. Family income accounted for 52 percent of the group difference. The quality of the home learning environment further reduced the ethnic difference by 28 percent. This means that an initially large group difference of 17.8 IQ points was reduced to a trivial IQ difference of 3.4 points when family variables were controlled.[44] Another study of elementary school children found that ethnic group differences in social skills and intelligence test scores are influenced by parental divorce and by sex. For intact families, there were almost no race differences. Among divorced families, blacks fared worse than whites on measures of IQ, social skills, and emotional adjustment. These differences were almost entirely attributable to greater vulnerability of black males than black females to the reduced parental investment associated with divorce.[45]

I recently performed an investigation of group differences in nonmarital pregnancy (or illegitimacy) between 1955 and 1994.[46] The aim was to find out whether ethnic group differences could be explained in terms of factors that affect parental investment. As for other social problems tracked by U.S.

government statisticians, people counted as "black" have a much higher rate of illegitimate births than people counted as "white." This difference, although it has diminished steadily over time, is still quite large and has persisted for every year of the study. In that sense, race is an extremely important variable, and if you include the effects of race with the impact of a very strong trend over time, it is possible to explain virtually all of the variance in illegitimate births. In everyday terms, this means that rates of illegitimacy fall into a near-perfect pattern. The illegitimacy rate for blacks and whites can be predicted for any year. Of course, the term "prediction" is used here in a technical sense referring to a pattern seen in the numbers for the past four decades. Unfortunately, it does not allow us to predict what will happen forty years down the road.

Superficially, this analysis explains everything about the numbers. In reality, it explains nothing. We do not know why the illegitimate birthrate has been surging steadily upward over time. Neither do we know why there is a difference in illegitimacy rates between whites and blacks.

What is really responsible for these trends? We know that for black women an intuitive connection has been made between their likelihood of nonmarital pregnancy and the availability of eligible black men. Moreover, it has been shown that black illegitimacy rates are highest in metropolitan areas having the greatest scarcity of marriageable men.[47] Could changes in the availability of suitable men be responsible for the strong trend of increase in illegitimacy during the second half of the twentieth century? Does the same principle apply to white women?

To conduct this test, the ratio of men to women between the ages of twenty-five and forty-four was used to measure marital opportunity separately for whites and blacks. Also included in the analysis were the percentage of women participating in the labor force, which is a direct measure of time investment in child care by mothers, and the proportion of families living in poverty, which indirectly assesses the availability of men who are economically viable marriage partners. As predicted, illegitimate births increased as the availability of men declined, as poverty increased, and as the proportion of women in the labor force increased. Together, these three variables explained 97 percent of the differences in teen pregnancy rates over time and across racial group.[48]

These results suggested that nonmarital birth, like teen pregnancy, is a response to poor marital opportunities for women. Increases in illegitimate birthrates are predicted by a declining control over the marriage market by women. Furthermore, between them, these variables largely explained ethnic group differences in illegitimacy rates. We know this because these environmental variables in the lives of women predicted 97 percent of the differences in illegitimacy rates, leaving only about 3 percent unexplained. Since this 3 percent must accommodate undetected environmental influences and error of measurement, it is clear that there is very little room for the possibility of genetic influence on group differences in illegitimacy rates.

Whether the same kind of analysis can account for group differences in criminality and other social problems remains to be seen. However, it is clear that what might look like a genetic difference can be explained in environmental terms if we look at those factors that affect parental investment. Conversely, if we do not investigate how the political circumstances of an ethnic group affect parental investment in families, we cannot hope to arrive at an environmental account of "race" differences. If the results for illegitimate births are reflected in other social problems, then we can forget about race as an entity and begin to investigate the environmental differences of which it is composed.

The conclusion that race differences are influenced by environmental factors related to parental investment is not only of great importance for explaining group differences in vulnerability to social problems but also suggests that the very substantial differences in social problems between blacks and whites are attributable to different interactions with parents. There could hardly be any more compelling evidence that what parents do matters for how their children turn out.

Chapter 10

Can You Increase Parental Investment?

The human brain is rather like a flower. Given the right kind of stimulation, it is programmed to open up in a way that delights and amazes us. Just as some flowers are particularly challenging to the gardener, so some children require a special effort from their parents. In some cases, children with sensory problems or developmental disabilities require a heroic commitment from specialists without which they have little prospect of anything approaching a normal life experience. We have all heard the moving account by Helen Keller of the tireless efforts through which her teacher aroused her slumbering brain to the delights of language. More recently, a training method developed by Ivor Lovaas has been used to release autistic children from their nonverbal prisons. These are dramatic examples of the benefits of increased "parental" investment for children who could not be reached by their own parents. Can parental investment be enhanced in the case of normal children who have been exposed to reduced parental investment in early childhood?

Parental investment matters a great deal for how children turn out. Different levels of parental investment not only explains why children in a family vary in academic potential and proneness to depression and delinquency but also accounts for differences in social problems associated with income and ethnic group. Moreover, it can explain why social problems change over time. If parental behavior is of such importance for child outcomes, it is important to know whether what parents do can be improved in order to head trouble off at the pass, by preventing juvenile delinquency and crime and by improving occupational success.

Whether parental investment can be increased is really a twofold question. The first part is scientific. If interventions that are designed to enhance, or to supplement, parental investment are implemented for at-risk children, are their outcomes better? The answer to this question rests on the outcomes of actual experiments that compare one group of parents who receive the intervention and a control group who does not. The second question is more difficult: Can the fundamental social conditions that undermine parental investment be improved? One is reminded of the biblical promise that "the poor you shall always have with you." Since extreme poverty currently undermines parental investment in different ways than before, this would imply the inevitability of serious social problems for at least a minority of the population. This question is taken up in more detail in the next and final chapter.

PARENTAL INVESTMENT IN AN INDIVIDUALISTIC SOCIETY

Before asking whether parental investment can be enhanced, it is useful to characterize some important influences on parental practices in our individualistic society. Our era is an extremely—and some might say excessively—child-oriented one. For children today it is both the best of times and the worst of times. It is the best of times because of unprecedented prosperity and the fact that nutrition and health services for children have never been better. On the plus side is the fact that families today are so small compared to what they were at the beginning of the twentieth century. Fewer slices of the pie of parental investment inevitably means larger portions. Parents, particularly fathers, expect to have closer relationships with their children and are highly motivated to devote their leisure hours to child-centered activities, such as getting up early on Saturday morning to bring their child to soccer practice.

This leads to the reasons why it is the worst of times. We live in a society obsessed with money and the pursuit of wealth. There is no fundamental reason that people cannot pursue wealth and invest in their children at the same time. In fact there is plenty of evidence that people who are successful in their professions are also committed and effective parents who enjoy close relationships with their children, which are irrigated by plenty of positive daily interactions. Yet there is an emotional conflict between extreme competitive materialism and parental investment, a problem dramatized by Arthur Miller in his play *Death of a Salesman*. One who values money a lot is likely to value interpersonal relationships less, or to interpret them in terms of their monetary implications. The Beatles were wiser than they knew when they sang, "money can't buy you love." In more specific terms, parents who emphasize a child's ability to compete on the sports field or in the classroom often communicate the message that love is conditional. Saying, "I really want you to come first in your class" tells a child that a lesser performance will provoke parental displeasure. The implication is that the love of the parent is conditional on the performance of the child.

Parents are understandably concerned that they should do everything to promote the success of their child. We know that parental attitudes towards achievement are transmitted to children and influence their adult social behavior and occupational striving in complex ways.

This phenomenon has been studied by psychologist David McClelland[1] in relation to differences between Protestants and Catholics, differences that have declined considerably in the past few decades in this country as Catholics have moved closer to a Protestant orientation. Protestantism emphasizes individual responsibility for salvation. In Catholicism, by contrast, Church institutions mediate between the individual and God. Given the ethic of individual responsibility, we might expect that people in Protestant nations would work harder, would be more entrepreneurial, and would enjoy higher industrial growth. McClelland used per capita consumption of electricity as an index of industrial development. In the year 1950, he found that the Catholic nations of the industrialized world used only 23 percent as much electricity per person as the Protestant ones.[2]

McClelland also conducted a fascinating study of children's literature over time to see whether changes in the kind of literature their parents selected for them was predictive of entrepreneurial behavior in adulthood. He conducted a historical study of achievement themes in British literature. He found that a peak in the amount of achievement imagery in fiction, poems, songs, and plays was followed approximately fifty years later by a peak in industrial growth. The rationale is that due to exposure to this literature, children learn to be high achievers. They are entrepreneurial and either start new businesses or expand old ones. Why there is a delay of half a century until the economy expands is not entirely clear. It may be that English entrepreneurs tended to reach a peak in productivity or wealth in their fifties. The environment of the parental home thus appears to be critical for the development of need for achievement, and contemporary children are being trained to be high on need for achievement. Of course, this makes adaptive sense because the society in which we live actually does provide good opportunities for high-achievers. It is also no accident that the rise of Protestantism in Europe coincided with the rise of capitalism, as sociologist Max Weber noted. (Previously, the wealthy aristocracy were wealthy because they had inherited tracts of land, and the notion of aggressive creation of large amounts of capital in the lifetime of an individual was new.)[3]

Religious differences in need for achievement provide a natural experiment showing that parental attitudes to material success are transmitted to children. Exactly how this happens is unclear, but it seems that Protestants inculcate high performance expectations from an early age. They expect children to develop competencies earlier than Catholic parents do, even to the extent of initiating potty training earlier.[4]

While Protestants tend to be more focused on occupational success, this focus exacts a price. Protestants tend to have weaker ties to the community and have less intense ties within their own families. At its simplest, this conflict can be reduced to a question of time budget. Parents who work long hours cannot have as much time or energy to devote to their families. This is consistent with the focus of Protestantism, as a religion, on individuality, while Catholicism focuses more on the individual's place in the community and the family. (It is probably no accident that the same difference in emphasis of community over individualism is typically found in less industrially developed countries.[5, 6])

Money may not be the root of all evil so far as parental investment is concerned, but it does not have simple consequences either. Clearly many of the experiences that go along with poverty tend to reduce parental investment, but more money does not mean more parental investment. Very rich people sometimes make appallingly bad parents and have unhappy, dysfunctional children that the press loves to write about. One such favorite subject was "poor little rich girl" Christina Onassis, whose parents rejected her as "an ugly duckling," a reaction which apparently motivated endless cosmetic surgeries.

Rich people have the option of handing off their child care responsibilities to hired servants, which may make the child feel rejected and abandoned. Conversely, the children may develop a very good relationship with the surrogate that is better than what they might have had with the mother herself. In either case, wealth is not the same as high parental investment, and the problems of impulse control among the unhappy children of neglectful wealthy parents bear a striking resemblance to the problems of impulse control among the children of neglectful poor parents.

Even though American children are often materially and intellectually enriched, it can be argued that they are at peril of emotional impoverishment. At the risk of misunderstanding, it could be argued that our society is somewhat more Protestant in its ethic than it is Catholic since the value of individual achievement is celebrated much more than the value of community. This ethic transmits a message of conditional love: the approval of parents is conditional on achievement. The expectation is fostered early in life by establishing firmer behavioral criteria. Children are expected to be more independent and more self-reliant at earlier ages, as McClelland's group found in their study of differing child-rearing practices of Catholics and Protestants—differences which have shrunk since 1955, when the study was published.[7]

Based on McClelland's work, it is clear that Protestant parents are more directive, or more demanding, in their child-rearing practices. This tends to make children more achievement oriented. At the same time, it tends to weaken their family ties. In other words, family is seen less as a haven from the external world of competitive business and more as contiguous with that world, with its inflexible demands on the skills, effort, time, and patience of the individual.

There is a very complex relationship between parental love and achievement. We know that infants who are securely attached to their mothers are more capable of exploring their environment and are better able to learn. They are likely to have strong egos in the sense of being ambitious and wanting to achieve. They are also better at learning to restrain their aggressive impulses, making them more popular with peers.[8]

Secure children learn early in life that they can gain satisfaction through their independent efforts and achievements. As a result, they tend to invest a great deal of effort in their careers and to seek emotional support from their occupational strivings rather than from their family of origin. Whether investment in a career at the expense of family can be considered a form of emotional deprivation is obviously a value judgment. People in some societies (mainly backward) would say that it is. People in other societies (mainly industrialized) would say it is not.

The real source of emotional impoverishment of contemporary childhood emanates from the relatively low level of emotional commitment between parents. When there is an excess of women to men in the population, women lose control over the marriage market and either (a) reproduce out of wedlock or (b) marry a man who is less than ideal and who does not offer a high level of commitment. These circumstances undermine parental investment, and this manifests itself in increased rates of social problems. This conclusion is based on the finding that criminality and illegitimate teen births are highly predictable based on the population sex ratio.

The argument that children today are emotionally impoverished is not just a theory. One of the more alarming manifestations is the emergence of widespread clinically diagnosed depression in teenagers and even young children for the first time. At the beginning of the twentieth century, far fewer people were depressed, and depression was unlikely to strike until a person reached his or her forties. One study of children born between 1972 and 1974 found that 7 percent had experienced a full-blown episode of depression by the time they were fourteen years old. Children are much more likely to be gloomy and pessimistic if their parents either fight a lot or are divorced. The reason for this connection is not hard to find. Children find conflict between the parents both deeply upsetting and outside their control. Basic research on animals, including dogs, rats, and monkeys, has found that repeated exposure to unpleasant, uncontrollable events causes depression, which has distinctive consequences for bodily health and behavior. The rats develop ulcers. The dogs become upset, and when they learn that the unpleasant events are outside their control, they become passive and helpless.[9]

Children whose parents are not deeply committed to each other are keenly sensitive to this lack of commitment, particularly if it is expressed in the form of open hostility, and are responding to the outward and visible signs of marital instability. In short, childhood pessimism and depression are a response to hostile family relationships, one of the central features of reduced-parental-investment homes. Sadly, this kind of emotional deprivation often occurs in homes that are materially and intellectually enriching. The successful pursuit of wealth is not equivalent to the successful pursuit of happiness.[10]

CAN INTERVENTIONS ENHANCE PARENTAL INVESTMENT?

One of the most puzzling features of modern life is the emergence of extremely antisocial adolescents in middle-class homes as reflected in the recent spate of high school shootings. While such individual actions can never be reduced to any simple explanation, most do illustrate a frightening lack of connection between the lives of adolescents and their parents. The Littleton, Colorado, and Paducah, Kentucky, episodes paint a picture of teens rehearsing their paranoid fantasies in public for several months, or years, without being noticed by their parents. In most cases, parents are acutely aware of the antisocial tendencies of their children because they make home life miserable. The question is whether that misery can be relieved through professional help.

Many researchers have designed experiments to investigate whether the behavior problems of children could be improved if the way in which parents interacted with children was altered. These experiments were not conducted with the intention of discovering whether parents matter for how children turn out; their intention was rather to find out if the behavior problems could be improved. Nevertheless, the results are directly relevant to the theme of this book.

At the outset, it must be acknowledged that not all such projects have met with success. This is hardly surprising. It may seem unlikely that the investment of a few hours of time by a researcher would be successful in overriding the effects of years of previous interactions between parents and children. Then again, not all such projects are equally well conceived. On the face of it, it seems unlikely that delinquency can be avoided through interventions that are designed to improve children's self-esteem, although at least one program is in existence that is partly based on this premise.[11]

Given these necessary qualifications, there is solid evidence that a very wide range of interventions that alter parent-child interactions have had remarkably strong and long-lasting effects. The same is true of community interventions in which some of the burden of parental responsibility has been borne by unrelated individuals and philanthropic organizations. All of the evidence suggests that children and teenagers are extremely receptive to the right kinds of parental intervention.

Studies on the training of Dutch mothers of irritable infants have shown the most spectacular results for a modest amount of time invested.[12] The implications are enormous:

- Many mothers are not prepared to handle difficult infants. A bad relationship with the mother develops, which predicts future behavioral problems.

- The majority of abused children are insecurely attached. Is the abuse undermining the formation of a secure relationship between the mother and child, or is the absence of a warm emotional relationship between child and mother causing the abuse? Both mechanisms are plausible.[13]

- The apparently inevitable increased risk of behavioral problems associated with growing up in poor homes may not be inevitable at all.

- Taking care of children is the most important responsibility of adults, but they receive virtually no formal training of any kind for this purpose. In the past, child care techniques were transmitted via extended families. Absent this kind of social support, mothers rely on personal empathy and intuition. In the case of difficult infants, this may not be enough.

- Like any other skill, caring for the psychological needs of an infant can be learned, easily and quickly.

Around the age of two years, most children are aware of themselves as individuals who have a distinctive behavioral agenda.[14] This often conflicts with the agenda of their parents, which provokes violent outbursts on the part of the child—the dreaded tantrums of the "terrible twos." While it is reasonable to see this difficult phase as something all children experience, and most grow out of, tantrums can also be used as a weapon against parents. This phenomenon can often be witnessed in the supermarket checkout where candy is temptingly displayed within reach of waiting children. Parents often want to resist this form of manipulation by the store owners and refuse to buy the child a treat. Meanwhile, the child might grab a favorite sweet. When told to put it back, there are wailing and tears followed by a great deal of whining and persuasion. If this is unsuccessful, the child may launch an all-out offensive by throwing himself on his back while bawling at the top of his lungs, arms flailing wildly and eyeballs rotating back in their sockets so that the pupils are obscured. This is an astonishing spectacle, and most parents consider that the cost of a small piece of candy is very little to pay to make the embarrassing spectacle go away. If they give in, however, they have made a bargain with the devil, and their weakness will return to haunt them as the child brings out its secret weapon the next time it is seriously frustrated.

Clearly, how a parent responds to objectionable aggressive behavior is of great importance. Instead of rewarding a child for throwing tantrums, parents should punish the child by withdrawing a privilege, making it very clear that they have a zero tolerance policy. When older children become so aggressive that they are considered to be out of control, it is clear that this is also largely the result of the home environment, which is not to deny that people differ on degree of aggressiveness for constitutional or biological reasons.

Study of the family dynamics of such conduct-disordered children has found some clear patterns. First, members of such families are constantly struggling against each other. They are reluctant to begin conversations and, when they do, the tone of the conversation is likely to be negative—designed to tease, annoy, threaten, or otherwise irritate a family member. Psychologist Gerald Patterson refers to such homes as "coercive" because one family member is constantly trying to force another to stop irritating him or her.[15] In coercive homes, the mother rarely uses reinforcements, such as praise and hugs, to strengthen a child's good behavior. Instead, she ignores proper conduct on the part of the child, focusing instead on suppressing bad behavior. Her tactics rely heavily on expression of anger and the use of punishment. Interestingly, when parents rely heavily on punishment to suppress the fighting of children, their efforts are usually unsuccessful. The child may be openly defiant and may immediately repeat the very action, such as hitting a sibling, for which he or she has just been punished. One reason is that this is an effective way of gaining the attention of an adult who rarely shows affection or rewards good behavior.

In addition to experiencing coercive parental tactics, Patterson concluded that problem children are often rejected by peers. They tend to be placed in classes or study groups with other academically deficient children. This means that they may form a deviant clique that scoffs at school work and encourages all manner of delinquent activities from drug use to vandalism to sexual misconduct to dropping out of school. There is no question that such peer groups can be a powerful source of influence in the lives of children even though their problems have much deeper roots in family interactions.[16, 17]

It is all very well to claim that delinquent children come from hostile, negative families and graduate to antisocial peer groups, but how do we know that it is the behavior of the parents that sets the ball rolling? After all, it might merely be the case that the conflict in the home is due to a heavy dose of "aggressive genes" that are shared by parents and children, thereby accounting for the volatile nature of their mutual interactions. The most convincing answer to this problem is to look upon psychological interventions designed to cope with conduct disorder as a natural experiment. That is, if changing how parents interact with their children lessens the aggression and defiance shown by the child, then we can be confident that parental behavior made a causal contribution to the problem in the first place.

Since oppositional conduct disorder arises in the context of a hostile, or coercive, family environment, some of the most successful interventions have focused on the family as a social system. Others, which have concentrated exclusively on the skills of parents in managing their problem children, have also produced good results.

Both kinds of intervention have produced surprisingly strong effects. An example of the parent-child approach is furnished by a study of two- to seven-year-old children who were referred to parent counseling because of disobedience to parents.[18] Researchers showed parents how to reinforce the child when he was behaving well and how to punish disobedient and aggressive behavior using time outs. A marked improvements in behavior of the children was seen after only eight to ten sessions at the clinic. Even short-term improvements can be considered a real break for the parents but do not amount to much of a boon to the community unless they have staying power. For this reason, the researchers did a follow-up study fourteen years later. When the participating children were contacted again they completed a number of questionnaires measuring delinquent behavior, relationship with parents, and psychological symptoms (such as anxiety and depression). Astonishingly, the treated children were no different than a control group of normal children on any of the measures. It is unlikely that the lasting improvement could have been due simply to the passing of time because untreated conduct disorders are quite stable through childhood development. Far from being a genetically determined characteristic, out-of-control behavior is a reflection of parental practices. This does not in any way minimize the greater challenge that some children pose to parental authority.

Proponents of the view that antisocial children are produced by coercive family environments like to work with the entire family. The objective is to modify the behavior of all family members so that the hostile tone of the household is reduced to the point where ordinary friendly interactions become possible. Patterson's group has produced good results largely by showing parents how to punish aggressive and coercive behavior of children (using time outs and loss of points that can be converted into prizes) while rewarding civilized behavior by demonstrating affection. These approaches produce immediate changes in some families but the improvement is more gradual in others. If progress bogs down, the therapist may visit to assess the cause of the difficulty and offer suggestions or retrain the parents to overcome it. These interventions produce excellent long-term results. It is thus clear that well-conceived psychological interventions that are primarily targeted at helping parents gain control over their children are remarkably successful even when dealing with the most difficult cases.[19, 20]

CAN CHILDREN'S NEED FOR ACHIEVEMENT BE BOOSTED?

When surveying the current epidemic of social problems, it becomes clear that the emotional fallout from reduced parental investment is enormous. Children from harsh, insensitive homes tend to be unhappy people as adults who are more vulnerable to the extreme unhappiness known as clinical depression. Apart from chemical interventions, which are always a mixed blessing, there are evidently no preventive programs designed to make people happier.

We tend to focus more on behavioral problems because these affect the community more directly. Of the behavioral problems, the most serious is the soaring crime rate. We know that the funnel of future criminal offenders is filled with juvenile delinquents. Juvenile delinquency can result from parental practices that inadvertently encourage oppositional behavior. Parenting practices can be improved, heading off delinquent behavior.

Apart from delinquency, the biggest concern in relation to the consequences of reduced parental investment is low educational and occupational attainment. This is a serious problem, not only because of the personal unhappiness of people who are not equipped to succeed in our society, but because lack of economic success contributes to the intergenerational cycle of poverty that spawns our most troubling social problems. In plainer terms, people who do not succeed economically fall into the underclass and have children who grow up in poverty, increasing the likelihood that they will be included in social problem statistics.

Low parental investment undermines occupational attainment in several ways, not all of which are reversible. For instance, it is clear that the amount of intellectual stimulation received by children in the first few years of life can affect their intelligence, as represented in IQ scores. We may presume that this is because there are windows of opportunity in respect to brain development during which certain types of stimulation have to be received if they are to boost the brain's capacity to handle these kinds of information in the future. In early life, the child's environment is greatly circumscribed by his or her relationship with the mother, and study of institutional children has revealed that maternal deprivation results in a fairly rapid loss of intellectual capacity beginning around the sixth month of life.

It might be presumed that an intellectually impoverished early life presents an insurmountable barrier to subsequent achievement, but this does not necessarily follow. James Flynn's study of the achievements of Chinese Americans clearly shows that any barrier that is normally associated with

IQ is actually quite permeable. Chinese Americans with an IQ of 100 produce occupational achievements equivalent to those of people in the rest of the population with an IQ of 120. This shows that even though IQ score does predict achievement, you do not need to have above-average IQ to have above-average occupational success.[21]

It has recently become clear that traditional Chinese child-rearing practices are very different from those of European Americans. During early childhood, an exceptionally close physical and emotional relationship between mother and child is emphasized. As the child matures, there is a great deal of emphasis on training (*chiao shun*) in which children are taught to adhere to socially desirable and culturally approved behavior. While this may look like extreme regimentation to an outsider, within Chinese culture, it is interpreted as the result of a great deal of devotion and self-sacrifice on the part of the mother. The success of the mother's efforts are gauged by the ability of the children to succeed in school.[22]

The relationship between the teacher and pupils in the Chinese classroom is also unique. The central cultural concept in their relationship is governance (*guan*). To govern a child has the same sort of positive connotation as training by the mother. Teachers in China continuously monitor and correct children's behavior. Children are given information about whether they are meeting the teacher's expectations and standards. As a part of this evaluation, they are explicitly compared with other children. While this is frowned upon in mainstream American education as excessively threatening to the self-esteem of the child, it has the advantage of clarifying for the child exactly what is expected.[23]

Given the central role of education and training in the socialization of Chinese children, it is hardly surprising to learn that they are successful in school and translate their developed capacity to live up to social expectations into occupational success. There is plenty of evidence that how children in other groups are treated by their parents affects their need for achievement and accomplishments. Even after people have grown up, their need for achievement and resulting accomplishments can be affected by training.

The research of David McClelland concluded that parents inculcate a high need for achievement by stressing the importance of children being able to do things for themselves at an early age. Subsequent researchers went even further in suggesting that parents actively train children to do things well. One team visited the homes of nine- to eleven-year-old boys who had scored either high or low on need for achievement. In the presence of their parents, the children were asked to perform difficult tasks such as building towers with irregularly shaped blocks while blindfolded and using only one hand. They found that both mothers and fathers of children with a high need for achievement were very concerned about the quality of the son's performance. They set high standards, gave many useful hints, were quick to praise their son for his successes, and did not dwell on failures. Parents of boys with a low need for achievement often told their sons how to perform the tasks but when the child experienced difficulty, they became irritated instead of providing useful hints about how to get around the problem. While boys were criticized for failures, successes were rarely praised. It is not hard to understand why children from such homes would tend to avoid challenges. Since success is not rewarded and failure is punished, these boys tended to shy away from challenges. Why take the risk of being belittled for failure when there is no reward for success?[24]

Finding that there is a correlation between how children are treated by their parents and their enthusiasm for taking on challenges is suggestive but certainly does not prove that a positive attitude towards achievement is produced by parental actions. After all, it might be purely a question of children inheriting the genes influencing achievement motivation from their parents. The most convincing evidence against this view comes from training programs in which people who are initially low achievers are trained to be high on need for achievement. This retraining process can be thought of as modifying, supplementing, or even reversing the achievement training received from parents. Two examples are the training of African-American college students to be more motivated for academic accomplishment and the training of Indian businessmen to be more entrepreneurial.

One reason African Americans are doing poorly in schools and colleges is that they have a low need for achievement. That is, they fear failure and are not strongly motivated for academic success. The evidence for a motivational problem is fairly compelling:[25]

- Even when academic ability and preparation are controlled by comparing those with the same SAT scores, black students tend to have lower college GPAs than whites (about half a letter grade) and have a higher dropout rate (70 percent versus 43 percent for whites at four-year colleges).

- These differences are not fixed. For example, in the 1950s blacks tended to improve their grades during the college years until they graduated within a hair's breadth of the averages. In the 1980s, there was a steady erosion of grades during the college years, and black students ended up doing very much worse than the college population. Some commentators explain these differing patterns as due to the overall political climate of the times. In the 1950s there was a Jackie Robinson spirit of proving that one was as good as everyone else.

- The single most persuasive piece of evidence that lack of achievement motivation is undermining the performance of black students at each level of the educational system is that where measures are taken to convince students that they can succeed, huge improvements in performance have resulted.

This phenomenon is portrayed in the movie *Stand and Deliver*, which depicts the successful struggle of Jaime Escalante to teach math to disaffected Chicano high schoolers in East Los Angeles. Analogous success stories have emerged from college education. P. Uri Treisman's Mathematics Workshop Program was designed to help black students do better in calculus at Berkeley. This program combined challenging work with a group approach in which every individual was required to participate. Not only did the black participants do better in calculus, but they graduated at the same rate as their white counterparts. It seems likely that succeeding in a difficult subject, such as mathematics, convinced the students that they could master other challenges as well. They lost their fear of academic failure and developed a higher need for achievement. This approach can be contrasted with affirmative action quota systems, which convey the implicit message of academic inferiority. By analogy, when you visit a hospital and are compelled to ride in a wheelchair, you are not likely to feel very good about your state of health.

A number of successful elementary school programs have also been implemented that enhance academic success by convincing students of their own value and academic promise. One example is James Comer's work in New Haven, Connecticut, where some of the worst schools in the system have been transformed into some of the best. Another is Harlem's Central Park East Elementary School where a similar transformation was effected. It can be inferred that the mainly poor children attending these schools do not have the kind of parents who encourage them to accept challenges.[26]

Just as poverty in families is associated with low need for achievement, so poverty in countries is associated with a relative lack of entrepreneurial spirit. David McClelland noticed that entrepreneurs have a high need to achieve. He predicted that if businesspeople could be taught to have high achievement motivation, they would become more entrepreneurial. A group of fifty businessmen from Hyderabad, India, were trained to think, talk, and act like people with a high need for achievement. The training program, which lasted only forty days, was an outstanding success. By many indices, the businesses of the trainees grew more than those of a comparison group that was not trained. For example, they had hired more than twice as many new employees. McClelland concluded that the training program had permanently increased the living standards of at least 4,000 people. All of these training programs establish without any ambiguity that need for achievement is determined by the social environment.[27]

Since these programs mimic naturally occurring differences in training practices in parents, it is obvious that parental behavior affects need for achievement. High-investing parents treat their children in ways that foster a high need for achievement. Even if the parental home has not fostered high levels of achievement motivation, parental influences can be supplemented by a good school system which encourages children to accept challenges. As far as achievement is concerned, parental investment can clearly be enhanced by schools.

THE ROLE OF COMMUNITIES IN SUPPLEMENTING PARENTAL INVESTMENT

Families are not islands, and the efforts of parents in training their children are to some extent constrained by the properties of the societies and local communities in which they exist. Of course, the degree of influence by the community depends on the level of parental investment within families. Children living in homes with harsh, insensitive parents have the most to gain from good schools and nurturant local communities. Conversely, children living in low-investment homes are most vulnerable to the antisocial influences they encounter in their local communities. Thus, parents who complain the most about the adverse effects of peers are probably not exercising much supervisory control over their child's choice of companions and have not done much to educate their child about how to resist harmful peer influences. Moreover, a child with a bunch of eerily antisocial friends is likely to have experienced social rejection by more "acceptable" peers because of hostile or aggressive behavior.[28]

There is no doubt that the social problems arising from low parental investment can be lessened by the efforts of local communities, which step in to provide supplemental quasi-parental investment in the case of at-risk teens. One example is the city of Boston where the number of killings of juveniles was reduced from a high of sixteen in 1993 to none in the first ten months of 1996. This result was due to efforts to prevent crime by children under seventeen.[29]

The primary inspiration behind this effort was the ancient idea that the devil finds work for idle hands. In order to rescue children from gang culture, they were provided with alternative activities of a more constructive nature. Local colleges helped out by adopting elementary school students into their scholarship programs. The dangerously idle summer months were passed by enrolling youths at risk for joining gangs into Boys and Girls Clubs and basketball camps. YMCA youth club memberships were provided for free.

A critical aspect of the program for potential gang members was a thirty-eight-week job training and life skills program that allowed them to acquire summer jobs and internships. Such experiences are helpful because they convince young people that they do have a place in the workforce. This removes one important motive for involvement in criminal gangs. Law enforcement officers also played a role in supplementing the supervisory activities of parents. Thus probation officers kept tabs on their charges using an unusual system of random checks.

Determined efforts to clean up local communities by removing criminals from the streets in large cities like New York and Los Angeles have been remarkably successful in reducing crime rates. It is clear that these community policing efforts play an important role in creating a more favorable environment for teens, which makes it less likely that they will be involved in criminal activities and enterprises. In this way, they help parents to raise children who are less exposed to criminals and are less tempted by the ill-gotten gains of criminal behavior.[30]

Chapter 11

Can High Parental Investment Produce a Civil and Enlightened Society?

Television journalism makes money by striking a chord of human sympathy. At its crudest, this involves attempting to get people to cry on camera. ("How did you feel when you discovered that your wife was having sex with the man next door, a man whom you considered to be your best friend in the whole world?") In this genre, there is no more tear-jerking interview than that with the mother of a teenager who has been condemned to die. No mother will agree that her child should be put to death. Neither can she feel personally responsible. She loved her child and did everything she could to help him to grow up into a happy and responsible adult.

Faced with such an affecting story, how can you begin to apportion blame or to say that the mother had not given enough? How can you castigate her life of heroic self-sacrifice for her children by describing her as a "low-investing" parent? My response to this is that assigning blame for bad outcomes is not a useful exercise for anyone. Even though good intentions do not always lead to good results, we do know that how children turn out is a function of how they were raised both by parents and also by supplementary forms of "parental" investment received from friends, relatives, teachers, and mentors. The most devoted mother living in a seedy neighborhood may end up raising a killer because her parental investment is not complemented by the efforts of others but is negated by them. Trying to raise good children in very adverse circumstances can be like trying to fill a sieve with water. In short, bad things may happen to good parents.

Throughout this book, the case has been made that what parents do for their children matters a great deal for how they turn out. Parental investment can affect most of the qualities of adults that matter to themselves and to their societies. Even basic temperamental traits, such as shyness, that have an inherited biological component can be modified by parental treatment. Shy children whose parents gradually, but firmly, encourage them to overcome their fears become less shy over time. Some shy people, such as Johnny Carson and Barbara Walters, even excel in professions that are normally the province of extroverts.[1] It is not so much that they lose their basic shyness but rather that they learn to live with it so that their lives are not crimped by social inhibitions.

In general, outcomes that we see as desirable are the product of high parental investment. Children of loving and competent parents are more likely to be happy, productive members of society. Children of neglectful, abusive, distant, or inconsistent parents are more likely to be unhappy and antisocial adults. The unhappiness and antisocial tendencies find expression in their personal lives and behavior. They have conflictual intimate relationships, tend to be low-investing parents, and leave their mark on social problem statistics including poverty, teen pregnancy, drug abuse, traffic accidents, and crime. They also tend to have poor health behavior, which leaves them at risk for illnesses related to lifestyle.

Not only do differences in parental behavior affect all of these outcomes when you compare the children of different families at the same period in time, but there is good evidence that changes in patterns of child-rearing over time are producing marked increases in social problems from crime to teen pregnancy to divorce rates, which are of concern to every thinking person.

If parental investment is so critical in determining the ebb and flow in rates of social problems over time, then increasing parental investment should result in declining social problems. We know that the outcomes of children raised in low-investment homes can be improved by the supplemental efforts of enrichment programs, parenting skills classes, achievement training, and so forth, as discussed in the last chapter. Determined efforts to increase parental investment should therefore produce a decline in social problems. Are such interventions likely to be widely used? If they were, would they produce a more civil and harmonious society? Can parental investment be boosted by legislation? These issues are addressed in the context of recent trends of decreasing social problems, the problems of African-American families, and the influence of government welfare policies in Sweden. Finally, the role of schools as supplemental sources of "parental" investment is discussed.

TURNING A CORNER IN SOCIAL PROBLEMS?

Many social scientists believe that poverty is at the root of social problems, from teen pregnancy to academic failure and crime. The twentieth century seems to contradict this view because there has been an unprecedented increase in social problems at the same time that there has been an unprecedented increase in national wealth and real wages. One solution to this conundrum is to recognize that increasing wealth of the country does not necessarily mean increasing wealth of individuals. In recent decades, the great increase in national wealth represented by the rising stock market has left most individuals out in the cold because they do not own stocks. Increases in wages also tell a mixed story because the greatest increases in salary have gone to those at the top. A hamburger flipper in the 1990s is probably not feeling more affluent than a hamburger flipper in the 1960s. Social problems are affected by the number of people living in poverty. While there has been a great increase in the number of people who are wealthy during this century, poverty rates have remained fairly high. For example, in 1970, the poverty rate for Americans families was 10.1 percent. In 1995, it stood at 10.8 percent, having risen as high as 12.3 percent in 1983.[2]

Among the problems that increased by at least a factor of five during the twentieth century were depression incidence, divorce rates, and illegitimate births. Yet no social trend moves forever in the same direction. There is evidence that for many problem statistics, the rate of increase has diminished and, in some cases, the graph has turned a corner and begun to move downward.

The illegitimate birthrate has continued to rise, but there is evidence that the graph is losing acceleration. Thus, the rate per thousand unmarried women rose from thirty-three in 1985 to forty-four in 1990 but only increased from forty-four to forty-six between 1990 and 1994. The illegitimate birthrate for African Americans declined from ninety-four per thousand unmarried women in 1990 to eighty-two in 1994. Births to teens actually declined from eighty-nine per thousand in 1960 to fifty-seven per thousand in 1995, but this is a misleading statistic because the proportion of these births that were nonmarital increased from 15 percent in 1960 to 75 percent in 1995. Nonmarital teen births are considered more of a problem because of their perceived role in perpetuating the cycle of poverty.[3, 4]

The divorce rate is an example of a problem statistic that has reached its peak and begun to decline (see Figure 2 in Chapter 7). Having risen steadily from a rate of 2.5 per thousand population in 1966 to a peak of 5.3 in both 1979 and 1981, the rate declined in the 1980s and leveled off at a rate of about 4.7 from 1988 to 1993.[5]

The number of families living in poverty has also shown an encouraging trend of recent improvement. For the population as a whole, the poverty rate peaked at 12.3 percent of families below the poverty line in 1983 and again in 1993. By 1995, the poverty rate had fallen to 10.8 percent. For blacks, there were peaks in 1982 (33.0 percent) and 1993 (31.3 percent), and by 1995 the rate had fallen to 26.4 percent.[6]

Crime rates also declined between 1980 and 1985. However, there has been an extraordinary increase in the number of people in U.S. prisons in the last decade. In the case of prisoners in state and federal prisons (who make up approximately half of the total number of prisoners, the rest being housed in local jails), the rate of incarceration for white men increased from 0.28 percent in 1985 to 0.49 percent in 1995. The corresponding rates for black men were 1.49 percent in 1985 and 2.95 percent in 1995. This means that during that decade the prison population almost doubled. The percentage of black males who were incarcerated, including in local jails, stood at the staggering figure of 6.9 percent in 1995.[7]

It is not clear why these figures have risen so alarmingly in such a short period, but the lucrative business of selling illegal drugs certainly plays a major role. Government efforts to prevent this trade have succeeded only in driving up the prices and thereby encouraging career criminals to specialize in it. Another factor in the increased rates of violent crime is the ready availability of handguns and assault rifles.

Even if crime rates have jumped up since 1985, they have not seen the same kind of long-term increase as other social problems. For example, incarceration rates in 1985 were slightly lower than they were in 1955. This indicates that the conditions favoring the contemporary increase are not part of a long-term trend. They may merely reflect the fact that it is easy to make a lot of money in a short period of time by selling crack cocaine. It is also easy to get arrested while attempting to do so.

Excluding the vagaries of the illicit drug trade, it is possible to draw the conclusion that many of the most troubling social problems (nonmarital pregnancy, divorce rates, poverty, and even some types of crime) have begun to turn a corner and move in the desired direction. Why have these improving trends occurred? The obvious answer is that the conditions of families have improved. Parental investment theory suggests two trends that are particularly favorable. The first is that the sex ratio of the population has risen. The second is that there has been a marked decline in family size.

The rising sex ratio means that for white women between the ages of twenty-five and forty-four, marital opportunities in 1995, when the sex ratio stood at 101.2, were much better than they were in 1965, when it stood at 97.0. Since there are now more men than women, women exert more control over the marriage market. This means that they can expect a higher level of emotional commitment from men as a precondition for marriage, that women will be more valued for their role as mothers, and that marriages will be more stable. Men will be less ready to initiate divorce because they will feel less confident in finding a desirable partner. Since there is now a relative scarcity of marriageable women (at least if we ignore the complication of sexual orientation), men are more likely to find themselves left out in the musical chairs of intimate relationships. The structure of the black population has gone in a similar direction but has moved less substantially. In 1965, for black women between the ages of twenty-five and forty-four, there were only 86.9 men of the same age for every 100 women. In 1995, there were 88.7 men per 100 women.[8]

Declining family size is also important for at least two obvious reasons. The first is that the fewer children there are, the less dilution of family resources occurs. From a formal statistical perspective, this means that poverty rates tend to decline. The second reason is that a greater proportion of the children are firstborns. Despite suggestions that parents are inexperienced in dealing with their first children, it is clear that firstborns receive a lot more attention from parents and that they identify more strongly with parental authority. The strongest objective evidence for this is that being firstborn is a protective factor resulting in an approximate 30 percent reduction in risk of being criminally active. Firstborns also receive more education, which reflects a willingness of parents to invest in their future. Children in small families also have higher IQ scores, which predicts that they should do better in school. This is important because school achievement is a negative predictor of many social problems including teen pregnancy, drug use, delinquency, and crime.[9]

AFRICAN AMERICANS, SEX RATIOS, AND PARENTAL INVESTMENT

It is often pointed out that the social problems of African Americans make a disproportionate contribution to the problems of the country as a whole. For instance, they make up half of the prison population even though they constitute only about one-eighth of the overall population. Nonmarital birthrates are about three times higher for African Americans, and the majority of blacks are raised out of wedlock.[10]

The problems of the black community are certainly not different in kind from those of the rest of the population. They are simply thicker on the ground. This book has made the case that social problems result from diminished parental investment. The greater incidence of social problems among African Americans reflects the fact that forces in the social environment have undermined parental investment to a greater extent for this ethnic group.

The primary difference is a scarcity of marriageable men in the black population. The causes of this scarcity are complex. However, since there is no scarcity in the early teens (when there are more males than females), a primary determinant is greater vulnerability of males to different causes of early mortality, including war deaths, illnesses, drug use, homicide, and accidents.[11]

Low sex ratios weaken the bargaining position of women in the marriage market. This means that they cannot expect a commitment of lifelong economic support in return for marriage. This translates into reduced parental investment in children for several reasons, including (a) lack of economic support for children, (b) the likely absence of the father from the home of children, and (c) a general air of conflict between men and women, which makes children more vulnerable to social and personal problems.

As Robert Staples[12] pointed out, the low sex ratio for African Americans greatly understates the marital difficulties of women because of the large number of men who are not suitable marriage material or are unavailable for marriage. The reasons include imprisonment, institutionalization, and homosexuality, all of which remove men from the marriage market. When you exclude those men who do not work for a living, those who are not counted by the census because they have no permanent address, and those whose income from work is below the poverty level, you arrive at an estimate of the number of marriageable black men. According to Staples's estimate, there is only about one marriageable black man for every two black women. Perhaps the most insidious, and important, aspect of low sex ratios for women is not just that they have less chance of being married but that when they do marry, the stability and trust within marriage tends to decline.[13]

Children raised in conflict-ridden homes in which separation and divorce are likely are at a greater risk of marital instability themselves. This means that contemporary changes in marriage and the family have a tendency to feed on themselves. Children raised without their fathers, due to parental divorce, are more likely to have impermanent marital relationships. The consequence is an acceleration of divorce rates and many of the undesirable correlates of this, such as increased rates of juvenile delinquency.[14, 15]

The solution to the marital difficulties of African-American women is to increase the number of potential husbands, which calls for increased parental investment in African-American males to help them be economically successful. It is clear that the economic difficulties of black men are due to changes in the economy, according to which the number of highly paid low-skill jobs has undergone a progressive decline. Without a good education it is extremely difficult to get a well-paid job. New jobs have been created in high-skill, technologically sophisticated fields and also in service industries, such as fast food restaurants where wages tend to hover just above the legal minimum. Black men tend to be squeezed out of the former type of occupation by educational difficulties and are not attracted to the latter because of low wages and lack of prestige. Simply raising the minimum wage is unlikely to help since this would merely reduce the number of hires of low-skill employees. It would neither produce a fundamental change in the way that these low-margin businesses operate nor help black men to succeed in more prestigious occupations.

Even philanthropically motivated jobs programs for inner-city youth have not been successful due to high attrition rates. It is believed that young men tend to drop out of such programs partly because of the more lucrative opportunities available in illegal occupations, such as drug trafficking.[16] They may also lack the kind of discipline and work ethic that are required to continue. We cannot easily change the economic landscape to fit the needs of African-American youths. Rather, it is they who will have to adjust to meet the needs of the job market. Recent improvements in academic performance suggest that this is already happening.

So far as the more fundamental question of scarcity of marriageable men is concerned, African-American women could opt to marry outside of their ethnic group. In fact, far fewer black women than men marry outside their ethnic group, which makes the sex ratio problem even worse. The reasons for this are poorly understood, and proposed explanations center around issues of social status and the notion that women are attracted to men whose skin tone is somewhat darker than their own.[17]

THE ROLE OF GOVERNMENT IN FAMILY STABILITY

Most students of the American family have been struck by the strength of the relationship between social problems and family structure. The absence of the father as a permanent resident in the familial home is a key predictor of vulnerability to becoming depressed, becoming pregnant as an unmarried teen, and committing crimes. Many commentators have jumped to the conclusion that the absence of the father from the home causes these problems instead of considering the possibility that both phenomena are caused by a third variable, namely a poor marriage market for women. Throughout this book, I have argued that marital relationships are unstable because women lose their bargaining power in the marriage market. This happens when the supply of marriageable women exceeds the demand by marriageable men. These marriage market conditions foster marital discord, divorce, and abandonment, and thereby reduce parental investment. Can government initiatives affect marital stability and single parenthood, thereby reducing social problems?

The assumption that fatherlessness causes social problems has led to some thoughtful books being written that ask what exactly it is that fathers do that is of such earth-shattering importance to their children and to society. This is a difficult question since many of the fathers of well-behaved children may actually play very little of a direct role in caring for them or providing advice or discipline. This is certainly changing with fathers becoming increasingly involved in the nurture of their children, even to the extent of becoming the primary care giver, which happens when fathers receive custody of their children following divorce. Most fathers still do less than mothers regarding the routine domestic chores such as organizing their children's meals, clothing, homework, leisure activities, bed time, and school lunches, even if the mother is in full-time employment. Their daily interactions with children are usually briefer than interactions of mothers with children, but these may have enriching consequences. Recent research has found that fathers are more involved with infants than previously believed, and this involvement is associated with elevated child IQ at the age of three years. Premature infants with highly involved fathers who played with them often had child IQ scores six points higher than infants whose fathers were less involved. Of course, this is potentially important because premature birth is a risk factor for low intelligence. It is interesting that father involvement peaked at around twelve months, when the brain undergoes rapid changes of the kind that allow infants to begin walking and talking. The verbal ability of young children is also predicted by how much their fathers talk to them and by the richness of the vocabulary used.[18, 19]

The presence of a paternal figure can have an important effect on the household, which ultimately translates into improved child socialization outcomes. For instance, the presence of fathers may help mothers to fulfill their roles as socialization agents. Fathers may provide emotional support and solidarity, which helps mothers to discover the firmness and resolve needed to discipline children. This argument is bolstered by evidence that single mothers of boys tend to become more permissive of aggressive behavior as the boys mature, suggesting that the rules are being bent by the unruly behavior of their sons. It is also very difficult for one person to monitor the whereabouts and activities of several children while engaged in some attention-requiring activity, such as cooking. Fathers also provide a model, or example, of how husbands interact with wives, which provides both a general idea of how adults interact with each other and a specific education in the relationships to be expected between husbands and wives. Children who are raised without the example of a cooperative marital relationship often have unstable interpersonal relationships when they grow up, possibly because they neither know nor feel what such intimate relationships require.[20]

Reasonable though these arguments may seem, the function of husbands can be pared away to its irreducible minimum, to the point that they are seen primarily as economic providers, an interpretation of fatherhood that is current in anthropology and was quite widely accepted in the United States up to the 1950s. The great advantage of thinking so simplistically is that our ideas can be easily tested to see whether they measure up to reality. One way of testing the extent to which fatherhood is reducible to provisioning is for government to artificially intervene by providing economic subsidies to pregnant women and continuing until the child has grown up, to see whether this affects the institution of fatherhood.

Unlikely as this experiment might seem, it has actually happened in Sweden where the welfare state took on most or all of the economic roles previously fulfilled by fathers. This produced some profound and unexpected changes for the social system, resulting in the decline of marriage as an institution and the unleashing of a trend of sexual liberation. These changes are partly due to the fact that women no longer rely on marriage as an economic strategy for supporting their children.[21]

Anthropologists interpret marriage as entailing a basic contract in which there is an exchange of economic goods (provided by the husband) for opportunity to reproduce (provided by the wife). Women who wish to enhance their value as wives must practice sexual restraint because this provides a guarantee of paternity to a potential husband. Thus, where women rely heavily on the wealth provided by husbands in order to raise their children, premarital chastity is inculcated. If they do not rely on male provisioning, then they do not need to seem chaste and sexually restrained because they are not in competition with other women to seem like the most desirable bride.[22, 23]

Since the welfare state instituted in Sweden guarantees women full support for their children, women do not need to be married to raise children successfully. The immediate consequence has been a decline in marriage rates and rising divorce rates. Without the shared economic commitment of caring for children, the permanence of marriage tends to be eroded. The rationale for this seems quite transparent. If a couple is experiencing conflict for any reason, then neither party has to swallow their hostility for the sake of the children. The marriage may be dissolved without worries, confident in the knowledge that any children will be well cared for by the Swedish welfare state.[24]

Changes in the state of Swedish marriage have had profound and complex effects on norms of sexual behavior. Since women do not have to compete for husbands, it is not necessary to advertise their value as wives by practicing sexual restraint. With the demise of sexual modesty, there has been an expansive sexual freedom involving unusual lifestyle experiments such as young men living with older women.

While the consequences of the Swedish system for marriage and sexual behavior are exactly what might have been predicted from a parental investment perspective, one interesting anomaly is that the surge in social problems that is connected to marital instability in the United States never occurred. This may be because the better economic conditions for women at the bottom of the ladder in Sweden allow for more effective socialization of children, which means that the extreme failure represented by arrest for serious criminal activities is far less likely to occur than is true for children raised in U.S. urban slums where crime, as it were, seeps into children from their gangland homes. Another interesting difference is that there has been a decline in teen births, which is attributable in part to a declining overall birthrate but also reflects good career opportunities for women. In short, Sweden does not have a large underclass in which the challenge to parental investment posed by marital instability is compounded by the effects of living in a slum.

The fact that the state's support of young mothers has not produced an increase in teen births in Sweden is unusual. A cross-national study of teen pregnancy in other developed countries, conducted by the Guttmacher Institute, has found that liberal government policies in relation to support of mothers with children goes along with increased teen pregnancy rates. This suggests that young women are more likely to become pregnant, or to carry their babies to term, if they are not overly concerned about issues of financial security. However, the possible effects of such government policies must always be weighed in the light of other factors affecting the reproductive decisions of young women. For instance, where there is a scarcity of potential husbands, women are much more likely to reproduce as teens. The underlying logic seems to be that their prospects for favorable marriage are bleak and unlikely to improve by delaying reproduction. In such a social environment, young women will tend to reproduce whether there are financial incentives from governments or not. Canceling such support programs also raises a difficult humanitarian issue because of the immediate impact of increasing the number of children living in abject poverty. Another important variable is the career opportunities available to young women. The evidence suggests that young women who have good career opportunities are much more likely to delay reproduction until after their careers have been established.[25]

In summary, although government policies can have profound effects on family structure, these effects are moderated by so many aspects of the marriage and job markets in specific countries that it is difficult to make firm generalizations. However, it appears that direct economic support for children by governments does weaken the social role of fathers, resulting in a decline in the importance and stability of marriage. Conversely, if governments want to strengthen the role of families and fathers in raising children, they can do so most effectively by policies designed to boost the incomes of men in low-paying jobs. Reducing income taxes for parents with low salaries would have this effect. Another possibility would be to link employment with housing credits, which would help poor families to buy their own homes.

THE ROLE OF SCHOOLS

One way to think of teachers and schools is as surrogate parents and families. There are many reasons for taking this analogy seriously. To begin with, formal schooling for young children is a comparatively recent phenomenon. Young children are plucked from the bosoms of their families at a tender age to learn how to fit in with the rules, routines, friendship alliances, and social hierarchy of a larger group. Inevitably, the needs of children for care and comfort dictate that the interactions of teachers with young children bear some resemblance to parent-child interactions. This connection is formalized in the institution of the kindergarten, which is essentially a day-care arrangement for older preschool children but also includes structured group activities, such as artwork and singing, that require the sort of attention, discipline, and group coordination typical of formal classroom activities.

Not only do teachers take on some of the child care roles of parents, but there is evidence that children may respond to their preschool teachers in much the same way that they respond to parents. One study looked at security of attachment between teachers and three- to five-year-old pupils and found that children who are securely attached to their teachers (as judged by a statement-sorting task, rather than the Strange Situation Test used for infants) also fare better in terms of their social development.[26] Children who were securely attached to their teachers were better behaved. They were happier, were more popular with peers, and had better social skills as assessed by the teacher. Furthermore, there was evidence that a secure attachment with the teacher could compensate somewhat for an insecure attachment with the mother. Children who were securely attached to the teacher, but not to their mothers, were happier and better behaved than children who were not securely attached to either mother or teacher.

This result not only clarifies the quasi-parental role of teachers of young children but also helps to explain why it is possible for children to spend so much time apart from their mothers in day-cares without experiencing social problems. The bottom line is that children are quite flexible in their social relationships. They are capable of responding to nonrelatives as though they were parents. In high-quality day-cares and kindergartens, there is a reasonably plentiful supply of nurturant individuals who are around long enough for children to get to know them and form attachments to them. That children are so flexible should not be surprising. We know that young children are sponges who attempt to soak the last drop of attention, effort, and investment out of their parents. In preschools, and possibly later, they evidently latch on to teachers as sources of emotional support and respond to them very much as surrogate parents.

The phenomenon of the remarkable success of Chinese-American children in schools and occupations makes the point that the process of socializing children is continuous between homes and schools, even if we do not always think of it in this way. Chinese child-rearing practices are specifically designed to help children to fit in and succeed in school. From the teacher's perspective, they have been softened up not only to accept but actually to welcome classroom discipline.[27]

Conversely, the much more permissive environment of the majority of American homes tends to work against inculcation of academic discipline. The declining academic standards of American schools at all levels, despite ever-increasing emphasis on the importance of education for occupational success, can be related to concurrent problems within families. Boldly stated, teachers do not expect a great deal from some pupils because they are not very well socialized by their parents to begin with. Such diminished expectations have had a pervasive effect on educational philosophy.

Since some children are not well prepared to receive a disciplined type of education, there has been a transformation in educational philosophy. All classroom activities have to be fun to coax reluctant and boredom-prone youngsters to become actively involved in learning. An emphasis on the positive aspects of the school experience also tends to avoid the kind of disciplinary conflict that might arise if undisciplined children were being compelled to learn something they did not enjoy, such as spelling words correctly or the multiplication tables, the staple components of basic literacy in a bygone era.

The contemporary philosophy is well illustrated by the "whole language" approach to learning to write English. Once they have learned to write their letters, second- and third-graders are encouraged to use their language to express themselves. This is often done by means of a daily journal in which children are encouraged to describe the significant events of their lives. The only criterion for this activity is that the children satisfy some arbitrary quota, such as filling the page or writing ten sentences.

The most remarkable feature of this exercise is that the journals are usually not corrected. Errors of spelling and grammar are left where they lie. The most that can be hoped is that the teacher might skim through the content, occasionally dispensing a "smiley face" to keep the child motivated. The rationale behind this is that correcting every niggling little error is too frustrating for the child. It would make him or her not want to write.

The downside of whole language is that children (a) learn that spelling and grammar don't matter and (b) become practiced in making errors of spelling and grammar that will haunt them later. Needless to say, the notion of formal language will have been entirely lost. The child will not grasp the difference between conversational and professional English. This will be quite evident thirty years later when the fifty recipients of a business memo come to fifty different conclusions about what it is supposed to say.

The more immediate concern is that some children go through elementary school without ever learning to spell correctly. The fact that the same is true of some high schools has resulted in the imposition of exit tests assessing basic literacy, a requirement in some states before a high school diploma can be obtained. These measures are a reflection of the desire of the electorates to ensure that schools fulfill their obligations in respect to basic literacy. The need for such tests is underscored by the embarrassing proliferation of remedial courses in mathematics and English at the college level. This is the loudest and clearest possible message that high schools have not been preparing their graduates adequately for a college education. Presumably this reflects, in part, the fact that the elementary schools have not emphasized basic academic skills.

Since schools can be considered in many ways a supplement to the education and training of children by parents, it is no surprise to learn that children who are well socialized tend to do well in school. Conversely, children from poor families and from conflictual homes tend to do more poorly because they are likely to suffer from cognitive deficits and conduct disorders. At an extreme, children with severe conduct problems become part of an antisocial high school subculture that scoffs at the value of education and engages in delinquent activities.[28]

For such problem teenagers, it is quite superficial and misleading to attribute their problems to having delinquent friends. The fundamental issue is that their parents did not prepare them well for succeeding in school. Since schools can only build upon the parental investment of parents, it is understandable, but unfortunate, that schools are failing to provide an education for some of the children who need it most.

THE CIVIL SOCIETY AND PARENTAL INVESTMENT

Just because dedicated mothers may raise criminal children does not mean that parents cannot help their children to avoid getting into trouble with the law. In fact, it is quite clear that the most important predictors of delinquency and crime are indices of low parental investment such as single parenthood, divorce, family size, late birth order, a poor marriage market for women, and poverty. The fact that poverty tends to be associated with insensitive and conflictual parental practices does not mean that money has any virtue in itself. Some poor people are high-investing parents, and they raise happy and successful children. Some rich people make neglectful and abusive parents. The fact that there are exceptions does not invalidate the general rule. Poverty is associated with elevated risk of all manner of social problems, and the reason is that it tends to go along with reduced parental investment.

Given the wealth of compelling scientific evidence that how parents treat their children affects how they turn out as adults, it is inconceivable that the extreme position taken by Judith Harris in *The Nurture Assumption*[29] could be correct. Her argument that it is all genetics and peer influence and that parental training matters little is mistaken in several fundamental ways, although her book will be a useful stimulus to socialization researchers in that it compels them to come up with more reliable research designs.

While peers can certainly be an important influence, their effect is greatest in the teen years after parents have had an extensive opportunity to mold the character of their children. Most teens go through a phase of adolescent revolt, which causes them to behave in reckless and delinquent ways. They may defy parental authority and fit in with peer group norms by smoking cigarettes, drinking alcohol, and using illegal drugs. Most of us pass through this rebellious phase and turn into solid citizens suspiciously like our boring old parents. While adolescence is certainly a risky time, peer influences can have prosocial consequences in the sense that identifying with our peers helps us to fit in with the norms of adult society. Peer influences are very threatening to parents only if they have not taken the opportunity to develop character in their children from an early age. Thus, teenagers who fall in with the most antisocial peer groups are the most antisocial to begin with, reflecting an absense of warmth in their relationships with parents.

Harris's whole argument relies on the premise that how we behave is determined by genetics. Nothing could be further from the truth. Behavior genetic studies have found that about half of the differences between individuals in personality traits and cognitive ability are explained by genes. Personality traits are based on the chemistry of the brain. To say that the chemistry of the brain is affected by genetics is not saying very much unless you happen to be a biochemist who is interested in showing how this happens. (Preliminary research in this area suggests that it is a brutally laborious task.[30])

To say that genes affect personality is another way of saying that they affect our behavioral tendencies. Do they affect behavior? Behavior genetic studies that have studied actual behavior have generally found very weak results. That is precisely because a host of environmental influences, including parental training, intervene between biological predispositions and actual behavior.

Another technical issue on which Harris's conclusions rest is the finding that parents do not make children more alike in personality, if you leave out the influence of genetics. Of course this does not mean that parents don't matter, even within the narrow domain of personality differences. Why not? Parents have socialization objectives that affect different children in different ways. For example, if one child is too reckless, parents try to rein her in. If another is too cautious, parents encourage her to be more adventurous. The average effect, in a behavior genetic study, looks like a zero contribution to adventurousness by parents. Just because parents do not push all of their children in the same direction does not mean that they do not affect them. The myth that parents treat all of their children the same has recently been exploded by findings that most of the differences in antisocial tendencies between sibling pairs are explained by different treatment from parents. Children who are harshly treated are much more likely to be antisocial, and their favored siblings are protected against conduct disorder and depression.

The view that parents do not shape their children flies in the face of basic principles of learning. If you can train a dog to herd sheep simply by talking to it, how likely is it that the social reinforcers and punishments we offer to our own children would be without effect? This notion not only contradicts the most fundamental principles of scientific psychology, but also ignores the wealth of conflicting evidence examined in this book. While some of the evidence is correlational and therefore open to alternative explanations, some of it rises to the highest level of scientific support since it is based on experiments that allow us to rule out other explanations (such as peers and genes). Some of the critical experiments are:

- the experimental establishment of secure attachment in Dutch mothers of irritable infants;
- the rehabilitation of institutionalized infants adopted into homes (technically a "natural experiment");
- the experimental manipulation of cognitive ability by altering maternal responsiveness to infants;
- Head Start programs begun early enough in life to boost IQ; and
- successful training of parents (and families) in correcting conduct disorders so that the problem children were later indistinguishable from normal children.

Of course, my conclusion that how children turn out, and by implication the civility of the society in which we live, is greatly affected by parents relies on a much richer body of evidence pointing in the same direction. These experiments are simply the most convincing kind of scientific evidence for what most of us have experienced in our own lives, namely that the love of parents can guide us safely through our darkest hours and deepest tribulations.

What About . . . ? Objections and Replies

This Appendix assembles some of the arguments that have been used in the technical literature or heard in popular debate that seem to challenge the important role of parental behavior in affecting how children turn out.

What about the possibility that children shape parental behavior more than parents shape children?

According to the conventional view of child socialization, difficult children are produced by harsh and inconsistent treatment from parents. The usual evidence for this is the fact that conduct disorders in children go along with harsh and insensitive parenting styles. This correlation is open to different interpretations, however. It is possible that harsh parenting causes difficult behavior in the child. It is equally possible that difficult behavior in the child brings out harsh parental behavior. After all, children who are temperamentally difficult from an early age for genetic reasons can be extremely frustrating to parents. School children identified with conduct disorders can also turn their families upside down and embitter their parents, thereby souring parent-child relationships, to put it mildly.

It seems unreasonable to insist that the inherited qualities of infants, from their physical cuteness to their irritability level, sociability, and so forth, may not affect the quality of the relationship with parents and to some extent determine how parents treat them. The important point is that biology is very far from being destiny in this respect. For example, children with a biological potential for shyness can become much more outgoing during early childhood if their parents both encourage them and challenge them to come out of their shell.

We know from the best kind of experimental evidence that parents can overcome the adversity of children having a genetic potential for behavior problems. This is true of irritable infants whose relationship with the mother improves dramatically after the mother is trained to be more sensitive to cues reflecting her infant's emotional state. It is also true of older children with conduct disorders. Increasing parental skills has been shown to produce excellent results so far as resolving the conduct problems is concerned. In the face of this kind of solid evidence, it is easy to conclude that parental behavior definitely influences child outcomes even though the arrow of causation may also go in the other direction.

What about father absence and the fact that visitation by the father after divorce has no effect on child outcomes?

In their book *Growing Up with a Single Parent: What Hurts, What Helps*, Sara McLanahan and Gary Sandefur found that contact with the father following divorce made little difference for the outcomes of children in respect to high school dropout, teen pregnancy, and risk of being unemployed.[1] This seems to suggest that contact with the father doesn't matter a great deal for postdivorce children. By implication, it might be concluded that fathers really don't matter very much in general. A number of qualifications are in order:

- Perhaps the most obvious is that there are many differences in the quantity, and quality, of contact from fathers following divorce compared to relations when the father lived permanently in the home. Clearly, there are also important differences between conflictual predivorce homes and more stable ones. Following divorce, visits from or to fathers (by children of whom the mother has custody) tend to be strained for various reasons. In particular, the child can become a vehicle for hostility between the parents, and arranging custodial visits can become a focus of discord.

- In controlling for race and sex, the researchers threw out the baby with the bath water. It turns out that divorce has more severe consequences for African Americans than the rest of the population and that black males are more adversely affected than black females.[2] Controlling for—or, in other words, ignoring—the effects of race on social problems is generally not a good idea because a lot of the differences between families regarding social problems are bound up with ethnic group classification. Instead of writing these differences off as due to "race," researchers should be trying to explain why they occur.

- Even if custodial visits were all that they could possibly be, it is hard to see why children who have experienced the trauma of parental disagreement and seen their parents separate would be entirely reassured about their family life by seeing their father once a week. One of the points made in this book is that a confictual home falls within the category of a low-parental-investment home because of the lasting consequences it has for social development of children.

What about the moral implications of parental investment theory?

Talking about the consequences of parental investment for children raises issues of responsibility and hence raises moral concerns. Single mothers are often blamed for the increased incidence of social problems found in their children. Yet there is nothing voluntary about the problems experienced by teen mothers and other groups whose children are at risk of turning out badly.

Mothers almost always do the very best that they can for their children, and the same is generally true of fathers as well. It is easy to stand back and say that children have better opportunities if their mothers postpone reproduction until after they have established careers or gotten married, or both. Most young women see these goals as desirable, but their prospects in both directions may be limited.

Thus, the high incidence of nonmarital births for African-American women is very often cast in moralistic terms. Just because this segment of the population is unlikely to marry before giving birth, the inference is often made that they do not want to marry. In fact, researchers who have looked at attitudes towards marriage among black women find that, if anything, they are more promarriage than white women. They fail to marry not because they do not value marriage but because, as a practical matter, it is extremely difficult for them to marry black men who have the potential to provide stable economic and social support to their households.

Similarly, in the case of unmarried teen mothers, young women who become pregnant and carry their infants to term are not deliberately destroying their career prospects and choosing a life of poverty for themselves and their descendants. For most, their pregnancy is preceded by such a dismal academic record so that career prospects seem quite dim and the positive aspects of motherhood are correspondingly more attractive. Even though teen motherhood carries with it a host of risks for children, it makes no more sense to say that mothers choose these risks for their children than it does to say that someone chooses to have an illness by living in a neighborhood in which the groundwater is chemically contaminated. Teen motherhood is not a moral choice so much as a practical response to adverse job markets and limited marital opportunity. Moralists who do not address these fundamental factors are wasting their breath.

What about the association between drug use and peer pressure?

Psychological development is analogous to an assembly line in which different functions are installed at different stages. When maturity is reached, most of the features that really matter for performance or behavior have already been fully installed. However, appearances, such as paint and upholstery, are left until close to the end. Teenagers can also change greatly in their dress fashions, mannerisms, and style of self-presentation.

Adolescent rebellion is possibly the most unrewarding and disheartening phase of being a parent. Parents often feel helpless and are even inclined to agree with the conclusion now being reached by a small, but growing, minority of academic psychologists—that parents really don't matter. Every time their teenage daughter comes home with a new hair color, a new tattoo, a new disgusting example of body piercing, or a new scary boyfriend, they may say to themselves: "Judith Harris is right, the darn peers are winning!"

While the impulse is understandable, Harris is not right. Astute readers will already know the direction of my response. It is that the parents have been (or should have been) more completely in control at the earlier stages of the assembly line. Either they have carefully tightened all of the bolts and closed all of the rivets, or they have sent someone out into the world who is going to leave a bitter taste in the mouth—they have assembled a lemon! Just as it takes more than a messy paint job to screw up a really good car, it takes more than a difficult adolescence to change the fundamental habits of self-discipline, decency, and goal-directedness that children acquire in high-parental-investment homes.

Most teens shake off the rebellious mannerisms of their adolescence just as soon as they become a social liability (e.g., when those mannerisms make it impossible for them to pass a job interview). Perhaps the longest period ever of adolescent revolt involved the hippie culture of the 1960s. During the 1980s, many Americans experienced quite a surprise when they recognized in the features of well-groomed, conservatively clad businessmen the former leaders of the student protests, such as Abbie Hoffman. They had gotten rid of the psychedelic paint job and now everyone could see that they had high-quality components under their hoods.

What about the finding from behavior genetics that parents do not make their children more alike?

There is a poison phrase that can kill every party. When you want to clear the room of zealous parents, behavior genetics has what it takes. The toxic aphorism is that when you subtract out the effect of shared genes, children growing up in the same family are little more similar than any two persons chosen from the population at random.

This would be beyond disheartening if it were true. As usual, the devil is in the details. What behavior geneticists have studied, for the most part, is responses on paper-and-pencil personality tests and IQ tests. When actual behavior is studied, one finds that genetics has little effect and occasionally no effect. There is a corresponding increase in the importance of the shared environment.

Given this inconsistency, one might well ask what personality tests really measure. Why do identical twins often score so closely on personality scales that it is as if the same person took the test on two different occasions? One plausible explanation is that personality tests are a fairly accurate, even if highly indirect, measure of brain chemistry.

Since aggressiveness is influenced by brain chemistry, for example, behavior geneticists find that there is a fairly high heritability for aggression as a personality trait (just under 50 percent). When they study aggressive behavior, the heritability is zero. This apparently reflects the fact that people with aggressive tendencies can succeed in controlling them. Anyone who has ever succeeded in stamping out tantrum behavior in a young child will know that this doesn't happen by accident.

The important point that is easy to miss from behavior genetics is that even though parents have little capacity to alter how children score on personality tests, which is another way of saying that they can do little to alter the chemistry of their child's brain, they can do a lot to alter their child's behavior. In particular, they can raise children who are well-behaved, well meaning, and hard working, or they can raise children who are delinquent, cynical, and lazy. If the children grow up to fulfill their social obligations and are productive, law-abiding citizens, we don't need to concern ourselves too much about the brain chemistry that determines their personality or about the genes that underlie that chemistry.

What about language development in immigrants and the theory that children are socialized primarily by peers?

One wit remarked that having blamed their parents for everything bad that went on in their lives, baby boomers went on to make poor parents, being a tad too self-absorbed to get really worked up about their children. Now that their own children have grown up and look like a mess, the happy truth has dawned that parents don't really matter at all. It is all about the gosh-darn peers.

It turns out that this claim is only true in a subliminal sense. When parents fail to provide a good sense of direction for their children, the children are certainly more likely to fall under the sway of antisocial peers. High school cliques of disaffected teens are certainly a force to be reckoned with, and parents who have let their children go in this direction have very good reason to be frightened for them and of them.

The question of good role models also arises in the very different context of language learning. Judith Harris makes a very big deal of the fact that when children learn English as a second language, they go for the better model provided by Americans instead of mimicking the broken English of their parents. She sees this as strong evidence for the view that children are more strongly influenced by "peers" than they are by parents.

Yet, this is an invalid generalization based on a selective example. These children acquire their English from other people around them because they notice that their parents are not good role models so far as their spoken language is concerned. The children become painfully aware that when they mimic their parents, no one understands them.

Of course the children will prefer a language medium that works over one that does not. After all, if you were learning to sing, you would be unlikely to prefer a teacher who couldn't sing in tune to one who sang beautifully. Just because children grow up speaking a different accent than their parents does not mean that they are not strongly influenced by them in other ways. Within the realm of language learning, the Hart and Risley study has shown that young children acquire almost all of their vocabulary from parents, as well as the emotional tone of their conversations.[3]

What about the fact that some families do not train their children to succeed in America?

The theory of parental investment developed in this book rests on the assumption that child training practices are adaptive in the sense that children are taught to behave in ways that increase their chances of social success. Yet we find that among certain demographic groups, such as the poor and African Americans, parents seem to be doing the opposite. That is, the fact that children do poorly in school, get in trouble with the law, and otherwise fail to fit in with their communities can be traced to a style of parenting that is referred to as low parental investment. Doesn't this falsify the adaptationist perspective on child-rearing?

Not necessarily. If you look at the specific example of achievement motivation, the case has been made that children are taught to be highly achievement-oriented in societies in which effort pays off in terms of increased wealth or enhanced social status, or both. This is essentially a feedback system in which parents whose own efforts are rewarded inculcate a high need for achievement in their offspring. If the parents have not experienced economic or social progress but have constantly struggled only to remain miserably poor all of their lives, then their own experiences will convince them of the futility of trying to better one's situation through personal effort.

In the particular case of poor African Americans, the lack of parental achievement inevitably places a damper on the prospects of the children.

Generalizing from their own experiences, parents may not have high expectations for their children and therefore are less likely to train them to be achievement-oriented. In that sense, growing up in the United States may not be so very different, for certain groups, from those growing up in a Third World country where the absence of prospects for economic progress engenders a more fatalistic outlook. One difference is that African Americans may be painfully aware of the comfortable affluence of other groups that may seem beyond their reach.

Of course, this answer has dwelt only on the motivational aspect of career striving. Even if you forget about whether people want or do not want themselves or their children to work hard and improve their economic status, there are social factors that tend to reduce parental investment. One of the most potent of these, which further establishes African Americans as a society apart from the mainstream, is the scarcity of marriageable men. It can therefore be argued that the social world in which black Americans are raised and to which they adapt is not the same as the America in which children learn to be high achievers.

What about the claim that current research does not establish that group socialization theory is wrong?

Judith Harris has proposed a group socialization theory that claims that peers are a much more potent influence on child socialization than parents are. She acknowledges that her theory has little direct evidence, which gives it unambiguous support. To remedy this situation, it would be necessary to do an experiment in which children were raised with appalling parents, just like Cinderella, but were fortunate enough to meet some decent peers, like Prince Charming and his courtiers. The basic prediction is that children who are raised in low-investing homes—however bad, so long as there is no actual brain damage—will turn into normal adults provided they have normal relationships with their peers. In other words, she is predicting that the quality of social outcomes will be positively related to the quality of peers and independent of the level of parental investment.

It is true that we have little information about the first prediction. Do children with normal peer relationships turn out fine regardless of the quality of their homes? This lack of information is attributable to the fact that antisocial family influences and antisocial peer influences tend to go together. This is partly attributable to the role parents play in determining the peer relationships of their children, something which Harris freely admits. This lack of independence between parental and peer influence may mean that the Cinderella experiment cannot be carried out.

However, it doesn't have to be for group socialization theory to be falsified. The theory has already been tested in its other prediction, namely that the behavior of parents makes no real difference to how children turn out.

While Harris argues that these tests are not conclusive because they did not manage to separate out genetic and environmental influences, she is making an error. Many actual experiments have been conducted that show, without ambiguity, that it is parental behavior and not genetics that affects how children turn out. Thus, when parents of children with conduct disorders are trained to be more effective parents, the conduct problem can be completely resolved. One wonders why Harris does not discuss such critically important evidence in her book.

In conclusion, the central prediction of group socialization theory has already been tested by the best possible kind of research. No reasonable person can examine this evidence without seeing in it an overwhelming confirmation of the ability of parents to affect the behavior of their children. This not only confirms our intuitions as children and as parents, but also confirms what we know from the technical field of learning psychology. Reinforcement and punishment are effective in modifying behavior. Parents, whether they are kind or abusive, always apply powerful reinforcement contingencies. For good or ill, all parents can strengthen some tendencies in their children and weaken others. We know this from science. We know it in our bones.

Notes

CHAPTER 1

1. Chernkovich, S. A., & Giordana, P. C. (1987). Family relationships and delinquency. *Criminology, 25,* 295–321.

2. Rankin, J. H., & Wells, L. E. (1990). The effects of parental attachment and direct controls on delinquency. *Journal of Research on Crime and Delinquency, 27,* 140–165.

3. Ceci, S. J., Rosenblum, T. B., & Kumpf, M. (1998). The shrinking gap between high- and low-scoring groups: Current trends and possible causes. In U. Neisser (Ed.), *The rising curve: Long-term gains in IQ and related measures* (pp. 287–302). Washington, DC: American Psychological Association.

4. Ramey, C. T. (1992). High-risk children and IQ: Altering intergenerational patterns. *Intelligence, 16,* 239–256.

5. Hauser, R. M. (1998). Trends in black-white test score differentials: 1. Uses and misuses of NAEP/SAT data. In U. Neisser (Ed.), *The rising curve: Long-term gains in IQ and related measures* (pp. 219–249). Washington, DC: American Psychological Association.

6. Lynn, R. (1991). Race differences in intelligence: A global perspective. *Mankind Quarterly, 31,* 255–296.

7. DeMause, L. (1974). The evolution of childhood. In L. DeMause (Ed.), *The history of childhood.* New York: The Psychohistory Press.

8. U.S. Department of Commerce. (1996). *Statistical abstract of the United States.* Washington, DC: U.S. Department of Commerce.

NOTES

9. U.S. Department of Health and Human Services. (1996). *Vital statistics of the United States, Vol. 3: Marriage and divorce*. Washington, DC: U.S. Government Printing Office.

10. Trivers, R. (1972). Parental investment and sexual selection. In B. Campbell (Ed.), *Sexual selection and the descent of man* (pp. 136–179). Chicago, IL: Aldine-Atherton.

11. Dawkins, R. (1976). *The selfish gene*. New York: Oxford University Press.

12. Alcock, J. (1989). *Animal behavior: An evolutionary approach* (4th ed.). Sunderland, MA: Sinauer Associates.

13. Creighton, J. C., & Schnell, G. D. (1996). Proximate control of siblicide in cattle egrets: A test of the food-amount hypothesis. *Behavioral Ecology and Sociobiology, 38*, 371–377.

14. Trivers (1972), Parental investment.

15. Barber, N. (1994). Machiavellianism and altruism: Effect of relatedness of target person on Machiavellian and helping attitudes. *Psychological Reports, 75*, 403–422.

16. Simmons, R. G., Klein, S. D., & Simmons, R. L. (1977). *Gift of life: The social and psychological impact of organ transplantation*. New York: Wiley.

17. Ellis, L. (1987). Criminal behavior and r/K selection: An extension of gene-based evolutionary theory. *Deviant Behavior, 8*, 149–176.

18. Fisher, D. G. (1984). Family size and delinquency. *Perceptual and Motor Skills, 58*, 527–534.

19. Tygart, C. E. (1991). Juvenile delinquency and number of children in a family: Some empirical and theoretical updates. *Youth and Society, 22*, 525–536.

20. Reiss, D., Heatherington, E. M., Plomin, R., Howe, G. W., Simmens, S. J., Henderson, S. H., O'Connor, T. J., Bussell, D. A., Anderson, E. R., & Law, T. (1995). Genetic questions for environmental studies: Differential parenting and psychopathology in adolescence. *Archives of General Psychiatry, 52*, 925–936.

21. Lykken, D. T. (1995). *The antisocial personalities*. Hillsdale, NJ: Lawrence Erlbaum.

22. Tuchman, B. W. (1978). *A distant mirror: The calamitous 14th century*. New York: Alfred A. Knopf.

23. Daly, M., & Wilson, M. (1983). *Sex evolution and behavior* (2nd ed.). Belmont, CA: Wadsworth.

24. U.S. Department of Health and Human Services. (1996). *Vital statistics of the United States, Vol. 2B: Mortality*. Hyattsville, MD: Author.

25. DeMasuse (1974), The evolution.

26. Tuchman (1978), *A distant mirror*.

27. Ibid.

28. Lancaster, J. B. (1987). The evolution history of human parental investment. In P. A. Gowaty (Ed.), *Feminism and evolutionary biology: Boundaries, intersections, and frontiers* (pp. 466–488). New York: Chapman and Hall.

29. Neisser, U. (Ed.). (1998). *The rising curve: Long-term gains in IQ and related measures*. Washington, DC: American Psychological Association.

30. Guttentag, M., & Secord, P. F. (1983). *Too many women: The sex ratio question*. Beverly Hills, CA: Sage.

31. Ibid.

32. South, S. J. (1993). Racial and ethnic differences in the desire to marry. *Journal of Marriage and the Family, 55,* 357–370.

33. Staples, R. (1985). Changes in black family structure: The conflict between family ideology and structural conditions. *Journal of Marriage and the Family, 51,* 391–404.

34. Flynn, J. R. (1991). *Asian Americans: Achievement beyond IQ.* Hillsdale, NJ: Lawrence Erlbaum.

35. Cavalli-Sforza, L. L., Menozzi, P., & Piazza, A. (1996). *The history and geography of human genes.* Princeton, NJ: Princeton University Press.

36. Flynn (1991), *Asian Americans.*

37. Hauser (1998), Trends.

38. Belsky, J., Steinberg, L., & Draper, P. (1991). Childhood experience, interpersonal development, and reproductive strategy: An evolutionary theory of socialization. *Child Development, 62,* 647–670.

CHAPTER 2

1. Kaplan, P. S., Bacharowski, J., & Zarlengo-Strouse, P. (1999). Child-directed speech produced by mothers with symptoms of depression fails to promote associative learning in 4-month-old infants. *Child Development, 70,* 560–570.

2. Shaffer, D. R. (1994). *Social and personality development* (3rd ed.). Pacific Grove, CA: Brooks/Cole.

3. Parten, M. (1932). Social participation among preschool children. *Journal of Abnormal and Social Psychology, 27,* 243–269.

4. Ainsworth, M.D.S., Blehar, M. C., Waters, E., & Wall, S. (1978). *Patterns of attachment: A psychological study of the strange situation.* Hillsdale, NJ: Erlbaum.

5. Ibid.

6. Ainsworth, M.D.S. (1979). Attachment as related to mother-infant interaction. In J. S. Rosenblatt, R. A. Hinde, C. Beer, & M. Busnel (Eds.), *Advances in the study of behavior, vol. 9* (pp. 2–51). Orlando, FL: Academic Press.

7. Alley, T. R. (Ed.). (1988). *Social and applied aspects of perceiving faces.* Hillsdale, NJ: Erlbaum.

8. van den Boom, D. C. (1990). Preventive intervention and the quality of mother-infant interaction and infant exploration in irritable infants. In W. Koops et al. (Eds.), *Psychology behind the dikes* (pp. 249–268). Amsterdam: Eburon.

9. Youngblade, L., & Belsky, J. (1989). Child maltreatment, infant-parent attachment security and dysfunctional peer relationships in toddlerhood. *Topics in Early Childhood Special Education, 9,* 1–15.

10. Starr, H. R. (1994). The lasting effects of child maltreatment. In L. Fenson & J. Fenson (Eds.), *Human development* (22nd ed.) (pp. 142–146). Guilford, CT: Dushkin.

11. Hazan, P., & Shaver, P. R. (1987). Romantic love conceptualized as an attachment process. *Journal of Personality and Social Psychology, 52,* 511–524.

12. Barber, N. (1998). Sex differences in disposition towards kin, security of adult attachment, and sociosexuality as a function of parental divorce. *Evolution and Human Behavior, 19,* 1–8.

13. Hill, E. M., Young, J. P., & Nord, J. L. (1994). Childhood adversity, attachment security, and adult relationships: A preliminary study. *Ethology and Sociobiology, 15,* 323–338.

14. Bowlby, J. (1969). *Attachment and loss, Vol. 1: Attachment.* London: Hogarth Press.

15. Copeland-Mitchell, J., Denham, S. A., & DeMulder, E. K. (1997). Q-sort assessment of child-teacher attachment relationships and social competence in the preschool. *Early Education and Development, 8,* 27–39.

16. Shaffer (1994), *Social.*

17. Teti, D. M., Sakin, J. W., Kucera, E., & Corns, K. M., et al. (1996). And baby makes four: Predictors of attachment security among pre-school age firstborns during the transition to siblinghood. *Child Development, 67,* 579–596.

18. Shaffer (1994), *Social.*

19. Bohannon, J. R., Dosser, D. A., & Lindley, S. E. (1995). Using couple data to determine domestic violence rates. *Violence and Victims, 10,* 133–141.

20. Harari, H., & Kaplan, R. M. (1982). *Social psychology: Basic and applied.* Monterey, CA: Brooks/Cole.

21. Vaughn, B. E., Kopp, C. B., & Krakow, J. B. (1984). The emergence and consolidation of self-control from eighteen to thirty months of age. *Child Development, 55,* 990–1004.

22. Mischel, H. N., & Mischel, W. (1983). The development of children's knowledge of self-control strategies. *Child Development, 53,* 603–619.

23. Shaffer (1994), *Social.*

24. Toner, I. J., Moore, L. P., & Emmons, B. A. (1980). The effect of being labeled on subsequent self-control in children. *Child Development, 51,* 618–621.

25. Harris, J. R. (1998). *The nurture assumption: Why children turn out the way they do.* New York: The Free Press.

26. Springer, S. P., & Deutsch, G. (1989). *Left brain, right brain.* New York: W. H. Freeman.

27. Maunders, D. (1994). Awakening from the dream: The experience of childhood in Protestant orphan homes in Australia, Canada, and the United States. *Child & Youth Care Forum, 23,* 393–412.

28. Hazan and Shaver (1987), Romantic love.

29. Ibid.

CHAPTER 3

1. Malsen, L. (1972). *Wolf children and the problem of human nature.* New York: Monthly Review Press.

2. Curtiss, S. (1977). *Genie: A psycholinguistic study of a modern-day "wild" child.* New York: Academic.

3. Rymer, R. (1993). *Genie: An abused child's flight from silence.* New York: HarperCollins.

4. Reynolds, A. G., & Flagg, P. W. (1983). *Cognitive psychology* (2nd ed.). Boston, MA: Little, Brown and Company.

5. Malsen (1972), *Wolf children.*

6. Ibid.

7. Ibid.

8. Provence, S., & Lipton, R. C. (1962). *Infants in institutions*. New York: International Universities Press.

9. Harlow, H. F. (1971). *Learning to love*. San Francisco, CA: Albion.

10. Vorria, P., Rutter, M., Pickles, A., Wolkind, S., & Hobsbaum, A. (1998). A comparative study of Greek children in long-term residential group care and in two-parent families. *Journal of Child Psychology and Psychiatry and Allied Disciplines, 39,* 225–236.

11. Fonagy, P., Target, M., Steele, M., & Steele, H. (1997). The development of violence and crime as it relates to security of attachment. In Joy D. Osofsky (Ed.), *Children in a violent society* (pp. 150–177). New York: The Guildford Press.

12. Cermak, S. A., & Daunhauer, L. A. (1997). Sensory processing in the postinstitutionalized child. *American Journal of Occupational Therapy, 51,* 500–507.

13. Provence & Lipton (1962), *Infants*.

14. Blakemore, C. (1974). Developmental factors in the formation of feature-extracting neurons. In F. G. Worden and F. O. Schmitt (Eds.), *The neurosciences: Third study program* (pp. 105–113). Cambridge, MA: MIT Press.

15. Cermak & Daunhauer (1977), Sensory processing.

16. Yarrow, L. (1961). Maternal deprivation: Toward an empirical and conceptual reevaluation. *Psychological Bulletin, 58,* 459–490.

17. Rosenzweig, M. R., Bennett, E. L., & Diamond, M. C. (1972). Brain changes in response to experience. *Scientific American, 226*(2), 22–29.

18. Ramey, C. T. (1992). High-risk children and IQ: Altering intergenerational patterns. *Intelligence, 16,* 239–256.

19. Barber, N. (1998). *Parenting: Roles, styles, and outcomes*. Commack, NY: Nova Science.

20. Harris, J. R. (1998). *The nurture assumption: Why children turn out the way they do*. New York: The Free Press.

21. Barber (1998), *Parenting*.

22. Resnick, M. D., Bearman, P. S., Blum, R. W., et al. (1997). Protecting adolescents from harm: Findings from the National Longitudinal Study on Adolescent Health. *Journal of the American Medical Association, 278,* 823–832.

23. Barber (1998), *Parenting*.

24. Fonagy et al. (1997), The development.

25. Resnick et al. (1997), Protecting.

26. Dodge, K. A. (1990). Mechanisms in the cycle of violence. *Science, 250,* 1678–1683.

27. Barber (1998), *Parenting*.

28. Shaffer, D. R. (1994). *Social and personality development* (3rd ed.). Pacific Grove, CA: Brooks/Cole.

29. Kandel, D. (1973). Adolescent marijuana use: Role of parents and peers. *Science, 181,* 1067–1070.

30. Stice, E., & Barrera, M. (1995). A longitudinal examination of the reciprocal relations between perceived parenting and adolescents' substance use and externalizing behaviors. *Developmental Psychology, 31,* 322–334.

CHAPTER 4

1. Symons, D. (1979). *The evolution of human sexuality*. New York: Oxford University Press.

2. Buss, D. M. (1994). *The evolution of desire: Strategies of human mating*. New York: Basic.

3. Amato, P., & Keith, B. (1991). Parental divorce and the well-being of children: A meta-analysis. *Psychological Bulletin, 110*, 26–46.

4. Wallerstein, J. S. (1998). Children of divorce: A society in search of policy. In M. A. Mason, A. Skolnick, and S. D. Sugarman (Eds.), *All our families: New policies for a new century* (pp. 66–94). New York: Oxford University Press.

5. Lykken, D. T. (1995). *The antisocial personalities*. Hillsdale, NJ: Lawrence Erlbaum.

6. Kurian, G. T. (1994). *Datapedia of the United States 1790–2000: America year by year*. Lanham, MD: Bernan Press.

7. Flynn, J. R. (1991). *Asian Americans: Achievement beyond IQ*. Hillsdale, NJ: Lawrence Erlbaum.

8. Staples, R. (1985). Changes in black family structure: The conflict between family ideology and structural conditions. *Journal of Marriage and the Family, 51*, 391–404.

9. South, S. J. (1993). Racial and ethnic differences in the desire to marry. *Journal of Marriage and the Family, 55*, 357–370.

10. McLanahan, S., & Sandefur, G. (1994). *Growing up with a single parent: What hurts, what helps*. Cambridge, MA: Harvard University Press.

11. Kurian (1994), *Datapedia*.

12. Cherlin, A. J. (1992). *Marriage, divorce, remarriage*. Cambridge, MA: Harvard University Press.

13. Kurian (1994), *Datapedia*.

14. Ellis, L. (1987). Criminal behavior and r/K selection: An extension of gene-based evolutionary theory. *Deviant Behavior, 8*, 149–176.

15. Fox, J. A. (1996). *Trends in juvenile violence: A report to the United States Attorney General on current and future rates of juvenile offending*. Washington, DC: United States Department of Justice.

16. Snyder, H. N., & Sickmund, M. (1995). *Juvenile offenders and victims: A national report*. Upland, PA: Diane Publishing Co.

17. Barber, N. (1998). *Predicting social problems from parental investment indicators at birth using U.S. population data*. Unpublished paper.

18. Hewlett, B. S. (Ed.). (1992). *Father-child relations: Cultural and biosocial contexts*. New York: Aldine de Gruyter.

19. Baxter, J. (1997). Gender equality and participation in housework: A cross-national perspective. *Journal of Comparative Family Studies, 28*, 220–247.

20. Perkins, H. W., & DeMeis, D. K. (1996). Gender and family effects on the "second shift": Domestic activity of college-educated young adults. *Gender and Society, 10*, 78–93.

21. Popenoe, D. (1996). *Life without father*. New York: Martin Kessler/Free Press.

22. Jones E. F. (1986). *Teen pregnancy in industrialized countries*. New Haven, CT: Yale University Press.

23. McLanahan & Sandefur (1994), *Growing up*.

24. Wallerstein (1998), Children.

25. Flynn (1971), *Asian Americans*.

NOTES

CHAPTER 5

1. Hardin, G. (1968). The tragedy of the commons. *Science, 162,* 1243–1248.

2. Teti, D. M., Sakin, J. W., Kucera, E., & Corns, K. M., et al. (1996). And baby makes four: Predictors of attachment security among preschool-age firstborns during the transition to siblinghood. *Child Development, 67,* 579–596.

3. Trivers, R. L. (1972). Parental investment and sexual selection. In B. Campbell (Ed.), *Sexual selection and the descent of man* (pp. 136–179). Chicago, IL: Aldine-Atherton.

4. Dawkins, R. (1976). *The selfish gene.* New York: Oxford University Press.

5. Creighton, J. C., & Schnell, G. D. (1996). Proximate control of siblicide in cattle egrets: A test of the food-amount hypothesis. *Behavioral Ecology and Sociobiology, 38,* 371–377.

6. Plomin, R. (1990). *Nature and nurture: An introduction to human behavioral genetics.* Pacific Grove, CA: Brooks/Cole.

7. Tellegen, A., Lykken, D. T., Bouchard, T., Jr., Wilcox, K. J., Segal, N. L., & Rich, S. (1988). Personality similarity in twins reared apart and together. *Journal of Personality and Social Psychology, 54,* 1031–1039.

8. Plomin (1990), *Nature and nurture.*

9. Harris, J. (1998). *The nurture assumption: Why children turn out the way they do.* New York: The Free Press.

10. Plomin (1990), *Nature and nurture.*

11. Asher, J. (1987). Born to be shy? *Psychology Today, 21*(4), 56–64.

12. Reiss, D., Heatherington, E. M., Plomin, R., Howe, G. W., Simmens, S. J., Henderson, S. H., O'Connor, T. J., Bussell, D. A., Anderson, E. R., & Law, T. (1995). Genetic questions for environmental studies: Differential parenting and psychopathology in adolescence. *Archives of General Psychiatry, 52,* 925–936.

13. Ernst, C., & Angst, J. (1983). *Birth order: Its influence on personality.* Berlin, Germany: Springer-Verlag.

14. Sulloway, F. (1996). *Born to rebel: Birth order, family dynamics and creative lives.* New York: Pantheon.

15. Harris (1998), *The nurture assumption.*

16. Somit, A., Arwine, A., & Peterson, S. A. (1996). *Birth order and political behavior.* Lanham, MD: University Press of America.

17. Ernst & Angst (1983), *Birth order.*

18. Harris (1998), *The nurture assumption.*

19. Sulloway (1996), *Born to rebel.*

20. McHale, S. M., Crouter, A. C., McGuire, S. A., & Updegraff, K. A. (1995). Congruence between mothers' and fathers' differential treatment of siblings: Links with family relations and children's well-being. *Child Development, 66,* 116–128.

21. Moore, G. A., Cohn, J. F., & Campbell, S. B. (1997). Mother's affective behavior with infant siblings: Stability and change. *Developmental Psychology, 33,* 856–860.

22. Tygart, C. E. (1991). Juvenile delinquency and number of children in a family. *Youth and Society, 22,* 525–536.

23. Glueck, F., & Glueck, E. (1950). *Unraveling juvenile delinquency.* New York: The Commonwealth Fund.

24. Robins, L. N., West, P. A., & Herjanic, B. (1975). Arrests and delinquency in two generations: A study of black urban families and their children. *Journal of Child Psychology and Psychiatry, 16,* 125–140.

25. Nye, I. F. (1958). *Family relationships and delinquent behavior.* New York: Wiley.

26. Wilkinson, K., Stitt, B. G., & Erickson, M. L. (1982). Siblings and delinquent behavior: An exploratory study of a neglected family variable. *Criminology, 20,* 223–239.

27. Brim, O. G., Jr. (1958). Family structure and sex role learning by children: A further analysis of Helen Koch's data. *Sociometry, 21,* 1–16.

28. Reiss et al. (1995), Genetic questions.

29. Ibid.

30. Geary, D. C. (1998). Male, female: The evolution of human sex differences. Washington, DC: American Psychological Association.

31. Dunn, J., & Plomin, R. (1990). *Separate lives: Why siblings are so different.* New York: Basic.

32. Plomin, R., Foch, T. T., & Rowe, D. C. (1981). Bobo clown aggression in childhood: Environment, not genes. *Journal of Research in Personality, 15,* 331–342.

33. Harris (1998), *The nurture assumption.*

34. Reiss et al. (1995), Genetic questions.

35. Asher (1987), Born to be shy?

36. Furstenburg, F. F., Jr., Brooks-Gunn, J., & Morgan, S. P. (1987). *Adolescent mothers in later life.* New York: Cambridge University Press.

37. Apfel, N., & Seitz, V. (1997). The firstborn sons of African American teenage mothers: Perspectives on risk and resilience. In S. S. Luthar, J. A. Burack, D. Cicchetti, and J. R. Weisz (Eds.), *Developmental psychopathology: Perspectives on adjustment, risk, and disorder* (pp. 486–506). New York: Cambridge University Press.

38. Ellis, L. (1987). Criminal behavior and r/K selection: An extension of gene-based evolutionary theory. *Deviant Behavior, 8,* 149–176.

39. Belmont, L., & Marolla, F. A. (1973). Birth order, family size, and intelligence. *Science, 182,* 1096–1101.

40. Ernst & Angst (1983), *Birth order.*

41. Barber, N. (1998). *Parenting: Roles, styles, and outcomes.* Commack, NY: Nova Science.

CHAPTER 6

1. Stone, L. (1977). *The family, sex and marriage in England 1500–1800.* New York: Harper & Row.

2. Ibid., p. 101.

3. Ibid., p. 99.

4. Lancaster, J. B. (1987). The evolutionary history of human parental investment. In P. A. Gowaty (Ed.), *Feminism and evolutionary biology: Boundaries, intersections and frontiers* (pp. 466–488). New York: Chapman and Hall.

5. Nightingale, C. H. (1993). *On the edge: A history of poor black children and their American dreams.* New York: Basic.

6. Snyder, T. D. (Ed.). (1993). *120 years of American education: A statistical portrait.* Washington, DC: National Center for Education Statistics.

7. Lamar, T. E., & Stafford, M. (1991). *American delinquency* (3rd ed.) (p. 89). Belmont, CA: Wadsworth.

8. Vaillant, G. E. (1983). *The natural history of alcoholism.* Cambridge, MA: Harvard University Press.

9. Hamer, D. H., & Copeland, P. (1999). *Living with our genes: Why they matter more than you think.* New York: Doubleday.

10. Argyle, M. (1994). *The psychology of social class.* London: Routledge.

11. Lykken, D. T. (1995). *The antisocial personalities.* Hillsdale, NJ: Lawrence Erlbaum.

12. Nightingale (1993), *On the edge.*

13. Hamer and Copeland (1999), *Living.*

14. Lykken (1995), *The antisocial personalities.*

15. Argyle (1994), *The psychology.*

16. Rowe, D. C., Rodgers, J. L., Meseck-Bushey, S., & St. John, C. (1989). Sexual behavior and nonsexual deviance: A sibling study of their relationship. *Developmental Psychology, 25,* 61–69.

17. Barber, N. (1998). The role of reproductive strategies in academic attainment. *Sex Roles, 38,* 313–323.

18. Goldin, C. (1995*). Career and family: College women look to the past.* National Bureau of Economic Research, Working Paper #5188. Cambridge, MA: National Bureau of Economic Research.

19. Astin, H. S. (1983). Gender roles in transition: Research and policy implications for higher education. *Journal of Higher Education, 54,* 309–324.

20. Call, G., Beer, J., & Beer, J. (1994). General and test anxiety, shyness, and grade point average of elementary school children of divorced and nondivorced parents. *Psychological Reports, 74,* 512–514.

21. Brubeck, D., & Beer, J. (1992). Depression, self-esteem, suicide ideation, death anxiety, and GPA in high school students of divorced and nondivorced parents. *Psychological Reports, 71,* 755–763.

22. Beer, J. (1989). Relationship of divorce to self-concept, self-esteem, and grade point average of fifth and sixth grade school children. *Psychological Reports, 65,* 1379–1383.

23. Forehand, R. (1992). Parental divorce and adolescent maladjustment: Scientific inquiry vs. public information. *Behavior Research and Therapy, 30,* 319–327.

24. Pittman, K., & Govan, C. (1986). *Model programs: Preventing adolescent pregnancy and building youth self-sufficiency.* Washington DC: Children's Defense Fund.

25. Barber (1998), The role.

26. Hart, B., & Risley, T. (1995). *Meaningful differences in the everyday experience of young American children.* Baltimore, MD: Paul H. Brookes.

27. Plomin, R., Fulker, D. W., Corley, R., & DeFries, J. C. (1997). Nature, nurture, and cognitive development from 1 to 16 years: A parent-offspring adoption study. *Psychological Science, 8,* 442–447.

28. Ramey, C. T. (1992). High-risk children and IQ: Altering intergenerational patterns. *Intelligence, 16,* 239–256.

29. Lazar, I., & Darlington, R. B. (1982). Lasting effects of early education: A report from the Consortium for Longitudinal Studies. *Monographs of the Society for Research in Child Development, 47*(2, sup. 3), 1–151.

30. Williams, W. E. (1998). Are we raising smarter children today? School- and home-related influences on IQ. In U. Neisser (Ed.), *The rising curve: Long-term gains in IQ and related measures* (pp. 125–154). Washington, DC: American Psychological Association.

31. Riksen-Walraven, J. M. (1978). Effects of caregiver behavior on habituation rate and self-efficacy in humans. *International Journal of Behavioral Development, 1,* 105–130.

32. Lancaster (1987), The evolutionary history.

33. Guttentag, M., & Secord, P. F. (1983). *Too many women: The sex ratio question.* Beverly Hills, CA: Sage.

34. Ibid.

35. Goldin (1995), *Career and family.*

36. Ibid.

37. Oliver, C. (1996, September 23). Why paychecks haven't kept up. *Investor's Business Daily* (1) 1, 4.

38. Ibid.

39. Barber, N. (1998). *Parenting: Roles, styles, and outcomes.* Commack, NY: Nova Science.

CHAPTER 7

1. Flynn, J. R. (1991). *Asian Americans: Achievement beyond IQ.* Hillsdale, NJ: Lawrence Erlbaum.

2. Goldin, C. (1995). *Career and family: College women look to the past.* National Bureau of Economic Research, Working Paper #5188. Cambridge, MA: National Bureau of Economic Research.

3. Barber, N. (1998). *Parenting: Roles, styles, and outcomes.* Commack, NY: Nova Science.

4. Youngblade, L., & Belsky, J. (1989). Child maltreatment, infant-parent attachment security and dysfunctional peer relationships in toddlerhood. *Topics in Early Childhood Special Education, 9,* 1–15.

5. U.S. Government Printing Office. (1993). *Economic report of the president.* Washington, DC: Author.

6. Aviezer, O., Van Uzendoorn, M., Savi, A., & Schuengel, C. (1994). "Children of the dream" revisited: 70 years of collective early care in Israeli kibbutzim. *Psychological Bulletin, 116,* 99–116.

7. Ibid.

8. Harris, J. R. (1998). *The nurture assumption: Why children turn out the way they do.* New York: The Free Press.

9. Bettelheim, B. (1969). *The children of the dream.* New York: Macmillan.

10. Aviezer et al. (1994), "Children."

11. Ibid.

12. Lee, R. B. (1979). *The !Kung San: Men, women, and work in a foraging society.* Cambridge, MA: Cambridge University Press.

13. Barber (1998), *Parenting.*

14. Belsky, J. (1990). Parental and nonparental child care and children's socioemotional development: A decade in review. *Journal of Marriage and the Family, 52,* 885–903.

15. Ibid.

16. Ibid.

17. Demarest, J. (1996, June). *Parental investment: "When mom can provide resources."* Paper presented to the Human Behavior and Evolution Society at Northwestern University.

18. Hazan, P., & Shaver, P. R. (1987). Romantic love conceptualized as an attachment process. *Journal of Personality and Social Psychology, 52,* 511–524.

19. Hazan, P., & Shaver, P. R. (1994). Love and work: An attachment theoretical perspective. *Journal of Personality and Social Psychology, 59,* 270–280. ✎

20. Barber, N. (1998). The role of reproductive strategies in academic attainment. *Sex Roles, 38,* 313–323.

21. Coley, R. L., & Chase-Lansdale, P. L. (1998). Adolescent pregnancy and parenthood: Recent evidence and future directions. *American Psychologist, 53,* 152–166.

22. Lykken, D. T. (1995). *The antisocial personalities.* Hillsdale, NJ: Lawrence Erlbaum.

23. U.S. Government Printing Office (1993), *Economic report.*

24. Kurian, G. T. (1994). *Datapedia of the United States 1790–2000: America year by year.* Lanham, MD: Bernan Press.

25. Ibid.

26. Ku, L., Sonenstein, F. L., & Pleck, J. H. (1993). Factors influencing first intercourse for teenage men. *Public Health Reports, 108,* 680–694.

27. U.S. Department of Commerce. (1950–1993). *Statistical abstract of the United States.* Washington, DC: U.S. Department of Commerce.

28. Guttentag, M., & Secord, P. F. (1983). *Too many women: The sex ratio question.* Beverly Hills, CA: Sage.

29. Harris (1998), *The nurture assumption.*

30. Werner, E. E. (1995). Resilence in development. *Current Directions in Psychological Science, 4,* 81–85.

CHAPTER 8

1. Baker, R. S., & Bellis, M. A. (1995). *Human sperm competition.* London: Chapman & Hall.

2. Laumann, E. O. (1994). *The social organization of sexuality: Sexual practices in the United States.* Chicago: University of Chicago Press.

3. U.S. Department of Commerce. (1975). *Historical statistics of the United States.* Washington, DC: U.S. Government Printing Office.

4. DeMause, L. (Ed.). (1974). *The history of childhood.* New York: The Psychohistory Press.

5. Tuchman, B. W. (1978). *A distant mirror: The calamitous 14th century.* New York: Alfred A. Knopf.

6. Ibid.

7. Illick, J. E. (1974). Child-rearing in seventeenth-century England and America. In L. DeMause (Ed.), *The history of childhood* (pp. 303–350). New York: The Psychohistory Press.

NOTES

8. Coley, R. L., & Chase-Lansdale, P. L. (1998). Adolescent pregnancy and parenthood: Recent evidence and future directions. *American Psychologist, 53,* 152–166.

9. Belsky, J., Steinberg, L., & Draper, P. (1991). Childhood experience, interpersonal development, and reproductive strategy: An evolutionary theory of socialization. *Child Development, 62,* 647–670.

10. Barber, N. (In press). On the relationship between marital opportunity and teen pregnancy: The sex ratio question. *Journal of Cross-Cultural Psychology.*

11. Barber, N. (2000). On the relationship between country sex ratios and teen pregnancy rates: A replication. *Cross-Cultural Research, 34*(1), 26–37.

12. Palmer, C. T., & Tilley, C. F. (1995). Sexual access to females as a motivation for joining gangs: An evolutionary approach. *The Journal of Sex Research, 32,* 213–217.

13. Hamer, D. H., & Copeland, P. (1999). *Living with our genes: Why they matter more than you think.* New York: Doubleday.

14. Surbey, M. K. (1990). Family composition, stress, and timing of human menarche. In T. E. Ziegler and F. Berkovitch (Eds.), *Socioendocrinology of primate reproduction* (pp. 11–32). New York: Wiley-Liss.

15. Garn, S. M., LaVelle, M., Rosenberg, K., & Hawthorne, V. M. (1986). Maturational timing as a factor in female fatness and obesity. *The American Journal of Clinical Nutrition, 43,* 879–883.

16. Barber, N. (1998). The slender ideal and eating disorders: An interdisciplinary "telescope" model. *International Journal of Eating Disorders, 23,* 295–307.

17. Barber, N. (1998). Secular changes in standards of bodily attractiveness in American women: Different masculine and feminine ideals. *The Journal of Psychology, 132,* 87–94.

18. Barber, N. (1995). The evolutionary psychology of physical attractiveness: Sexual selection and human morphology. *Ethology and Sociobiology, 16,* 395–424.

19. Seligman, M.E.P. (1993). *What you can change and what you can't.* New York: Fawcett Columbine.

20. Ibid.

21. Barber, N. (1998). The role of reproductive strategies in academic attainment. *Sex Roles, 38,* 313–323.

22. Wallerstein, J. S. (1998). Children of divorce: A society in search of policy. In M. A. Mason, A. Skolnick, and S. D. Sugarman (Eds.), *All our families: New policies for a new century* (pp. 66–94). New York: Oxford University Press.

23. McGue, M., & Lykken, D. T. (1992). Genetic influence on risk of divorce. *Psychological Science, 3,* 368–373.

24. Barber, N. (1998). *Predicting social problems from parental investment indicators at birth using U.S. population data.* Unpublished paper.

25. Belsky et al. (1991), Childhood experience.

26. Coley & Chase-Lansdale (1998), Adolescent pregnancy.

27. Plomin, R. (1990). *Nature and nurture: An introduction to human behavioral genetics.* Pacific Grove, CA: Brooks/Cole.

28. van den Boom, D. C. (1990). Preventive intervention and the quality of mother-infant interaction and infant exploration in irritable infants. In W. Koops et al. (Eds.), *Psychology behind the dikes* (pp. 249–270). Amsterdam: Eburon.

29. Long, P., Forehand, R., Wierson, M., & Morgan, A. (1994). Does parent training with young noncompliant children have long-term effects? *Behavioral Research and Therapy, 32,* 101–107.

30. Ramey, C. T. (1992). High risk children and IQ: Altering intergenerational patterns. *Intelligence, 16,* 239–256.

31. Hart, B., & Risley, T. R. (1995). *Meaningful differences in the everyday experience of young American children.* Baltimore, MD: Paul H. Brookes.

32. Shaffer, D. R. (1994). *Social and personality development* (3rd ed.). Pacific Grove, CA: Brooks/Cole.

33. Barber (1998), The role.

34. Plomin (1990), *Nature and nurture.*

35. Asher, J. (1987). Born to be shy? *Psychology Today, 21*(4), 56–64.

36. Lykken, D. T. (1995). *The antisocial personalities.* Hillsdale, NJ: Lawrence Erlbaum.

37. Musick, J. S. (1993). *Young, poor, and pregnant: The psychology of teenage motherhood.* New Haven, CT: Yale University Press.

38. Ibid., 181–182.

39. Pittman, K., & Govan, C. (1986). *Model programs: Preventing adolescent pregnancy and building youth self-sufficiency.* Washington, DC: Children's Defense Fund.

40. Coley & Chase-Lansdale (1998), Adolescent pregnancy.

41. Musick (1993), *Young, poor, and pregnant.*

42. Ibid., 183, references omitted.

43. Guttentag, M., & Secord, P. F. (1983). *Too many women: The sex ratio question.* Beverly Hills, CA: Sage.

44. U.S. Department of Commerce. (1960–1997). *Statistical abstract of the United States.* Washington, DC: U.S. Department of Commerce.

45. Ibid.

46. Ventura, S. J., Curtis, S. C., & Mathews, T. J. (1998). *Teenage births in the United States: National and state trends 1990–1996.* Hyattsville, MD: National Center for Health Statistics.

CHAPTER 9

1. Lawson, E., & Thompson, A. (1991). Historical and social correlates of African American divorce: Review of the literature and implications for research. *The Western Journal of Black Studies, 18,* 100.

2. Empey, L., Stafford, L. T., & Stafford, M. C. (1991). *American delinquency: Its meaning & construction* (3rd ed.). Belmont, CA: Wadsworth, 89.

3. Ibid., 95.

4. Flynn, J. R. (1991). *Asian Americans: Achievement beyond IQ.* Hillsdale, NJ: Lawrence Erlbaum.

5. Steele, C. M. (1994). Race and the schooling of black Americans. In E. Krupat (Ed.), *Psychology is social* (pp. 54–66). New York: HarperCollins.

6. D'Souza, D. (1995). *The end of racism: Principles for a multiracial society.* New York: The Free Press.

7. Rushton, J. P. (1995). *Race, evolution, and behavior.* New Brunswick, NJ: Transaction.

8. Ibid.

9. Ellis, L. (1987). Criminal behavior and r/K selection: An extension of gene-based evolutionary theory. *Deviant Behavior, 8,* 149–176.

10. Kagan, J., Arcus, D., Snidman, N., Feng, W.-U., et al. (1994). Reactivity in infants: A cross-national comparison. *Developmental Psychology, 30,* 342–345.

11. Ibid.

12. Rushton (1995), *Race.*

13. Cavalli-Sforza, L. L., Menozzi, P., & Piazza, A. (1996). *The history and geography of human genes.* Princeton, NJ: Princeton University Press.

14. Furstenberg, F., & Hughes, M. E. (1995). Social capital and successful development among at-risk youth. *Journal of Marriage and the Family, 57,* 580–592.

15. Barry, H., Child, I., & Bacon, M. (1959). Relation of child training to subsistence economy. *American anthropologist, 61,* 51–63.

16. Berry, J. W. (1967). Independence and conformity in subsistence-level societies. *Journal of Personality and Social Psychology, 7,* 415–418.

17. Low, B. (1989). Cross-cultural patterns in the training of children. *Journal of Comparative Psychology, 103,* 311–319.

18. Ibid.

19. Flynn (1991), *Asian Americans.*

20. Ramey, C. T. (1992). High-risk children and IQ: Altering intergenerational patterns. *Intelligence, 16,* 239–256.

21. Plomin, R., Fulker, D. W., Corley, R., & DeFries, J. C. (1997). Nature, nurture, and cognitive development from 1 to 16 years: A parent-offspring adoption study. *Psychological Science, 8,* 442–447.

22. Schultz, D. P., & Schultz, E. S. (1987). *A history of modern psychology* (4th ed.). San Diego, CA: Harcourt Brace Jovanovich.

23. Linn, R. L. (1982). Ability testing: Individual differences, prediction, and differential prediction. In A. Wigoder & W. Gardner (Eds.), *Ability testing: Uses, consequences, and controversies* (pp. 335–388). Washington, DC: National Academy Press.

24. Flynn (1991), *Asian Americans.*

25. Ibid.

26. Ibid.

27. Sowell, T. (1978). Three black histories. In T. Sowell (Ed.), *Essays and data on American ethnic groups* (pp. 7–64). Washington, DC: The Urban Institute.

28. Moynihan, D. P. (1986). *Family and nation.* San Diego, CA: Harcourt Brace Jovanovich.

29. D'Souza (1995), *The end.*

30. Flynn (1991), *Asian Americans.*

31. U.S. Department of Justice (1996). *Sourcebook of criminal justice statistics.* Washington, DC: U.S. Government Printing Office.

32. Sowell (1978), Three black histories.

33. Ibid.

34. Flynn (1991), *Asian Americans.*

35. Sowell (1978), Three black histories.

36. South, S. J. (1993). Racial and ethnic differences in the desire to marry. *Journal of Marriage and the Family, 55,* 357–370.

37. Barber, N. (1994). The evolutionary psychology of physical attractiveness: Sexual selection and human morphology. *Ethology and Sociobiology, 16,* 395–424.

38. Flynn (1991), *Asian Americans.*

39. Staples, R. (1985). Changes in black family structure: The conflict between family ideology and structural conditions. *Journal of Marriage and the Family, 51,* 391–404.

40. Kurian, G. T. (1994). *Datapedia of the United States 1790–2000: America year by year.* Lanham, MD: Bernan Press.

41. U.S. Department of Commerce (1994). *Statistical abstract of the United States.* Washington, DC: U.S. Department of Commerce.

42. Shipman, P. (1994). *The evolution of racism.* New York: Simon and Schuster.

43. Plomin, R. (1990). *Nature and nurture: An introduction to human behavioral genetics.* Pacific Grove, CA: Brooks/Cole.

44. Brooks-Gunn, J., Klebanov, P. K., & Duncan, G. J. (1996). Ethnic differences in children's intelligence test scores: Role of economic deprivation, home environment, and maternal characteristics. *Child Development, 67,* 396–408.

45. Jenkins, J. E., & Guidubaldi, J. (1997). The nature-nurture controversy revisited: Divorce and gender as factors in children's racial group differences. *Child Study Journal, 27,* 145–160.

46. Barber, N. (1998). *Parental investment and ethnic differences in social problems: Environmental explanation of "race" differences.* Unpublished manuscript.

47. Fossett, M. A., & Kiecolt, K. J. (1991). A methodological review of the sex ratio: Alternatives for comparative research. *Journal of Marriage and the Family, 53,* 941–957.

48. Barber (1998), *Parental investment.*

CHAPTER 10

1. McClelland, D. C., Atkinson, J. W., Clark, R. W., & Lowell, E. L. (1976). *The achievement motive.* New York: Irvington.

2. Woytinski, W. S., & Woytinski, E. S. (1953). *World population and production.* New York: Twentieth Century Fund.

3. McClelland, D. C. (1964). *The roots of consciousness.* Princeton, NJ: Van Nostrand.

4. McClelland, D. C., Rindlisbacher, A., & de Charms, R. C. (1955). Religions and other sources of parental attitudes toward independence training. In D. C. McClelland (Ed.), *Studies in motivation.* New York: Appleton-Century-Crofts.

5. Weber, M. (1930). *The Protestant work ethic* (translated by Talcott Parsons). New York: Scribners.

6. Mook, D. G. (1987). *Motivation: The organization of action.* New York: W. W. Norton.

7. McClelland et al. (1995), Religions.

8. Waters, E., Wippman, J., & Sroufe, L. A. (1979). Attachment, positive affect, and competence in the peer group. *Child Development, 50,* 821–829.

9. Seligman, M.E.P. (1993). *What you can change and what you can't.* New York: Fawcett Columbine.

10. Slater, P. E., & Gitlin, T. (1990). *The pursuit of loneliness.* Boston, MA: Beacon Press.

11. Harvey, A. R., & Coleman, A. A. (1997). An Afro-centric program for African-American males in the criminal justice system. *Child Welfare, 76,* 197–211.

12. van den Boom, D. C. (1990). Preventive intervention and the quality of mother-infant interaction and infant exploration in irritable infants. In W. Koops et al. (Eds.), *Psychology behind the dikes* (pp. 249–268). Amsterdam: Eburon.

13. Youngblade, L., & Belsky, J. (1989). Child maltreatment, infant-parent attachment security and dysfunctional peer relations in toddlerhood. *Topics in Early Childhood Special Education, 9,* 1–15.

14. Lewis, M., & Brooks-Gunn, J. (1979). *Social cognition and the acquisition of self.* New York: Plenum.

15. Patterson, G. R. (1982). *Coercive family processes.* Eugene, OR: Castilia Press.

16. Ibid.

17. Patterson, G. R., DeBaryshe, B. D., & Ramsey, E. (1989). A developmental perspective on antisocial behavior. *American Psychologist, 44,* 329–335.

18. Long, P., Forehand, R., Wierson, M., & Morgan, A. (1994). Does parent training with young noncompliant children have long-term effects? *Behavioral Research and Therapy, 32,* 101–107.

19. Patterson, G. R. (1981). Mothers: The unacknowledged victims. *Monographs of the Society for Research in Child Development, 45* (5, Serial No. 186).

20. Shaffer, D. R. (1994). *Social and personality development* (3rd ed.). Pacific Grove, CA: Brooks/Cole.

21. Flynn, J. R. (1991). *Asian Americans: Achievement beyond IQ.* Hillsdale, NJ: Lawrence Erlbaum.

22. Chao, R. K. (1994). Beyond parental control and authoritarian parenting style: Understanding Chinese parenting through the cultural notion of training. *Child Development, 65,* 1111–1119.

23. Ibid.

24. Rosen, B. C., & Dandrade, R. (1959). The psychological origins of achievement motivation. *Sociometry, 22,* 185–218.

25. Steele, C. M. (1994). Race and schooling of black Americans. In E. Krupat (Ed.), *Psychology is social* (pp. 54–66). New York: HarperCollins.

26. Barber, N. (1998). *Parenting: Roles, styles, and outcomes.* Commack, NY: Nova Science.

27. McClelland, D. C., & Winter, D. G. (1971). *Motivating achievement motivation.* New York: Free Press.

28. Shaffer (1994), *Social.*

29. Fields, G. (1996, October 25). Boston hasn't had a juvenile homicide in '96. *USA Today,* 3A, 2.

30. Barber (1998), *Parenting.*

CHAPTER 11

1. Asher, J. (1987). Born to be shy? *Psychology Today, 21*(4), 56–64.

2. U.S. Department of Commerce (1996). *Statistical abstract of the United States.* Washington, DC: U.S. Department of Commerce.

3. Kurian, G. T. (1994). *Datapedia of the United States 1790–2000: America year by year.* Lanham, MD: Bernan Press.

4. Ventura, S. J., Curtis, S. C., & Mathews, T. J. (1998). *Teenage births in the United States: National and state trends 1990–1996.* Hyattsville, MD: National Center for Health Statistics.

NOTES

5. U.S. Department of Health and Human Services. (1988). *Vital statistics of the United States, Vol. 3: Marriage and divorce*. Washington, DC: U.S. Government Printing Office.

6. U.S. Department of Commerce (1996), *Statistical abstract*.

7. U.S. Department of Justice (1996). *Sourcebook of criminal justice statistics*. Washington, DC: U.S. Government Printing Office.

8. U.S. Department of Commerce (1967/1996). *Statistical abstract of the United States*. Washington, DC: U.S. Department of Commerce.

9. Barber, N. (1998). The role of reproductive strategies in academic attainment. *Sex Roles, 38,* 313–323.

10. Ventura et al. (1998), *Teenage births*.

11. Guttentag, M., & Secord, P. F. (1983). *Too many women: The sex ratio question*. Beverly Hills, CA: Sage.

12. Staples, R. (1985). Changes in black family structure: The conflict between family ideology and structural conditions. *Journal of Marriage and the Family, 51,* 391–404.

13. Barber, N. (1999). Women's dress fashions as a function of reproductive strategy. *Sex Roles,* 40, 459–471.

14. Barber, N. (1998). *Parenting: Roles, styles, and outcomes*. Commack, NY: Nova Science.

15. Lykken, D. T. (1995). *The antisocial personalities*. Hillsdale, NJ: Lawrence Erlbaum.

16. Flynn, J. R. (1991). *Asian Americans: Achievement beyond IQ*. Hillsdale, NJ: Lawrence Erlbaum.

17. Frost, P. (1988). Human skin color: A possible relationship between its sexual dimorphism and its social perception. *Perspectives in Biology and Medicine, 32,* 39–58.

18. Yogman, M. W., Kindlon, D., & Felton, E. (1995). Father involvement and cognitive/behavioral outcomes of preterm infants. *Journal of the American Academy of Child and Adolescent Psychiatry, 34,* 58–66.

19. Popenoe, D. (1996). *Life without father*. New York: Martin Kessler/Free Press.

20. Lykken (1995), *The antisocial personalities*.

21. Buss, D. M. (1994). *The evolution of desire: Strategies of human mating*. New York: Basic.

22. Ibid.

23. Daly, M., & Wilson, M. (1983). *Sex evolution and behavior* (2nd ed.). Belmont, CA: Wadsworth.

24. Buss (1994), *The evolution*.

25. Jones, E. F., et al. (1986). *Teenage pregnancy in industrialized countries: A study sponsored by the Alan Guttmacher Institute*. New Haven, CT: Yale University Press.

26. Copeland-Mitchell, J., Denham, S. A., & DeMulder, E. K. (1997). Q-sort assessment of child-teacher attachment relationships and social competence in the preschool. *Early Education and Development, 8,* 27–39.

27. Chao, R. K. (1994). Beyond parental control and authoritarian parenting style: Understanding Chinese parenting through the cultural notion of training. *Child Development, 65,* 1111–1119.

28. Brown, B. B., Mounts, N., Lamborn, S. D., & Steinberg, L. (1993). Parenting practices and peer group affiliation in adolescents. *Child Development, 64,* 467–482.

29. Harris, J. (1998). *The nurture assumption: Why children turn out the way they do.* New York: The Free Press.

30. Hamer, D. H. & Copeland, P. (1999). *Living with our genes: Why they matter more than you think.* New York: Doubleday.

APPENDIX

1. McLanahan, S. & Sandefur, G. (1994). *Growing up with a single parent: What hurts, what helps.* Cambridge, MA: Harvard University Press.

2. Jenkins, J. E., & Guidubaldi, J. (1997). The nature-nurture controversy revisited: Divorce and gender as factors in children's racial group differences. *Child Study Journal 27,* 145–160.

3. Hart, B., & Risley, T. (1995). *Meaningful differences in the everyday experience of young American children.* Baltimore, MD: Paul H. Brookes.

Index